SAP on Azure Implementation Guide

Move your business data to the cloud

Nick Morgan

Bartosz Jarkowski

BIRMINGHAM - MUMBAI

SAP on Azure Implementation Guide

Copyright © 2020 Packt Publishing

All rights reserved. No part of this book may be reproduced, stored in a retrieval system, or transmitted in any form or by any means, without the prior written permission of the publisher, except in the case of brief quotations embedded in critical articles or reviews.

Every effort has been made in the preparation of this book to ensure the accuracy of the information presented. However, the information contained in this book is sold without warranty, either express or implied. Neither the authors, nor Packt Publishing or its dealers and distributors, will be held liable for any damages caused or alleged to have been caused directly or indirectly by this book.

Packt Publishing has endeavored to provide trademark information about all of the companies and products mentioned in this book by the appropriate use of capitals. However, Packt Publishing cannot guarantee the accuracy of this information.

Acquisition Editor: Ben Renow-Clarke
Acquisition Editor – Peer Reviews: Suresh Jain
Content Development Editor: Dr. Ian Hough
Technical Editor: Gaurav Gavas
Project Editor: Janice Gonsalves
Proofreader: Safis Editing
Indexer: Tejal Daruwale Soni
Presentation Designer: Sandip Tadge

Production reference: 2120520

Published by Packt Publishing Ltd.
Livery Place
35 Livery Street
Birmingham B3 2PB, UK.

ISBN 978-1-83898-398-7

www.packt.com

packt.com

Subscribe to our online digital library for full access to over 7,000 books and videos, as well as industry leading tools to help you plan your personal development and advance your career. For more information, please visit our website.

Why subscribe?

- Spend less time learning and more time coding with practical eBooks and Videos from over 4,000 industry professionals
- Learn better with Skill Plans built especially for you
- Get a free eBook or video every month
- Fully searchable for easy access to vital information
- Copy and paste, print, and bookmark content

Did you know that Packt offers eBook versions of every book published, with PDF and ePub files available? You can upgrade to the eBook version at www.Packt.com and as a print book customer, you are entitled to a discount on the eBook copy. Get in touch with us at customercare@packtpub.com for more details.

At www.Packt.com, you can also read a collection of free technical articles, sign up for a range of free newsletters, and receive exclusive discounts and offers on Packt books and eBooks.

Contributors

About the authors

Bartosz Jarkowski is a SAP Technical Expert with over 12 years of experience working and leading complex technical projects in a variety of businesses and industry sectors. He has a deep working knowledge of SAP NetWeaver, SAP HANA, and Microsoft Azure. Bartosz works as a trusted advisor at Microsoft, offering thought leadership to global companies to improve the management and resilience of their SAP landscapes. Bartosz is an active contributor on SAP Community, where he answers questions and publishes technically-related blogs and articles.

Nick Morgan is a highly experienced IT infrastructure architect, who, for the last 18 years has focused on architecting solutions for SAP. He helped design some of the earliest virtualized SAP environments using Solaris Containers, and then in 2011 moved on to virtualizing SAP on VMware based platforms. Since 2017, Nick has worked for Microsoft as part of their Global SAP practice, helping customers with moving their SAP workloads to Azure. Nick also regularly speaks on behalf of Microsoft at SAP events in the UK.

> Writing a book was much harder than we initially thought. It wouldn't be possible without the support and continuous encouragement of our wives, Sarah and Kamila. Many evenings, weekends and even holidays were taken up with writing this book. Thank you!
>
> To the fantastic SAP team at Microsoft that we are honored to be part of. This book wouldn't be possible without the experience and knowledge from all our colleagues who are part of that team!
>
> —Nick and Bartosz

Credits

Sanjeev Kumar

Naga Surendran

Sarah Johnson

Juergen Thomas

John Chien

Ross LoForte

Divya Swarnkar

Skyler Hartle

Siddhartha Rabindran

Table of Contents

Chapter 1: Cloud Readiness   **1**
Why Azure for business-critical systems?   **1**
Customer stories   **3**
Why is Azure the best cloud platform for all SAP workloads?   **6**
   Azure compliance and security   6
   Azure scalability   9
   System availability   11
   Business continuity/disaster recovery   15
   Microsoft Cloud Adoption Framework for Azure   17
   Automation   18
   Insights and innovation   20
   Partnership   22
   Common misconceptions   24
   Conclusion   25
Migration readiness   **26**
   When to migrate   26
   Migration order   28
   Types of SAP migration to Azure   29
   Migration strategies   31
Non-NetWeaver applications   **34**
Successful work team   **34**
   Internal resources   35
   Partners   37
   Microsoft   38
Summary   **38**

Chapter 2: Architect SAP on Azure — 41
Landscape planning — 41
Azure landing zone — 42
Network connectivity — 44
Management groups, subscriptions, and resource groups — 47
Sizing — 48
Rehosting and replatforming — 49
New installations — 51
Other sizing considerations — 52
Virtual machines and storage — 53
Virtual machine size — 53
Virtual machine storage — 54
Cost considerations — 61
Resilience — 64
Planned and unplanned downtime — 64
SAP NetWeaver high availability — 66
Disaster recovery — 75
Backup — 85
Disaster recovery versus backup — 85
Filesystem backup — 85
Disk snapshot — 86
Database backup — 86
Database snapshot — 87
Database streaming backup — 88
Azure Backup — 88
Third-party backup solutions — 89
Azure Blob Storage for backup — 90
Monitoring — 91
Azure Diagnostics extension — 92
Azure Enhanced Monitoring Extension for SAP — 92
Azure Monitor — 93
Activity Logs — 94
Alerts — 94
Dashboards — 95
Azure Advisor — 95
SAP NetWeaver-based systems — 96
Supported platforms — 97
Sizing SAP systems — 99
CPU and memory — 99
Storage sizing — 101
Network sizing — 103
System deployment — 105
Standalone installation — 106
Distributed installation — 106
Highly available installation — 107
Multiple SAP databases running on one server — 109
Multiple components on one system (MCOS) — 109

Central services instance stacking	110
Additional considerations	**112**
SAP Business Suite	112
SAP S/4HANA and SAP Fiori	112
SAProuter and SAP Cloud Connector	114
SAP HANA	**115**
Supported platforms	**115**
Why SAP HANA certified platforms?	115
SAP HANA sizing	**116**
CPU and memory requirements	116
Network requirements	119
Storage requirements	120
System deployment	**125**
Standalone HANA deployment	125
HANA multiple components on one system (MCOS)	125
HANA multitenant database containers (MDC)	126
HANA scale-up and scale-out	127
SAP HANA resilience	**128**
SAP HANA high availability	129
HANA disaster recovery	136
HANA database backup	**139**
HANA backup to a filesystem	139
Azure Backup for SAP HANA	140
HANA backup using filesystem snapshot	141
HANA Backup using third-party tools	141
Monitoring and performance optimization	143
SAP Data Hub	**143**
Supported platforms	**144**
System sizing	**145**
System deployment	**145**
SAP Hybris commerce	**149**
Summary	**153**
Chapter 3: Migrate SAP to Microsoft Azure	**155**
Exploring migration	**155**
Planning	**158**
Interfaces	159
Move groups	159
Preparing the environment in Azure	160
Housekeeping and archiving	160
Data transfer	161
Transfer data using Azure Data Box	161
Network-based data transfer	161
Landscape review	**163**
Choosing the right migration method	**164**

Homogenous migration	164
Migration using backup/restore	164
Downtime-optimized backup/restore	166
Migration using DBMS replication	166
Migration using Azure Site Recovery	167
Heterogenous migration	**168**
Classical migration	168
Performance optimization	170
Execute System Export Preparation ahead of time	170
Export/import process optimization	170
Database Migration Option (DMO) with System Move option	175
Sequential data transfer	178
Parallel data transfer	178
Near-Zero Downtime Migration with DMO	180
Third-party options	180
Summary of migration options	181
Summary	**182**
Chapter 4: Transforming SAP in Azure	**183**
Identity and access management	**183**
SAP Single Sign-On with Azure AD	186
Data platform	**190**
Storage types in Microsoft Azure	193
Data extraction	194
Finding a use case	195
Data exploration	195
Data security	196
Delta extracts	196
Schedule	196
The right tool	197
Azure Data Factory	197
SAP connectors in Azure Data Factory	198
Big data analytics	201
Azure HDInsight	202
Azure Databricks	203
Integration between SAP HANA and Hadoop	204
Data visualization and business intelligence	208
Azure Data Catalog	211
Integration	**213**
Internet of Things	**218**
Summary	**220**
Index	**223**

1
Cloud Readiness

Why Azure for business-critical systems?

Many **Information Technology** (**IT**) executives, be they **Chief Information Officer** (**CIO**), **Chief Technology Officer** (**CTO**), or **Chief Digital Officer** (**CDO**), are under pressure from their business to consider cloud computing. In many sectors organizations are seeing increased competition from new entrants to their market, whose IT systems show a level of agility and flexibility with which they simply cannot compete. At the same time, they are concerned about whether they can really move their business-critical systems into the Cloud; can the cloud offer the security, scalability, and availability that their business requires?

The answer to that is simple: yes it can. Like all new technologies, the cloud has taken time to mature, but it has now reached a level where even the most critical business systems can run in the cloud. As examples, the first **Software as a Service** (**SaaS**) offerings were made available to customers in late 1999, which is 20 years ago, with the first **Platform as a Service** (**PaaS**) offerings arriving as long ago as 2002. The first **Infrastructure as a Service** (**IaaS**) offerings including compute and storage were released in 2002, and Microsoft itself announced the Windows Azure platform in October 2008, which became commercially available in February 2010, and now offers over 600 services across SaaS, PaaS, and IaaS.

For most organizations SAP is the key business system. If SAP is unavailable for any reason then potentially your business stops, or at least your ability to respond to your customers' needs is impacted. Because of this, it is understandable that you will be concerned whether such a critical system can run in the public cloud. However, the days when you truly ran your IT system on-premises have long since gone. Most organizations have been getting rid of their own data centres and are increasingly moving to co-location facilities.

Additionally, in many cases the management and operation of this IT has been outsourced to third parties. In this context the public cloud is nothing more than one or more additional virtual data centers connected to your existing wide area network.

So why should you move to cloud? In March 2019 Forrester published their report The Total Economic Impact™ of Microsoft Azure for SAP[1]. This report identified the following quantified benefits:

- Avoided cost of on-premises hardware of $7.2M
- Faster time-to-market for SAP releases worth $3.3M
- Avoided cost of overprovisioned hardware of $3.1M
- Avoided cost of reallocation of staff required to manage SAP infrastructure worth $1.2M
- Avoided cost of physical data center space valued at $1.1M

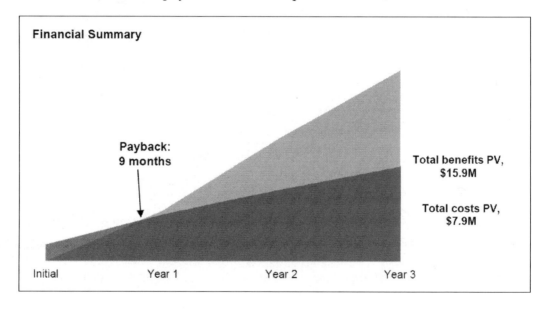

With overall benefits of $15.9M over three years versus costs of $7.9M, moving to Azure provides a **net present value (NPV)** of $8.0M and a **return on investment (ROI)** of 102%.

---

1 The Total Economic Impact™ of Microsoft Azure for SAP – a commissioned study conducted by Forrester Consulting, 12 April 2019:
https://azure.microsoft.com/en-gb/resources/sap-on-azure-forrester-tei/

For some, cost savings are one of the key drivers for moving SAP to Azure, while for others, aspects such as faster time to market are as important, if not more so. For many organizations, rather than driving innovation and change IT has in fact struggled to keep pace. By embracing Azure your IT department can become far more responsive and not only keep pace with the demand for change but become leaders in driving forward new innovations with data-driven insights. We will explore this in more detail later in this book.

Whatever your reasons for considering moving SAP to Azure, our purpose is to address your concerns and demonstrate that running SAP on Azure is not only possible but actually highly desirable. You should be reassured that you are not alone. At the time of writing in September 2019, over 800 organizations are at various stages of their journey to SAP on Azure. Some are fully productive, some with parts of their estate productive, and others are in various stages of migration. Of these, more than 80 are deploying SAP S/4HANA either as a conversion from ECC or as a net new implementation. Importantly, one of the largest customers for SAP on Azure is in fact Microsoft itself, who completed their migration to Azure in February 2018 and are now embarking on their journey to S/4HANA.

While this book focuses on SAP-supplied software and applications, it is important to remember that many SAP estates also include a number of third-party applications that are an integral part of the overall SAP application estate. These will also need to be moved. In general, the same approach can be taken to moving third-party applications as for SAP applications themselves. You do need to check that these applications are supported in Azure, and if there are any specific version, operating system, or database management system requirements to run in Azure. Most software vendors are less prescriptive than SAP, so moving to Azure is less likely to be a problem.

One final point to make is that this book only provides a high-level overview of each topic. Further information is publicly available on Microsoft websites such as docs.microsoft.com[2], with more detailed descriptions, best practices, and how-to guides. As Microsoft Azure is a constantly evolving platform, it is important to regularly check the documentation to find out about the latest features and how they can be used to run SAP on Azure.

Customer stories

Before delving into the details as to why Azure is the best cloud platform for all your workloads, let's start by looking at some of the existing customers that have already moved some or all of their SAP estate to Azure.

---

2   Use Azure to host and run SAP workload scenarios: `https://bit.ly/2PdICHQ`

Carlsberg Group[3] has been brewing since 1847 and is now the world's fourth largest beer manufacturer with 150 brands in more than 100 countries, and with net revenues in 2018 of DKK 62 billion (USD 9.4 billion). Some of Carlsberg's growth has come from acquisition, and this created IT challenges as each acquired company had its own IT systems. As part of a widescale corporate strategy (called SAIL'22), Carlsberg is embracing the cloud and digital technologies to drive product innovation and better experiences for customers.

Carlsberg's existing SAP estate was mostly running on IBM Power/AIX servers with an older version of the IBM DB2 database, except for SAP Business Warehouse, which was running on SAP HANA on SUSE Linux. As part of the migration to Azure Carlsberg migrated the AIX/DB2 SAP systems to Windows Server 2016 and Microsoft SQL Server 2016, and BW on HANA to Azure Large Instances. The solution is designed for both **high availability (HA)** and **disaster recovery (DR)** with failover to a secondary region. This whole migration was completed in six months.

In addition, Carlsberg has implemented the **Carlsberg Analytics Platform (CAP)** in Azure, which utilizes **Azure Data Factory (ADF)**, **Azure Data Lake Store Gen2 (ADLS Gen2)**, Azure Databricks, Azure SQL Data Warehouse, and Microsoft Power BI. CAP provides a unified platform for data analytics with the aim of allowing business analysts to gain new and improved insights from the structured and unstructured data that is now available.

As Sarah Haywood, Chief Technology Officer and Vice President of Technology of Carlsberg Group says: "*We're seeing a huge benefit in terms of scalability. We build out resources in the cloud as we need them, in a way that would have been impossible in a physical datacenter. We also trust in the security of Azure, which is important for any business site.*"

For Daimler AG[4] the challenge was to implement a **new procurement system (NPS)** to help the company transform its procurement services by providing greater transparency in contracts and unifying procurement processes across different business units and geographies. NPS was required to replace a legacy procurement system developed by Daimler in the 1990s that had become difficult to refresh, with the IT team only able to release new features a couple of times a year.

---

3 Customer Stories, Carlsberg Group: https://bit.ly/387ZQyU
4 Customer Stories, Daimler entrusts SAP HANA–based global procurement system to Microsoft Azure:
https://customers.microsoft.com/en-gb/story/daimler-manufacturing-azure

The new solution is based on SAP **Supplier Relationship Management (SRM)** on HANA with SAP S/4HANA and the **Icertis Contract Management (ICM)** platform. Daimler had already used Azure to deliver connected car, truck, and van projects to outfit its vehicles with **Internet of Things (IoT)** intelligence and remote monitoring capabilities, while ICM is natively architected on Microsoft Azure. As part of this solution SAP HANA runs on multiple large Azure M-series virtual machines.

Using Azure, Daimler was able to transform a key operational system months faster than it would have by using traditional on-premises methods. *To launch a project of this magnitude previously would have required up to 12 months just to acquire the necessary hardware*, says Dr. Stephan Stathel, Operations Lead for New Procurement System and Team Lead for the Build2Run Team at Daimler AG. *In Azure, we had the complete hardware set up in 12 weeks, which allowed development to start much sooner. We went live with NPS in just three months, which is unheard of by historic Daimler standards.*

Coke One North America (CONA) is a platform that provides each of the 12 largest Coca-Cola Company bottling partners in North America with tools they need to collaborate as one company. CONA Services LLC manages the solution specifically to support bottlers in North America. For CONA Services one of their biggest challenges was that if the migration was successful then they would have migrated the biggest SAP HANA instance to Azure at that time. Their aim was to migrate a SAP **Business Warehouse (BW)** on HANA system to SAP HANA on Azure Large Instances with SAP HANA in a scale-out 7+1 node configuration; 1 master node, 6 worker nodes, and 1 standby node. The SAP HANA database has a size of more than 12TB on disk, with 28TB of total memory on the active nodes.

Working with their partner and Microsoft CONA Services was able to complete the migration in just seven months, from initial planning to full production. The entire CONA platform now runs on Azure, making it easily accessible and scalable for bottlers and distributors. *We get cost value with Azure right now, and we're starting to clearly see increased performance*, says Brett Findley, Chief Services Officer at CONA Services. *Plus, we now have a base we can build on to provide greater capabilities in analytics and machine learning – so the results will only get better.* The new CONA Azure platform handles roughly 160,000 orders a day, which represents an annual $21 billion of net sales value. The company's bottlers use it to help them improve operations, speak the same technical language, and thrive in the digital age of bottling.

Hopefully these customer stories will reassure you that when you choose to move SAP to Azure you will not be the first. These are just some examples from the 800 (and that figure is growing) customers that have either moved to Azure or are in the process of moving.

Why is Azure the best cloud platform for all SAP workloads?

For most customers considering moving SAP to Azure there will be a number of key considerations:

- **Security**: Will my data be secure in Azure?
- **Scalability**: Will Azure have the performance and scalability to run my critical SAP workloads?
- **Availability**: Will Azure deliver the service levels that my business requires?
- **Disaster Recovery**: Will Azure deliver the business continuity my organization requires?
- **Cloud Adoption**: What do I need to do to move to Azure?
- **Automation**: How can I utilize cloud capabilities such as automation to be more agile?
- **Insights and innovation**: How can I leverage cloud-native services to enhance SAP?
- **Microsoft and SAP Partnership**: How closely are Microsoft and SAP aligned?
- **Responsibilities**: How do my responsibilties change when moving to Azure?

In this section we will look at each of these topics in turn. If you are already running other workloads in Azure then it is likely that you will already have addressed some of these topics, in which case please skip over those and jump to the topics that remain a concern.

Azure compliance and security

Compliance and security are normally the two main concerns for organizations when considering moving to the cloud; will I be able to comply with legal and industry-specific requirements, and will my data be safe? Because of this, these were also two of the main concerns for Microsoft when developing Azure.

When it comes to compliance Microsoft has the greatest number of compliance certifications of any public cloud, providing customers with the assurance they require to run their IT systems in Azure. Microsoft Azure has more than 50 compliance certifications specific to global regions and countries, including the US, the European Union, Germany, Japan, the United Kingdom, India, and China. In addition, Azure has more than 35 compliance offerings specific to the needs of key industries, including health, government, finance, education, manufacturing, and media. Full details are available on the Microsoft Trust Center[5].

When it comes to security there are still a lot of common misconceptions. The cloud does not mean that all your applications and data need to be exposed to the public internet; on the contrary most customers running applications in Azure will access them through private networks, either via **Virtual Private Networks (VPNs)** or, for business-critical applications such as SAP, by connecting **Wide Area Network (WAN)**, such as **multiprotocol label switching (MPLS)**, to Azure ExpressRoute. Essentially you can connect to systems and data in Azure in the same way that you connect to them today, whether running on-premises, in a **colocation (Colo)** data center, in a managed hosting environment, or in a private cloud.

Of course, you can provide public internet access to your systems in Azure when required, in a similar way to how you would when not in the cloud. You will typically create a **Demilitarized Zone (DMZ)** in Azure, protected by firewalls, and only expose those external-facing services that need to be accessed from untrusted network such as the internet. Many customers when starting to migrate workloads to Azure will in fact use their existing DMZ to provide external access, and simply route traffic via their WAN to the workloads running in Azure.

Many people are also concerned about the security of their data in Azure, where their data will be located, and who has access to that data. When it comes to data residency then when using Azure IaaS it is you who decides in which Azure Regions you want to deploy your workloads, and to where, if anywhere, that data will be replicated.

One of the currently unique features of Azure is that with a couple of minor exceptions Microsoft builds its Azure Regions in pairs. Each pair of regions is within the same geopolitical area so that from a customer perspective if your business requires true Disaster Recovery then you can replicate your data between two Azure Regions without needing to go outside your chosen geopolitical area.

---

5   Microsoft Trust Center:
https://www.microsoft.com/en-gb/trust-center/product-overview

In North America there are currently eight general purpose regions along with additional regions for the US Government and US **Department of Defense (DoD)**, Canada has East and Central, Europe West and North, the UK South and West, Asia East and Southeast, and so on. For some organizations this is essential if they are to be able to use the public cloud.

Once you have chosen the Azure regions in which you wish your data to reside, the next question is how secure is that data? All data stored in Azure is always encrypted while at rest by Azure **Storage Service Encryption (SSE)** for data at rest. Storage accounts are encrypted regardless of their performance tier (standard or premium) or deployment model (Azure Resource Manager or classic). All Azure Storage redundancy options support encryption, and all copies of a storage account are encrypted. All Azure Storage resources are encrypted, including blobs, disks, files, queues, and tables. All object metadata is also encrypted.

The default for Azure Storage Service Encryption is to use Microsoft-managed keys, and for many customers this may meet your requirements. However, for certain data and in certain industries it may be required that you use customer-managed keys, and this is supported in Azure. These customer-managed keys can be stored in the Azure Key Vault, and you can either create your own keys and simply store them in Key Vault, or use the Azure Key Vault API to generate the keys.

On top of the Azure Storage Encryption, you can choose to use Azure Disk Encryption to further protect and safeguard your data to meet your organizational security and compliance commitments. It uses the BitLocker feature of Windows and the DM-Crypt feature of Linux to provide volume encryption for the OS and data disks of Azure **virtual machines (VMs)**. It is also integrated with Azure Key Vault to help you control and manage the disk encryption keys and secrets, and ensures that all data on the VM disks are encrypted at rest while in Azure Storage. This combination of Azure Storage Service Encryption by default with the optional Azure Disk Encryption should meet the security and compliance needs of all organizations.

In addition to Storage and Disk Encryption you may wish to consider database-level encryption. All the SAP-supported **Database Management Systems (DBMS)** support some form of encryption: IBM DB2, Microsoft SQL Server, Oracle Database, SAP ASE, and SAP HANA. The exact details do vary by DBMS, but these are the same capabilities that are available in on-premises environments. One point to note is that it is not generally recommended to combine both Azure Disk Encryption with DBMS encryption, as this may impact performance.

Then there is the matter of encryption in transit. In order to encrypt traffic between the SAP application server and the database server, depending on the DBMS and version you can use either **Secure Sockets Layer (SSL)** or **Transport Layer Security (TLS)**. In general TLS is the preferred solution, as it is newer and more secure; however, where you have older DBMS versions in use then they may only support SSL. This may be a reason to consider a DBMS upgrade as part of the migration, which will normally provide other benefits such as enhanced HA and DR capabilities as well.

If you are using SAP GUI then you will also want to encrypt traffic between SAP GUI and the SAP application server. For this you can use SAP **Secure Network Communications (SNC)**. If you are using Fiori, then you should use HTTPS to secure the network communication. Many of you will already be using this today, so this should not be anything new.

Finally it is worth mentioning how **Azure Active Directory (AAD)** can be used to provide **Identity and Access Management (IAM)** for SAP applications. Whether a user is using the traditional SAP GUI, or they are use more modern web-based user interfaces such as SAP Fiori, AAD can provide **Single Sign-On (SSO)** for these applications[6]. In fact AAD provides SSO capabilities for most SAP applications including Ariba, Concur, Fieldglass, SAP Analytics Cloud, SAP Cloud for Customer (C4C0, SAP Cloud Platform, SAP HANA, and SuccessFactors. Many organizations are already using AAD to control access to solutions such as Office 365, and if it is already in place, extending its use to provide SSO across the SAP portfolio is very easy. This means not only can you use SSO, but you can also leverage other AAD capabilities such as **Conditional Access (CA)** and **Multi-Factor Authentication (MFA)**.

Azure scalability

For those with large SAP estates, and particularly some very large instances, then there may be concern about whether Azure can scale to meet your needs. This is a fair question as in the early days of Azure the IaaS service was primarily aimed at supporting smaller workloads or new cloud-native applications that are typically horizontally scalable. These applications require many small VMs rather than a few large VMs. Even in the world of SAP, the application tier can scale horizontally, but in general terms the database tier needs to scale vertically; while horizontally scalable database technologies such as **Oracle Real Application Cluster (RAC)** and SAP HANA Scale-Out are supported with SAP, they don't suit all SAP applications.

---

6   Tutorial: Azure Active Directory single sign-on (SSO) integration with SAP Fiori: `https://bit.ly/2s0dhA9`

SAP has been officially supported on Azure since May 2014 when SAP Note 1928533 was released with the title "SAP Applications on Azure: Supported Products and Azure VM types." To be fair, in the first version of that note support was fairly limited, with support for Microsoft SQL Server 2008 R2 or higher running on Microsoft Windows Server 2008 R2 or higher, and with a single supported Azure VM type of A5 (2 CPU, 14 GiB RAM, 1,500 SAPS). However, over the coming months and years support for a complete range of DBMSes and OSes was added rapidly with a wide range of Azure VM types supported. Now all the major DBMSes are supported on Azure for SAP – on Microsoft Windows Server, Oracle Linux (Oracle Database only), Red Hat Enterprise Linux, and SUSE Enterprise Linux operating systems[7]. As for supported VMs, these now scale all the way from the original A5 to the latest M208ms_v2 (208 CPU, 5.7 TiB RAM, 259,950 SAPS), with M416ms_v2 (416 CPU, 11.7 TiB RAM) announced and due for release before the end of 2019. Are you still concerned about scalability?

The next significant announcement came in September 2016 when Microsoft first announced the availability of Azure SAP **HANA Large Instances** (**HLI**). These are physical servers (sometimes referred to as bare metal servers) dedicated to running the SAP HANA database. As with VMs, HLI have continued to grow over the years and Microsoft now have SAP HANA Certified IaaS Platforms up to 20 TiB scale-up, and 60 TiB scale-out. Under the SAP HANA **Tailored Datacenter Integration** (TDI) Phase 5 rules, scale-up to 24 TiB and scale-out to 120 TiB is supported. Essentially Azure can support the same scale-up and scale-out as customers can achieve on-premises, as HLI leverages essentially the same servers as a customer can buy, but hosted and managed by Microsoft, and now within an Azure data center.

Some customers do question how a physical server can really be considered as a cloud solution. The reality is that physical servers will generally be one step ahead of any virtual servers because the physical server comes first. For any hypervisor developer new servers with more CPU and memory are required before they can test the new more scalable hypervisor, so physical will always come first. In addition, with only a very small number of customers requiring such large and scalable systems the economics of globally deploying hundreds or thousands of these servers in advance and hoping that the customers come really does not stack up. There are probably less than 1% of SAP customers globally that require such large systems.

---

7   Azure uses server hardware based on x86-64 architecture processors from Intel and AMD. As such Azure cannot support IBM AIX/Power, Hewlett Packard Enterprise HP-UX/Intel Itanium, or Oracle Solaris/SPARC workloads, and these must be migrated to Windows Server or Linux.

Ultimately these HLI systems address the edge case of the largest global SAP customers, meeting their needs for massive scalability, and enabling them to migrate the whole of their SAP estate to Azure. Without HLI they could not do this. For most customers one or two HLI will be used for their largest scale-up workload, normally ECC or S/4HANA, and their largest scale-out workload, normally BW or BW/4HANA.

In conclusion, whether you are running traditional SAP NetWeaver applications such as ECC, CRM, SRM, and so on, AnyDB (SAP's collective term for IBM DB2 UDB, Microsoft SQL Server, Oracle Database, SAP ASE, SAP HANA, SAP liveCache, and SAP MaxDB), or the latest S/4HANA and BW/4HANA, Azure has the scalability to meet your needs.

System availability

The third key concern of most people when considering the migration of SAP to Azure is availability.

Azure has been designed with availability in mind and there are multiple ways to provide HA for VMs in Azure.

At its simplest every VM in Azure is protected by Azure Service Healing, which will initiate auto-recovery of the VM should the host server have an issue. All VMs on the failing host will automatically be relocated to a different healthy host. The SAP application will be unavailable while the VM restarts, but typically this will complete within about 15 minutes. For some people this may be adequate, and many may already be familiar with and using this sort of recovery, as most hypervisors provide a similar capability in the on-premises environment.

The second Azure solution for HA is availability sets[8], which ensure that where two or more VMs are placed in the same availability set, these VMs will be isolated from each other.

---

8   Configure multiple virtual machines in an availability set for redundancy: https://bit.ly/362PAG9

Availability sets leverage two other Azure features as shown in *Figure 1-1*:

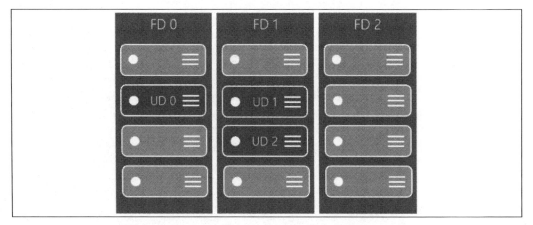

Figure 1-1: Azure fault and update domains

- **Fault domains (FD)** define a group of physical hosts that share a common power source and network switch. Potentially all the hosts within a fault domain could go offline if there is a failure of the power supply or network switch.
- **Update domains (UD)** define a set of hosts within a fault domain that may be updated at the same time, which could in some cases require the VMs to reboot.

When you create VMs in an availability set they will be placed in separate fault domains and update domains to ensure that you will not lose all the VMs if there is a fault or an enforced host reboot. Because there are only a finite number of fault and update domains once they have all been used, the next VM that is created in the availability set will have to be placed in the same fault and update domain as an existing VM.

When using availability sets the recommended solution is to create a separate availability set for each tier of each SAP application: the database tier, the (A)SCS tier, the application tier, and the web dispatcher tier. This is because if the total number of VMs exceeds the total number of fault domains then VMs will have to share the same FD. This will ensure that two database VMs in a cluster, or the (A)SCS and ERS in a cluster, will be placed in separate update domains in separate fault domains. Mix all the tiers together and there is the risk that these resilient pairs of VMs will be co-located in the same fault and/or update domain.

The final Azure solution for HA are availability zones, which are currently available in some but not all Azure regions. Where they are available each region will have three zones, with each zone having one or more separate data centres, each data centre having its own power, cooling, and network. This is shown in *Figure 1-2*[9]:

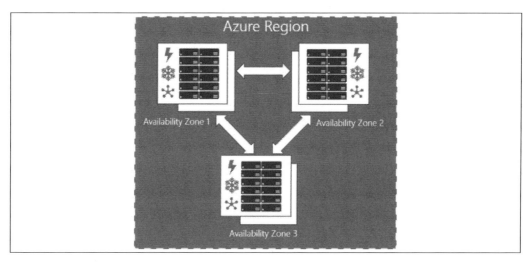

Figure 1-2: Azure availability zones

Availability zones provide a higher level of isolation than availability sets, as availability sets may be deployed within a single data centre, whereas availability zones span multiple data centres. With availability sets if something impacts the whole data centre then potentially all the VMs will be lost, whereas with availability zones multiple data centres would need to be affected before all the VMs are lost.

Based on these different solutions Microsoft Azure provides a **Service Level Agreement (SLA)** for Virtual Machines. The following financially backed guarantees are provided[10]:

- For any Single Instance Virtual Machine using premium storage for all Operating System Disks and Data Disks, we guarantee you will have Virtual Machine Connectivity of at least 99.9%;
- For all Virtual Machines that have two or more instances deployed in the same availability set, we guarantee you will have Virtual Machine Connectivity to at least one instance at least 99.95% of the time;

---

9   What are availability zones in Azure: `https://bit.ly/2RjH819`
10   SLA for Virtual Machines, Last updated: March 2018: `https://bit.ly/2rfPHj4`

- For all Virtual Machines that have two or more instances deployed across two or more availability zones in the same Azure region, we guarantee you will have Virtual Machine Connectivity to at least one instance at least 99.99% of the time.

It is important to note that this is an infrastructure SLA and is not the same as an application SLA. For example, if a virtual machine is restarted then as soon as the VM has restarted and a user can connect to the VM at operating system level, the downtime is considered to be finished. The application itself may take some more minutes to start, and if it is a VM running a large HANA database it could take many tens of minutes to fully reload memory.

So how do we use these availability options with SAP? For some customers Azure Service Healing will be sufficient to meet their HA needs as it will reboot VMs in the event of a host failure. In fact Azure Service Healing offers more than this, as it uses Machine Learning to predict potential hardware failures and will try to live migrate[11] VMs prior to a failure occurring to avoid any downtime. If your current on-premises landscape is already virtualized you may be relying on simple VM auto-restart to provide HA today, in which case Azure Service Healing offers better functionality than you currently have. However, it is important to know that Azure will very occasionally need to reboot VMs to make certain updates or patches, and while customers will be given warning of this and the opportunity to perform their own planned reboot, if this is not completed before the published deadline then your VMs will undergo a forced reboot.

If your SAP system is considered business-critical then it is very likely that you currently use some form of clustering to protect the database layer and the SAP (A) SCS (ABAP SAP Central Services/SAP Central Services for Java), and you may want to continue with this in Azure. There are some differences between clustering in an on-premises environment and clustering in Azure, but importantly clustering is fully supported.

The first difference is that Azure does not currently support the concept of shared disk storage for VMs, neither block storage nor file storage. This means that DBMS clustering solutions that rely on shared storage cannot be supported in Azure. However, SAP with its SAP HANA database has popularized the approach of shared-nothing clustering, where synchronous DBMS replication is used to keep two database instances fully synchronized, allowing failover between a primary and its standby to happen in seconds.

---

11   Live migration: https://bit.ly/368gPPV

In fact, this type of replication was not new as Microsoft introduced database mirroring with SQL Server 2008, and has continued to enhance the capabilities into what is now called SQL Server Always On Availability Groups. Similar solutions are also available with IBM DB2 LUW, Oracle Database, and SAP ASE; so all the mainstream-supported SAP DBMSes can provide a similar capability.

The second difference is that traditional operating system clusters generally rely on virtual IP addresses that can be migrated with a service when they are failed over from one machine to another. This type of floating virtual IP address is not supported in Azure. However, the functionality can be replaced by using Azure Load Balancers in front of each clustered service so that any process communicating with the clustered service always uses the Azure Load Balancer IP address, and in turn the Azure Load Balancer will route traffic to the currently active service. As with shared storage, there is a solution in Azure that meets the requirements to create a clustered solution.

While Azure provides the infrastructure and components to build a clustered solution, the actual responsibility for detecting a fault and initiating failover of a service, be it the database or SAP central services, falls to the operating system. All the supported operating systems can provide this capability, Microsoft Windows Server with Windows Server Failover Clustering, Red Hat, and SUSE Linux with Pacemaker, and for Oracle Linux a third-party product called SIOS Lifekeeper can be used. While there are some differences in capability all these clustering solutions have been enhanced to operate in Azure.

In conclusion it is possible to build the same type of highly available clustered solution for SAP in Azure as it has been historically on-premises. Some customers will deploy a range of solutions based on the criticality of individual SAP applications, rather than simply applying the same solution to every application.

Business continuity/disaster recovery

While High Availability addresses the issue of failure of infrastructure within an Azure region, most customers for whom SAP is business critical will also want a solution for **Disaster Recovery (DR)** should there be a whole Azure region-level failure. While you may consider the loss of an entire Azure Region to be highly unlikely, it is nonetheless possible and important to plan for what to do in such an event, were it to happen.

To support DR, with one or two exceptions Microsoft builds Azure Regions in pairs. These pairs of regions are in the same geopolitical area, allowing you to ensure that your data is kept within a particular jurisdiction. Azure is currently the only hyperscale cloud vendor to do this. Certain Azure services are inherently linked to these paired regions, such as **geo-redundant storage (GRS)**. In addition, Microsoft will only ever perform maintenance on one region within a pair to ensure that should the maintenance cause any problems and customers need to failover workloads to the other region in the pair then that region will not be undergoing any maintenance.

At a very minimum for DR you should plan to replicate backups to another Azure region. This will ensure that you have a copy of all data in an off-site location. It may take days to rebuild the infrastructure and restore data from backup, but at least the data is secure. Most customers pursuing this approach will build a minimal landing zone in the second region, with basic networking and security in place ready to start the rebuild process. This is not an ideal solution but where cost is critical, and where your business can survive without SAP for a number of days, then this may be adequate.

Where SAP is critical to your business it is likely that you will want a full-blown DR solution, with minimal data loss and the ability to recover service within a few hours. It is quite likely that you have agreements with your business to provide specific **Recovery Point Objectives (RPO)**, which define the acceptable level of data loss, and **Recovery Time Objectives (RTO)**, which define the time allowed to recover SAP. As for high availability you can use similar techniques in Azure for DR to those routinely used in the on-premises world. In this case you will build the complete foundation services in both regions so that all capabilities to run the complete production environment, as a minimum, are available in both regions.

The Azure regions are situated sufficiently far apart with the aim of ensuring that no single event will impact both regions in a pair. For example, you may consider 100 miles (160 kilometres) to be a safe distance between two data centres for DR purposes, but if they are both on the same river flood plain, or earthquake fault line, or hurricane path, then that is not adequate. Microsoft takes all this into account when deciding where to position regions, and which ones to pair. To ensure resilience, the regions are typically hundreds of miles apart, which means that only asynchronous replication is supported.

The most important first step is to protect the database, which you can do using DBMS asynchronous replication. The DBMS will replicate the data continuously, but by running asynchronously the latency and throughput of the network will not impact the performance of the primary database. This asynchronous replication can be supported alongside the synchronous replication used for HA, so that HA and DR can coexist.

For the application tier an Azure-native service called **Azure Site Recovery (ASR)** can be used to replicate the app server VMs. This takes regular snapshots of the VMs in the primary region and replicates them to the second region. ASR can provide either crash-consistent or application-consistent snapshots. By default, crash-consistent snapshots are taken every 5 minutes while application-consistent snapshots are taken every 60 minutes, although these defaults can be changed. For the SAP application, server VMs crash-consistent snapshots are adequate as there is no user data that needs to be protected.

ASR uses Recovery Plans to allow the sequencing of the way in which VMs are restored. You can also add your own scripts to ASR and these can include a pre-action script, for example, to failover the DBMS and promote the DR copy to active, and a post-action script, for example, to attach a load balancer to any clustered VMs once they have been failed over.

The final element of the SAP application that needs to be protected is the SAP (A)SCS. If the (A)SCS is part of an HA cluster with the **Enqueue Replication Server (ERS)** in the primary site then they will be using a file share, either SMB for Windows or NFS for Linux, to share files between the two VMs. Because of this, replication with ASR is not currently supported. The recommended solution is to create an (A)SCS VM in the secondary region and replicate any changes on the shared file systems using a scripted copy for Windows or Linux rsync.

Microsoft Cloud Adoption Framework for Azure

If you are already using Azure for other non-SAP workloads then it is likely you have a cloud foundation in place, in which case you can skip this section, but if you are uncertain or this is your first deployment in Azure then please read on. The Microsoft **Cloud Adoption Framework (CAF)** for Azure[12] is based on Microsoft's experience of working with a wide range of customers over the last several years as they have deployed workloads into Azure. To quote from CAF, *The framework gives enterprise customers tools, guidance, and narratives that help shape technology, business, and people strategies for driving desired business outcomes during their adoption effort.* The CAF builds on earlier Microsoft documentation such as the Azure Enterprise Scaffold[13] and the Cloud Operating Model[14].

---

12   Microsoft Cloud Adoption Framework for Azure:
https://docs.microsoft.com/en-us/azure/architecture/cloud-adoption/
13   Azure Enterprise Scaffold: https://bit.ly/2ORCCWj
14   Cloud Operating Model: https://bit.ly/34OJ7i8

The easiest way to understand the CAF is to think of it as providing the foundation for running your business in Azure. It covers the complete adoption life cycle from defining your strategy, through planning and readiness, to migration and innovation, and ultimately to management and operation. Like the foundations of any building, it may not be the most exciting aspect of the project, but it is probably the most essential. Put the right foundations in place and it becomes relatively easy to move new workloads to Azure and to ensure that your governance and security policies will be met. Fail to do this and the potential for problems to occur later in the project are high.

The only time you probably don't need to consider CAF is where you are working with a partner who will deliver **SAP as a Service (SAPaaS)** under the Microsoft **Cloud Service Provider (CSP)** model. In this case you will simply consume SAP applications under some form of pay as you go model, and the CSP will be responsible for the cloud foundation.

Automation

If you are to gain the full benefits of Azure, then it is essential that you embrace automation. How much automation will depend on your individual circumstances, and finding the right balance is key. At first glance it is easy to look at the Azure Portal and think to yourself, "this makes configuring resources so easy, why would I bother to invest in automation? To provision a new VM takes only a few minutes, only requires you to answer a few questions, and the hard work is handled by Azure." However, this tends to forget that people are generally poor at achieving repeatability.

In general SAP landscapes involve a relatively small number of relatively large VMs, which tends to feed the assumption that automation is not important. However, anyone with experience of SAP will be familiar with the challenges created by configuration drift between your development, QA/Test, Pre-Production, and Production environments. This can make it very difficult to diagnose and debug problems, where you think all the environments are the same when in reality they are not.

From experience working with a number of customers, there are three main approaches to automation:

1. **Empower the user**: Make it simple for the person requesting the resource to provision the resources that they require. This needs to ensure that all the security and governance rules are automatically applied, along with an approval process to limit who can provision what and when. In the world of SAP this will generally provision and configure the infrastructure but leave it to the SAP specialist to install and configure the required SAP software.

For a SAP BASIS administrator to know they can get the resources they need in a matter of a few minutes or even a few hours is a major step forward and supports the move towards a more DevOps culture for SAP development.

2. **Empower the infrastructure team**: Make it even easier for the person requesting the resource, while empowering the infrastructure team to deliver a fully working system. In this scenario the requestor outsources the whole responsibility to the Azure team, who not only use automation to build the infrastructure but also to install and configure the SAP application as far as possible, with potentially a few manual steps. For an SAP developer this takes delivery to the next level as they simply request the application that they want and wait to be told when it is available.

3. **None of the above**: Use minimal or no automation and the infrastructure team simply continues to build every VM manually via the Azure portal, Azure CLI, Azure PowerShell, or Azure Cloud Shell.

Unfortunately, option 3 is all too common and is what leads to mistakes and configuration drift. There are several reasons for this. Firstly, there are often time pressures to get the infrastructure built as quickly as possible. By the time you have made the decision to move to Azure most projects are already running behind schedule. Then you have no history of using automation in your on-premises world, and the basic Azure tools for manually building infrastructure are probably light years ahead of what you have been used to, so it is tempting just to wade in and get building. Finally building out the required automation requires you to learn new skills and takes time, providing rewards later in the project life cycle but potentially delaying the start. The answer is potentially to manually build the initial VMs while in parallel developing the automation skills, so that by the time you get to provisioning preproduction and production, the automation skills are in place.

The level of automation you should implement will depend on many factors. If SAP is to be your only workload in Azure, and you run a very static environment, then creating some basic ARM templates to improve consistency may meet all your needs. If, however, you are embracing Azure as part of a business transformation program, with a cloud-first strategy and a desire to drive business growth through IT innovation, then it makes sense to invest and build a more sophisticated solution.

The ultimate goal of automation is to deliver Infrastructure as Code, to allow infrastructure to be delivered quickly and consistently while complying with all the required governance. A number of enterprise customers have totally embraced automation. All requests for services in Azure are initiated through an IT Service Management request, which handles the approvals process. If approved the required infrastructure will be automatically provisioned and configured and the software installed.

The infrastructure is guaranteed to conform to all policies and will be correctly tagged to ensure full financial control. Finally, a **configuration management database** (**CMDB**) is updated to track all the assets and software licences to ensure full auditability. For non-production systems the infrastructure may even have a time limit, so that once expired the infrastructure will automatically be deleted again; the requestor will be notified before this and can request an extension if needed.

One of the more recent innovations is Azure Blueprints[15]. Blueprints provide a declarative way for you to define and deploy a repeatable set of resources that adhere to the requirements, standards, and patterns of your organization. Importantly, Blueprints are stored within Azure and globally distributed and can contain Azure resource templates as artifacts. Azure Blueprints is still in preview at the time of writing (October 2019) but should be generally available in the coming months.

If all this sounds quite daunting then there are a number of partners who have developed specific skills around the automation of Azure in general, and some with a particular focus on the automation of SAP in Azure. They can either provide you with automation as a service, whereby you simply consume their tooling to automate deployments into Azure, or in some cases will help you to develop the tooling that you require, and then hand it over to you to maintain and enhance as required.

Insights and innovation

For many organizations the motivation for moving SAP to Azure is part of a wider strategy of IT transformation, aimed at gaining greater insights and using these to drive innovation. While not an essential pre-requisite it makes sense to put SAP, the core system of record, into the same cloud that will be used for insights and innovation.

While most SAP customers have been using SAP BW to support both operational reporting and analytics, with a few exceptions BW has primarily been used for data sourced from other SAP applications. With the rapid growth of **Advanced Analytics** (**AA**) and **Machine Learning** (**ML**) there is a much greater need to take data from multiple sources, both structured and unstructured, to be used to support AA and ML, and ultimately **Artificial Intelligence** (**AI**). Because of the different types of data and the sheer volume, most organizations are looking to do this in hyperscale cloud.

---

15   Overview of the Azure Blueprints service:
https://docs.microsoft.com/en-us/azure/governance/blueprints/overview

Microsoft Azure has a whole range of native services available to support advanced analytics on big data[16], as well as being able to utilize a wide range of third-party solutions running in Azure. A common solution is to use ADF to extract data from SAP and store it in **Azure Data Lake Storage** (**ADLS**), where the data can be prepared and blended ready for analysis using tools such as Databricks. One of the benefits you enjoy is the ability to consume these Azure services as required and only pay for what you use. Many of you are probably still at the experimental stage, and the ability to rapidly stand up a solution in Azure, test it, and then either productionize it or tear it down and start again is a major benefit.

When it comes to SAP data there is often tension between the data scientists and the SAP team. The data scientists will generally start from the position of "give me all the data and I will decide what to do with it later," and for some data sources this may be fine. If you are extracting sentiment data from social media, then the data is already public and retrieving and storing it for future analytics may make sense. However, the data inside an SAP system is often more sensitive and is not generally in the public domain, or even widely available within your organization. SAP has a very sophisticated security model that ensures that users can only see the data that they need to see in order to fulfill their role in the organization.

While attitudes will change and evolve over time, the most successful projects currently begin with the end in mind[17]; that is, they start with a business outcome in mind and work back from that to determine the data required to deliver that outcome. In this way when it comes to extracting data from SAP there is a clear objective in mind, and you only need to extract the data required to deliver that outcome. In many cases the data required may not be considered highly sensitive, or if necessary sensitive data can be masked in such a way that the objective can still be achieved.

Using these data-driven insights you can start to drive innovation within your business, which is at the top of the agenda for many at the CxO level. With new startup disruptors appearing in many industries the ability to adapt and innovate has never been more pressing. Most of these start-ups are born in the cloud and have been leveraging advanced analytics as an integral part of their business model from the start. Traditional organizations must adopt similar strategies, but have the opportunity to mine the vast amounts of historical data that they hold to get even greater insights and to compete successfully.

---

16   Advanced analytics on big data: `https://bit.ly/2YkmcsE`
17   A slight misappropriation from The 7 Habits of Highly Effective People, Covey, Stephen R., Simon and Schuster

Partnership

Microsoft and SAP have a partnership that goes back as far as 1993, and the release of SAP R/3. This early relationship was primarily a technology one, the two companies working together to ensure that SAP technologies would support and integrate with Microsoft technologies. The relationship really started with SAP R/3 and the SAP GUI for Windows and then moved forward with the support for SAP R/3 running on Microsoft Windows NT Server and Microsoft SQL Server.

The partnership was strengthened when more than 20 years ago Microsoft chose to deploy SAP as the core ERP system to run its business. Microsoft was now both a partner and a customer. Over the years Microsoft's SAP system has grown to be one of the largest SAP ERP systems globally. As of May 2019, the size of this ERP/ECC system is as follows[18]:

- 16 TB of compressed database (equivalent of 50 TB uncompressed)
- 110,000 internal users
- 6,000 named user accounts
- 300,000 monitored jobs per month
- Up to 270 million transaction steps per month
- Up to 10 million dialog steps per day

However, ERP/ECC is only one of the SAP applications used by Microsoft; others include E-Recruiting, GRC, GST, CPM, SCM, OER, MDG, and SMG. In total the SAP estate comprises more than 600 servers, which between 2017 and February 2018 were moved entirely to Azure VMs. Microsoft now runs SAP 100% in Azure and is embarking on the first phase of its move to S/4HANA, also now deployed in Azure.

As part of this ongoing partnership, in November 2017 SAP announced[19] that it would move some of its key internal business-critical systems to Azure. As part of a further announcement in June 2018[20] Thomas Saueressig, CIO of SAP, shared an update on progress with this migration:

---

18   Building an agile and trusted SAP environment on Microsoft Azure: https://bit.ly/34SSk8W
19   Microsoft and SAP join forces to give customers a trusted path to digital transformation in the cloud, 27 November 2017: https://bit.ly/2DLglTo
20   Offering the largest scale and broadest choice for SAP HANA in the cloud, 5 June 2018: https://bit.ly/2LoNDwa

> *"In 2017 we started to leverage Azure as IaaS Platform. By the end of 2018 we will have moved 17 systems including an S/4HANA system for our Concur Business Unit. We are expecting significant operational efficiencies and increased agility which will be a foundational element for our digital transformation."*

In September 2018 Microsoft, Adobe, and SAP announced the **Open Data Initiative (ODI)**[21] with the objective of unlocking the data held in applications from all three entities, and potentially other third-party software, by combining that data in a data lake where AI can be used to derive insights and intelligence. In an update in March 2019[22] it was announced that:

> *"… the three companies plan to deliver in the coming months a new approach for publishing, enriching and ingesting initial data feeds from Adobe Experience Platform, activated through Adobe Experience Cloud, Microsoft Dynamics 365, and Office 365 and SAP C/4HANA, into a customer's data lake. This will enable a new level of AI and machine learning enrichment to garner new insights and better serve customers."*

As part of that November 2017 news release the availability of SAP **HANA Enterprise Cloud (HEC)** on Microsoft Azure was announced, enabling customers that want the SAP-managed cloud service to also leverage Azure hyperscale cloud. This is all part of SAP's wider strategy of making its "as a Service" offerings available on hyperscale cloud. Today this includes Ariba, Data Custodian, C/4HANA, SuccessFactors, and SAP Cloud Platform, all of which are available in certain Azure Regions.

Further strengthening this partnership in February 2019, SAP unveiled SAP Leonardo IoT[23] at Mobile World Congress in Barcelona. At the same time SAP announced that SAP Leonardo IoT will interoperate with Microsoft Azure IoT Hub and that SAP Leonardo IoT Edge **essential business function (EBF)** modules are planned to run in containers on Microsoft Azure IoT Edge.

---

21   Adobe, Microsoft and SAP announce the Open Data Initiative to empower a new generation of customer experiences, 24 September 2018: https://bit.ly/363LHRl
22   Adobe, Microsoft and SAP announce new Open Data Initiative details, 27 March 2019: https://bit.ly/2rjr6tJ
23   SAP Leonardo IoT Helps Shape the Intelligent Enterprise, 25 February 2019: https://bit.ly/2Rm8La7

Further details of this integration are covered in a Microsoft blog post[24]. Through this interoperability SAP Leonardo IoT will be able to leverage the market-leading secure connectivity and powerful device management functionality provided by Azure IoT Services, and stream data back to SAP's business applications. By running Leonardo EBF modules on Azure IoT Edge key business processes at the edge and avoid issues with network connectivity, latency, and bandwidth.

Most recently in May 2019 SAP announced project "Embrace,"[25] a collaboration between SAP, the hyperscale cloud providers, and some of SAP's **global strategic service partners** (**GSSPs**). The aim is to help customers move to S/4HANA in the cloud following market-approved journeys, which provide you with a blueprint for your journey towards an intelligent enterprise. At the same time Microsoft announced[26] that it is the first global cloud provider to join this project.

Common misconceptions

There are some common misconceptions about the cloud in general and running SAP on Azure in particular. As already mentioned, when you run SAP in Azure you are utilizing Azure IaaS, primarily VMs, storage, and networking. As such it is your responsibility to create the infrastructure, install and configure the SAP software, configure SAP for HA and DR, and manage your own backups. None of this happens automatically.

At the heart of the confusion is how IaaS is different to both PaaS and SaaS. With SaaS in particular you simply consume the application without any need to install any software, or concern yourself with matters such as HA, DR, and backup. You will have a SLA for the application and it is up to the application provider to take the necessary steps to deliver the SLA. Similarly, when consuming PaaS services in general the level of availability you require is something you choose when initiating the service, and the software provides the capability seamlessly.

---

24   MWC 2019: Azure IoT customers, partners accelerate innovation from cloud to edge, 25 February 2019: https://bit.ly/2OQ4kCz
25   SAP Partners with Ecosystem to Guide Customers to the Cloud, 9 May 2019: https://bit.ly/2PdJNXM
26   Microsoft partners with SAP as the first global cloud provider to launch Project Embrace, 9 May 2019: https://bit.ly/2sMBf2t

As an example of an Azure PaaS service, with Azure SQL Database you can choose different service tiers – general purpose, business critical, and hyperscale – which offer different levels of availability and redundancy. In addition, backups are taken automatically, written to **read-access geo-redundant storage (RA-GRS)** so that the backups are available even if the region becomes unavailable, and there is an option to configure long-term retention. All of this is handled automatically by Azure with minimal input required once the service has been created.

Further confusion arises from the fact that SAP has their own cloud offering called SAP HEC[27]. This combines cloud hosting with a range of HEC Standard Services, HEC Optional Services, and HEC **Enhanced Managed Services (EMS)**[28]. Even the HEC Standard Service provides most of the day-to-day services required to keep an SAP system running. As described elsewhere you can now combine these two worlds by choosing HEC on Azure, where SAP provides the HEC Services offering but utilizes Azure IaaS. As an aside, despite the name, HEC allows SAP customers to run any SAP application running on any SAP DBMS (HANA, ASE, MaxDB, and so on). It is not exclusively restricted to applications running on HANA.

When you deploy SAP in Azure it does not become either a PaaS or a SaaS offering; you are simply utilizing Azure IaaS. This is further brought home by SAP's recent naming convention, where for SAP S/4HANA you deploy the On-Premises Edition even when the deployment is going into a hyperscale cloud such as Azure, or into SAP's own HEC. S/4HANA Cloud Edition is only available as a Service from SAP and cannot be downloaded and installed elsewhere.

If what you want is a fully managed SAP service – SAP as a Service – then you can either opt for SAP HEC on Azure or work with one of the many partners that Microsoft has that can offer such a service, which includes **Global Systems Integrators (GSI)**, **National Systems Integrators (NSI)**, and local SAP Services Partners.

Conclusion

In this section we have covered a range of subjects related to running SAP on Azure. Hopefully this has addressed any fears or concerns that you may have and helped to convince you that there are no technical limitations to running SAP on Azure. In the next section we will look at how to migrate SAP to Azure.

---

27 SAP HANA Enterprise Cloud:
https://www.sap.com/uk/products/hana-enterprise-cloud.html
28 SAP HANA Enterprise Cloud (HEC) Services Documentation:
https://www.sap.com/about/agreements/policies/hec-services.html?tag=language:english

Migration readiness

This section will cover the various ways in which you can prepare to migrate your SAP workloads over to Azure. Let's begin with the first thing to consider: when should you migrate?

When to migrate

There are three main factors that determine when is a good time to migrate your SAP workloads to Azure, and for many customers it may be some combination of all three:

1. Your existing infrastructure is due for a refresh, and you must decide whether to refresh what you have today or use this as an opportunity to migrate to Azure.

2. Your existing outsourcing, hosting, or co-location contract is up for renewal and this provides an opportunity to look at different hosting options, such as Azure.

3. You are planning a migration to SAP Business Suite on HANA, SAP S/4HANA, SAP BW on HANA, or SAP BW/4HANA, and you want to avoid the capex cost of purchasing new infrastructure to run SAP HANA, and also want the agility and flexibility offered by Azure.

Ultimately every customer that plans to continue to run SAP must plan to move to SAP S/4HANA before the deadline of 31st December 2025, which is the current end of support for SAP Business Suite 7 core application releases and SAP Business Suite powered by SAP HANA[29]. Whether you are ready to move today, or planning to move in the next few years, moving your existing SAP estate to Azure now will provide much greater flexibility for the future.

From an infrastructure perspective one of the biggest challenges for customers when moving to SAP HANA is that the hardware required to run SAP HANA is very different to that required for AnyDB. SAP HANA is an in-memory database, which by default loads all HANA table data into memory at startup and requires additional temporary memory as working memory to allow the table data to be processed; for example, for table joins. While a VM with 64 GiB memory may be adequate to run a productive AnyDB instance with 2 TiB of data on disk, to run that same database on HANA could require up to 4 TiB memory; 2 TiB for table data and 2 TiB for temporary memory, based on SAP recommendations. In reality there will generally be some reduction in size of the data when migrating to SAP HANA, and potentially even more when migrating to SAP S/4HANA, so 2 TiB or even 1 TiB of memory may prove sufficient, but still that is a lot more than 64 GiB.

29   SAP Support Strategy, Maintenance 2025:
https://support.sap.com/en/offerings-programs/strategy.html

By moving to Azure when your next hardware or data centre refresh comes around allows you to better prepare for the migration to SAP HANA. If you make another Capex investment, then that will generally be depreciated over three to five years. If during this time you decide to move to SAP HANA then you will need to purchase new hardware for SAP HANA, while still depreciating the hardware you already have for AnyDB. This can play havoc with budgets, particularly if you decide to buy the new SAP HANA hardware as a further Capex investment. By moving to Azure you can instead stand up today the VMs you need for AnyDB, and when the time is right to move to SAP HANA simply stand up new larger VMs for SAP HANA, and once the migration is complete, shutdown, delete, and stop paying for the AnyDB VMs.

If you are running SAP on-premises and considering a migration to SAP HANA today, then once again deploying SAP HANA in Azure has many benefits. Firstly if you are still depreciating the existing hardware for your on-premises AnyDB then deploying SAP HANA in Azure will normally be classed as Opex, so will not impact your Capex budget in the same way, although this may depend on internal accounting practices along with local regulations. This may well reduce some of the financial challenges.

Also, customers moving to SAP HANA are often uncertain as to the exact size that their databases will be. If it is a net new implementation, for example a greenfield implementation of SAP S/4HANA or SAP BW/4HANA, then it can be hard to size the initial system and also predict future growth, although the SAP Quick Sizer can help here. If it is a migration to SAP HANA or a conversion to S/4HANA or BW/4HANA, then SAP do provide reports that you can run to estimate the future size of your SAP HANA database[30]. But even then, this is just an estimate, and predicting future growth can be challenging.

In most cases if you are deploying SAP HANA on-premises then you will use an SAP HANA Certified Appliance[31]. With any capex investment in hardware for SAP it is normal practice to try and predict the size that you will require for the depreciation life of the hardware; typically you are predicting three or even five years ahead. With all the uncertainty over initial sizing and future growth you must choose between choosing a larger appliance and simply accept the high cost, to minimize the risk of outgrowing the appliance, or choose a smaller lower-cost option and risk running out of capacity.

---

30   SAP Notes 1872710 – ABAP on HANA sizing report (S/4HANA, Suite on HANA…) and 2610534 – HANA BW Sizing Report (/SDF/HANA_BW_SIZING)
31   Certified and Supported SAP HANA Hardware Directory, Certified Appliances: https://bit.ly/387B1mQ

To make matters worse most appliance vendors have to switch server models as the memory grows, so expansion part way through the life of an appliance may in fact mean purchasing a net new appliance.

With Azure these problems mostly go away. With SAP HANA certified Azure VMs you can start with what you need today, and simply resize the VM as and when it is required. This keeps your initial costs lower, by not over provisioning, but still allows you to scale as the database grows. In addition, you can easily scale up the SAP application tier, adding additional application server VMs to address peak workloads, and shut them down again when not required.

In addition, most customers know that they should right size before migrating to SAP HANA, reducing capacity through data archiving or deletion, but the reality is this may not be possible. SAP has always recommended that customers implement Information Life cycle Management for data held in SAP to improve performance, reduce infrastructure costs, and provide governance, risk, and compliance for enterprise data. However, many organizations fail to do this, because no data retention policies exist, and for many years now infrastructure has become faster and cheaper, so it has not been essential.

SAP HANA does change the economics of this as the cost per TB of storing data in memory rather than on disk is typically an order of magnitude higher. It does not take as long to build a compelling business case for archiving when the additional infrastructure costs for SAP HANA are considered. While the project timescales may make right sizing before migration impossible, in Azure it is much easier to stand up an oversized VM for the initial migration, then archive, delete, and right size the VM once the data is in Azure.

Migration order

You may be asking whether SAP should be the first workload that you migrate to Azure, or whether you should leave it until later in your cloud migration strategy, or even right to the end. The answer is that there is no right or wrong answer, and we see customers where SAP is first and others where it is towards the end: it normally depends on the compelling event.

Some of you will have already started to deploy other workloads in Azure, having your cloud adoption framework in place, when the compelling event to migrate SAP to Azure comes along. While the foundations may be in place, for many of you SAP will still be the largest and most critical workload that you have yet moved to Azure. So, all the issues around security, scalability, and availability still need to be addressed with respect to SAP before the migration can begin. However, hopefully at least some of the work will have already been undertaken. What is important is that having the Azure foundation in place should speed up the migration process.

Others may be yet to deploy any workloads into Azure when a compelling SAP event arrives. This means a steeper learning curve for you, because you need to understand a lot more about how SAP runs in Azure before you can make the decision that you want to migrate your SAP workloads. For those in this position, this book should help. Starting with SAP does add an additional step to the process because you will need to build the bare bones of an Azure foundation before you can start to deploy SAP in Azure. You wouldn't build a house without first putting in the foundations, so you shouldn't deploy workloads in Azure without first building the foundations.

Types of SAP migration to Azure

Migrating SAP to Azure is no different to any other type of SAP migration. Many customers will already have undertaken a SAP migration whether it be migrating from a traditional Unix operating system such as AIX, HP-UX, or Solaris to Linux or Windows, or migrating from one data centre to another; from old to new on-premises, or on-premises to co-location, managed hosting, or similar. The migration approaches are very similar when Azure is the target; essentially Azure is just another data centre connected to your corporate WAN.

There are two main types of SAP migration to Azure:

- **Brownfield**: Where you have existing SAP workloads you want to migrate from on-premises to Azure, potentially with an OS or database migration, and maybe an upgrade or conversion
- **Greenfield**: Where you plan to start afresh in Azure with a new implementation of SAP, whether or not you have existing SAP workloads on-premises

Brownfield migrations are by far the most common, and these in turn fall into four main categories as shown in *Figure 1-3*:

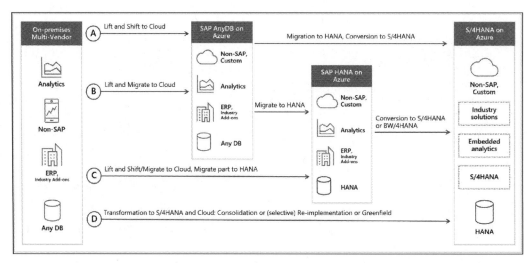

Figure 1-3: Options for SAP migration to Azure

- **Lift and Shift to Cloud**: Where the existing OS and DBMS used on-premises are supported in Azure, and you have no plans to migrate to HANA at this time, a lift and shift or rehosting is possible. This is normally referred to as an SAP Homogeneous System Copy and is the simplest type of migration.

- **Lift and Migrate to Cloud**: Where the existing OS is not supported in Azure – HPE HP-UX/IA64 or HP-UX/PA-RISC, IBM AIX/Power, Oracle Solaris/SPARC, or Solaris/x64 – or there is a desire to change the DBMS, then a lift and migrate or replatforming is the solution. This is normally referred to as an SAP Heterogeneous System Copy and while it is more complicated than lift and shift, there is a well-proven path using tools such as SAP R3load or the SAP **Database Migration Option (DMO)** of the **Software Update Manager (SUM)** where the target DBMS is SAP HANA.

- **Lift and Shift/Migrate to Cloud, migrate part to HANA**: Particularly if facing an OS/database migration this may be a good time to consider migrating at least part of the SAP landscape to SAP HANA, if you have not already done this. Migrating BW on AnyDB to BW on HANA will provide an immediate performance boost and will allow you to start to get familiar with SAP HANA before you migrate to S/4HANA. Importantly, if you are currently using BW Accelerator then that is not supported in Azure and a migration to SAP HANA is the recommended route forward from SAP.

- **Transformation to S/4HANA**: If facing an OS/database migration, then this could be an excellent time to consider a conversion from ECC to S/4HANA. A basic conversion can be done with minimal disruption to end users and will ensure you are ready for 31st December 2025.

For some of you the move to S/4HANA represents an opportunity to get rid of years of customizations and to standardize business processes possibly using the SAP Model Company. When you originally implemented SAP those customizations may have been essential to meet your business requirements, but as SAP has evolved the functionality has increased and now the standard functionality may better meet your business needs. If this is the case, then you may prefer a greenfield migration.

Microsoft has several customers globally either live with greenfield S/4HANA implementation, or in the process of deployment. A small number are net new SAP customers, but the majority are customers that have been using SAP for 10, 15, or even 20 years, but want to start afresh with S/4HANA. They are deploying S/4HANA in Azure for all the reasons stated above, because they may still be finalizing the sizing, want to start small and grow with their data, and do not want to make large upfront capex investments in the hardware needed to run the SAP HANA database than underpins S/4HANA.

Migration strategies

When it comes to brownfield migrations it is important to plan the order in which the migrations will take place. To some extent this will depend on whether you are planning a homogeneous or an heterogeneous migration, and also the downtime window available for the migration.

A homogeneous migration, or in SAP terminology a homogeneous system copy, is one where there is no change to either OS or DBMS. For SAP workloads in Azure the supported operating systems are Microsoft Windows Server, **Red Hat Enterprise Linux (RHEL)**, **SUSE Enterprise Linux (SLES)**, and Oracle Linux; the latter only for Oracle DBMS. If you are currently running SAP on any other operating system, then you will need to undertake a heterogeneous system copy.

A heterogeneous system copy is one where either the OS, the DBM, or both are changed. This is a well-proven path and SAP have several tried and tested tools for carrying out such migrations. If you need to undertake a heterogeneous migration because you must change the operating system, then this also provides an opportunity to consider changing the DBMS as well.

Cloud Readiness

While SAP used to advise against combining multiple changes into one, it is now common for customers to combine a SAP application upgrade with an OS and/or DBMS migration into a single delivery. If there are problems it can make diagnosing the cause more difficult – was it the software upgrade, the OS migration, or the DBMS migration? – but in terms of testing effort and business disruption it is generally preferred.

Homogeneous migrations are the simplest and offer the most migration options. The simplest solution will be a simple backup and restore, taking a full system backup on-premises, copying over the backup files, and then restoring them into Azure. Where downtime needs to be minimized then DBMS replication can be used to set up a new database instance in Azure and add it as a replication target to the primary on-premises. Because there is no change to the OS or DBMS there will be no compatibility issues.

In contrast heterogeneous migrations, while well proven, are more complicated and will normally require more downtime. The standard SAP tool for this is known as R3load, which exports data from the source database into flat files and then imports the flat files into the target database. While SAP now refer, to using **Software Provisioning Manager (SWPM)** and **Database Migration Option (DMO)** of SAP **Software Update Manager (SUM)** for heterogeneous system copies, in reality R3load remains at the heart of the actual migration process.

When it comes to the order in which to migrate an SAP estate there are two main options as shown in *Figure 1-4*[32]:

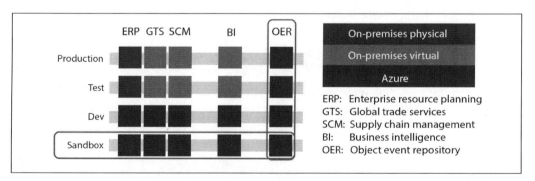

Figure 1-4: Horizontal versus vertical migration

---

32 Strategies for migrating SAP systems to Microsoft Azure: `https://bit.ly/2rRNTg5`

With horizontal migrations each landscape is moved one environment at a time. For example, you may move all the Development environments into Azure, then the QA/Test environments, followed by the Pre-Production environments, and finally the Production environments. In general, this method only makes sense for homogeneous migrations, otherwise you will have incompatibility between the new environments in Azure and the old environments still on-premises; for example, running AIX/DB2 on-premises and SLES/DB2 in Azure.

For heterogeneous migrations it is more normal to use a vertical approach, moving all the environments for a given SAP application at one time. This avoids any issue of compatibility between the Development, QA/Test, Pre-Production, and Production environments. In some cases, you will use a mix of horizontal and vertical approaches, as some SAP applications may undergo a homogeneous migration while others undergo a heterogeneous migration.

Where you have a large and complex SAP estate it may well not be possible to migrate all the SAP applications at once. In this case it is important to carefully plan the order in which the applications are migrated. While you can maintain network connectivity between the applications that have been migrated to Azure and those still running on-premises, in most cases network latency will increase. If you have SAP applications that are closely coupled and highly interactive, then it is desirable to migrate them together as part of the same move group. When planning move groups it is important not just to consider the SAP applications themselves but also any third-party applications that are an integral part of the SAP landscape and may also be closely coupled and highly interactive, as these will need to form part of the same move group.

If the migration is to be phased using move groups, then you will need to plan the order in which to migrate each group. In general, it is better to start with the smaller, simpler, and least critical SAP applications to prove the migration strategy and to gain confidence with operating SAP applications in Azure. The final SAP applications to move should generally be the largest and most critical. The process does not need to be entirely sequential, as for the largest SAP applications you are likely to need to run multiple test migrations to develop the best approach to minimize downtime and complete the process within the allowed downtime window. Resources permitting, this can run in parallel with migrating some of the smaller less critical SAP applications.

As previously mentioned there are now over 800 customers at various stages of deploying SAP in Azure, with some having their full SAP landscape in production. While a few have been new installations of SAP, either because this is the first time they have implemented SAP or because they have chosen the greenfield migration option, in the majority of cases the customer has migrated from on-premises to Azure using one of the methods described here. There is now a wealth of experience within the partner community of managing such migrations.

This section has so far focused on the traditional SAP NetWeaver-based applications, but not every SAP application uses the NetWeaver stack.

Non-NetWeaver applications

The main focus of this book is on traditional SAP applications based on the NetWeaver stack and written in ABAP or Java, along with the newer applications such as SAP S/4HANA, which since release 1809 uses the ABAP Platform for S/4HANA rather than the NetWeaver stack. However, there are also SAP applications that are not based on this technology, the most notable being SAP hybris.

The company hybris was founded in 1997 in Switzerland and developed an omnichannel commerce platform. SAP acquired hybris in 2013, and has gradually integrated it into their product portfolio. However, hybris continues to use its own quite different technology stack, written in Java and supported on either VMs or Containers, and supporting a number of database management systems including Microsoft SQL Server and SAP HANA.

Today SAP hybris is available as both a SaaS offering under the name SAP C/4HANA as well as an on-premises edition that can leverage Azure IaaS and PaaS services, such as **Azure Kubernetes Service (AKS)**. Further details on running SAP hybris on Azure are given in the later chapters of this book.

Having discussed how you can migrate both SAP NetWeaver-based applications as well as non-NetWeaver applications, let us now discuss who should carry out the migration.

Successful work team

When moving workloads to any cloud it is important to think about how this will affect your organization, and how you leverage partners to support you in this journey. As described earlier in this chapter, while many of the responsibilities remain unchanged, in a software-defined data centre individual roles may need to change if you are to take full advantage of the flexibility and agility provided by Azure. These roles and responsibilities will also be different when considering consuming IaaS, PaaS, and SaaS offerings.

In the case of running SAP on Azure we are mostly considering the use of Azure IaaS services, but most customers will also need to consider how these integrate with native Azure PaaS services, such as AKS for hybris, SAP PaaS services such as **SAP Cloud Platform (SCP)**, as well as SAP SaaS services such as Ariba, Concur, Fieldglass, and SuccessFactors.

For most of you, it is unlikely that you have all the skills in-house to manage the migration of SAP to Azure. Most projects are delivered by a combination of customer, partner, and Microsoft resources. While some tasks can only really be performed by internal resources, such as user acceptance testing, others may be better oursourced to partners who have experience in such migrations. Most customers will only ever perform one SAP migration to Azure, while some partners will have completed tens or hundreds of such migrations. We will now look at some of the roles and responsibilities for each group in more detail.

Internal resources

It is important to realize that when running SAP on Azure you are primarily using Azure IaaS offerings. This removes the need for you to be concerned with the physical assets such as data centres, servers, storage arrays, network switching, and cabling, and replaces all those with virtual assets that are fully software defined, and configured through a portal, command-line, scripts, or automation. You remain fully responsible for configuring the required resources, ensuring data and applications are secure, and configuring and managing backup/restore, high availability, and business continuity/disaster recovery. In that sense there is very little change to your responsibilities.

The first and most important question is, who in your organization owns responsibility for Azure? While the technical responsibilities may not have changed, the financial governance is potentially totally different. If your users are to take full advantage of the agility provided by Azure, they will need to be empowered to consume what they need when they need it. However, giving them this freedom will impact your costs and without good financial governance the costs of Azure can quickly exceed expectations. Historically those responsible for provisioning infrastructure were not typically responsible for the financial governance; they would simply provision what someone else in the organization had procured. In Azure they have access to essentially limitless capacity, and you need to decide who can provision what and when.

Azure has built-in capabilities to provide the required financial governance. Azure Cost Management provides a complete solution to monitor resource usage and manage costs across Azure and other clouds, implement financial governance policies with budgets, and cost allocation and chargeback, and supports continuous cost optimization.

However, it still requires you to plan how you want to use financial governance and then implement a strategy to deliver it. The main question is, who within your organization owns responsibility for this?

After financial governance the other big area of change is the use of automation in Azure. You may already be using tools such as Ansible, Chef, or Puppet to automate software deployment and configuration, in which case you are well placed to adopt automation of Azure and to deliver end-to-end solutions using **Infrastructure as Code** (**IaC**). You will have people with the required skill set to embrace technologies such as **Azure Resource Manager** (**ARM**) templates to automate Azure deployments, or to use other tools such as Terraform.

However, if you are not using any automation tools today then this is a big area of change and you will need to identify people with the right skills to handle automation. In general, they require good programming skills as they will essentially be modifying or developing code to automate deployments. It may be tempting to take the view that with only a few hundred VMs to build for SAP on Azure, and with a wide variance of configurations, it is hardly worth investing in automation. For all the reasons given previously this tends to lead to poor-quality deployments with lots of variance between VMs that should be similar, and many configuration errors. As an example, Microsoft recommends enabling Azure **Accelerated Networking** (**AN**) for VMs running SAP, but much of the value is lost if AN is enabled on the database server VMs but not on the application server VMs, or worse still on some application server VMs but not others. You might not believe it, but these mistakes are made.

When it comes to security it is likely that you already have a team responsible for security within your existing data centres. They will need to extend their existing security model to encompass Azure and define the policies that are to be implemented. These policies can be instantiated through the Azure Policy Service and monitored using Azure Security Center. Arguably there are far better tools available natively in Azure than you probably have available on-premises today, but if you don't use them then you won't gain the benefit. The security team will also need to consider when and where to use technologies such as firewalls, and whether to use native solutions such as Azure Firewall, or to continue with the same products as used today on-premises but implemented in Azure as **Network Virtual Appliances** (**NVA**). Their responsibilities do not change significantly, but some of the tools they use will.

The biggest area of change is within core infrastructure management. The role of server, storage, or network administrator will change significantly; there are no physical assets to manage, but there are their virtual equivalents. Their role becomes one of defining policies as to what resources should be configured when and how, and is closely linked to the topic of automation.

As an example, when a user requires a new SAP application server VM the automation should ensure that only SAP-certified VMs can be chosen, that the disk storage is configured appropriately for SAP, that the VM is joined to the correct VNet, and that the VM uses the correct OS image. The code to create the VM will configure all these aspects, which means the server, storage, and network teams must work together to define these and implement the policies. This team may have the skills and ambition to take on responsibility for all aspects of automation.

Unless you have been lucky enough to recruit a team with previous experience of Azure, then training needs to be factored into your plans. However willing and able your staff may be, best practice in Azure is not the same as best practice in the on-premises world. There are differences in how things are done in Azure, and if your project teams are to be effective then they need to understand these differences. As you might imagine, Microsoft, in conjunction with its training partners, offers a variety of Azure training and certifications[33]. It is highly advised that you ensure that staff that will be involved with the migration to Azure receive the necessary training and certification.

Partners

Of course, you may decide that rather than try and take on all this work in-house you would rather entrust it to partners. In this case you will need to decide whether to work with your existing incumbent partners if you have any, or look to new partners. The key question needs to be, do your existing partners have the required skills? As Azure becomes more pervasive skills in both Azure IaaS and SAP on Azure are becoming more common; however, you still need to ensure that the resources allocated to your project have these skills. In most cases by definition the partner team currently managing your on-premises environment are unlikely to have the required Azure skills.

Microsoft is by its nature a partner-centric company and relies on its partners to deliver customer projects. For this reason, Microsoft has been encouraging its traditional partners to develop the core Azure skills required to deliver the Azure cloud foundations, and at the same time working with the GSI, NSI, and local SAP Services Partners to build the skills around SAP on Azure. Where SAP is the lead project migrating to Azure then some customers will use one partner to build the Azure cloud foundations because of their deep expertise and experience in core Azure, and use a separate partner to handle the SAP migration to Azure, based on their expertise and experience of SAP migrations. There is no right or wrong solution; it is a question of leveraging the right skills at the right time in the project.

---

33   Microsoft Azure Training:
https://www.microsoft.com/en-us/learning/azure-training.aspx

Microsoft

Whether or not you choose to use a partner to deliver your project, you will have access to certain Microsoft resources. The first level of assistance is FastTrack for Azure[34], which provides you with access to Azure engineering resources with real-world customer experience to help you and your partners. These engineers cover a wide range of Azure areas from the basic Azure cloud foundations through to SAP on Azure. The FastTrack service is delivered remotely using Teams.

For larger projects it is likely you will have access to Microsoft **Cloud Solution Architects (CSAs)**. They provide similar capabilities to the FastTrack engineers but generally support a smaller number of concurrent projects and will provide support both remotely and on-site. As with FastTrack there are CSAs who specialize in the core aspects of Azure and also those with specific SAP on Azure skills. It is important to understand that both FastTrack engineers and Cloud Solutions Architects act in a purely advisory capacity: they are not a consulting organization and are not indemnified to carry out work within the customer's own Azure subscriptions.

Finally, if what you really want is a one-stop shop then **Microsoft Consulting Services (MCS)** can provide this capability. They are the consulting services division of Microsoft and can deliver whole cloud migration projects. Unlike some software companies Microsoft does not see consulting services as a major revenue-generating arm; MCS exists primarily to enable customers to adopt and deploy Microsoft technologies. MCS will provide overall program management and have the required skills in-house to deliver the Azure cloud foundations, but will leverage accredited partners to deliver the SAP migration to Azure.

Summary

The first objective of this chapter was to explain why Azure is the best cloud for SAP and to reassure you that any concerns you may have can be addressed. Whether it be security, availability, or scalability, hopefully you will now see that it is possible to run even the largest and most business-critical SAP systems in Azure. Microsoft has invested heavily to enhance the capabilities of Azure to meet the specific demands of enterprise-scale SAP systems, with technologies such as Mv2-series virtual machines offering up to 11.4 TiB of memory, Azure SAP HANA Large Instances, and Proximity Placement Groups.

---

34   FastTrack for Azure:
https://www.microsoft.com/en-us/fasttrack/azure

The second objective was to highlight some of the areas that need to be considered when moving SAP workloads to Azure. If you are already running other workloads in Azure then it is likely that much of the Azure foundations are already in place. If not, this will need to be done before embarking on moving the SAP workloads. We also looked at how important it is to have the right team in place to deliver the project. In most cases bringing in partners with previous experience of moving SAP workloads to Azure will accelerate the move process and ensure a better overall project outcome.

In the following chapters we will look into some of these areas in more detail, to help you better understand how to deploy SAP in Azure. It is important to remember that Azure is constantly evolving and thus as you plan a project you should follow the links in the book to access the latest documentation. This book can only be a snapshot in time.

"If you are interested in speaking to Microsoft about migrating your SAP workloads to Azure, you can reach out via this link: `https://aka.ms/contact_Azure_for_SAP`"

2
Architect SAP on Azure

This chapter will walk you through the steps required to plan your SAP on Azure architecture. As the title suggests, the focus is on the what and the why, how you architect SAP in Azure, not the how of building it, which is in the following chapter. Depending on where you are on your journey to Azure may influence which sections you need to read. We'll begin from the initial planning stage – landscape planning, where we design the structure of basic cloud artifacts. We'll call it the landing zone. It's a set of Azure resources that allows your company to build solutions in the cloud. It includes virtual networks and connections to your on-premises data centers but also the hierarchy of resources for effective management and simplified billing.

Landscape planning

If SAP is the first or only workload in Azure, then this project will need to consider all aspects of governance, security, network design, cost management, monitoring, and so on. If your organization is already running other workloads in Azure, then most if not all this work will already have been completed, and SAP will become just another workload in Azure conforming to the standards already agreed. That said, as always SAP is slightly different to many other workloads, and we will cover some of those difference as the chapter progresses.

Most organizations will have teams of people in IT responsible for each of these areas, and it will be for those teams to make many of the decisions. If SAP is the first workload, then you will need to work with all the relevant teams to create your initial migration landing zone, what Microsoft used to call the *Azure enterprise scaffold*.

If your landing zone is already in place, then you may want to skip the first few sections and jump straight to sizing. However, you may still find value in reading them, as you may find that there are SAP-related considerations that may not have been fully catered for when the landing zone was created.

For those for whom SAP is the first workload that is being moved to Azure, Microsoft has published the Microsoft **Cloud Adoption Framework (CAF)** for Azure[1]. This is a best practice guide to the process of cloud adoption in Azure, and should be reviewed before you start your journey. While it is a general guide, not specific to SAP, it identifies a lot of areas that you need to consider. Rather than repeat the content that is contained in the CAF, in this chapter we will focus more on the essential areas that need consideration if you are moving SAP to Azure.

Azure landing zone

An Azure landing zone is the foundation for deploying workloads in Azure. It should provide a structure that allows you to implement the security, governance, and management controls that you require. It is important to get the basic structure in place before you start deploying workloads into Azure, as it can be difficult or impossible to retrofit it later.

As mentioned in *Chapter 1, Cloud Readiness*, you can use Azure Blueprints to help deploy the Azure landing zone in a consistent and repeatable way. While you may question whether investing in developing the blueprint is worthwhile, most organizations will deploy into at least two Azure Regions for protection against disasters. Larger global organizations will often deploy into many more Azure Regions, deploying some workloads close to the end users, while others may be global systems deployed into a single or pair of regions. In addition, you should use Azure Policy to implement the governance model that you require when running workloads in Azure. These are powerful Azure-native tools, and ones generally not deployed in the on-premises world; if you do not use them you are missing out on a great opportunity to enforce your organization's policies in Azure.

From a security, governance, and management perspective, one of the de facto standards that has developed is to deploy a hub and spoke network topology as shown in *Figure 2-1*:

---

1   Microsoft Cloud Adoption Framework for Azure:
https://docs.microsoft.com/en-us/azure/architecture/cloud-adoption/

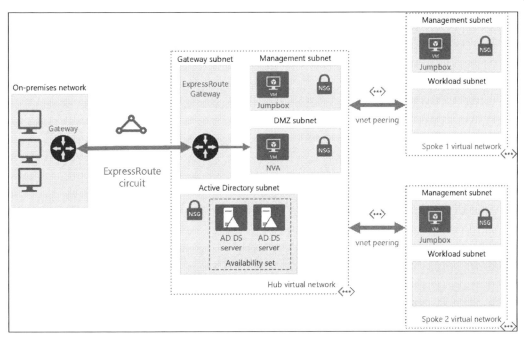

Figure 2-1: Azure hub and spoke network topology[2]

The hub provides the connection point for network connectivity between your existing network and Azure. It is also where you will deploy security services such as firewalls, either using a third-party **Network Virtual Appliance (NVA)** firewall or using the cloud-based Azure Firewall. It is also where you will normally deploy directory services by extending your on-premises Active Directory into Azure.

As you start to deploy workloads into Azure, you are likely to find other shared services that are best placed into the hub. You are likely to want Jumpbox servers to help provision and manage your workloads; these can go into the hub alongside other services such as DNS, IDS, and NTP.

---

2 Hub-spoke network topology with shared services in Azure: `https://bit.ly/38ett1m`

The spoke virtual networks are where you will deploy SAP and other workloads. You may use separate spokes for production and non-production workloads, and restrict end user access so that they can only access the production spoke, while developers and testers have access to the non-production spoke. In many cases you may outsource the management of different workloads deployed in Azure to different service providers. Similarly, you can restrict the service provider access so that they can only have access to the spokes that contain the workloads that they manage. We will look at these in more detail in a later section of this chapter.

The Jumpbox in the hub is generally used to manage the overall deployment in that region, with access restricted to specific users. The Jumpboxes in the spokes would be used by people managing specific resources within that spoke, who may well not be permitted access to the Jumpbox in the hub.

Network connectivity

As we have just seen, the hub provides the connection point between your on-premises network and Azure. There are two main ways to connect from your network to Azure:

- **Site-to-site (S2S) VPN**[3]: This connects a VPN device on your on-premises network via the public internet to a VPN gateway in Azure
- **ExpressRoute**[4]: It creates a private network connection between your on-premises network and Azure data centers

The S2S VPN has the benefit of being quick to set up compared with ExpressRoute. For this reason, many customers start with an S2S VPN while they plan their ExpressRoute connectivity, and work with their telecommunications provider to get the required connectivity in place. While Microsoft strongly recommends using ExpressRoute for production SAP workloads, if you are using S2S VPN today to access your SAP systems then you may consider it adequate when SAP is hosted in Azure.

---

3   Connect an on-premises network to a Microsoft Azure virtual network: https://bit.ly/2OSG178
4   ExpressRoute connectivity models: https://bit.ly/2sQUwjj

The main benefits of ExpressRoute over S2S VPN are that it offers better reliability and higher security, may offer lower latency, and can support higher throughputs than an S2S VPN. SAP is a critical application for many customers, and having a reliable private network connection that provides consistent performance will be preferred.

If you already have workloads running in Azure, then you may already have ExpressRoute connectivity in place between your on-premises landscape and the cloud. You can re-use it for SAP, but you should ensure the existing bandwidth is sufficient. However, if you don't have ExpressRoute in place, then you need to work with your Telco provider to get the required connectivity established as early as possible, as it can take a few weeks or months to get the necessary circuits established between your on-premises network and an Azure network peering partner.

There are three main ways to establish an ExpressRoute connection:

- **Any-to-any (IPVPN) Connection**: This is the most common connection method, normally using **Multiprotocol Label Switching (MPLS)** VPN. You simply establish an additional MPLS connection to an ExpressRoute peering partner[5].
- **Cloud Exchange Co-location**: If you are already co-located in a facility with a cloud exchange, or you have connectivity to such a facility for connection to other clouds, then you can order a cross-connection to the Microsoft cloud.
- **Point-to-point Ethernet Connection**: This option is being increasingly offered by telecommunications providers.

An ExpressRoute circuit provides a level of redundancy as it consists of two connections to two **Microsoft Enterprise Edge (MSEE) routers**. An ExpressRoute connection also provides access to all the Azure Regions within a geopolitical region. If you need to extend ExpressRoute across geopolitical boundaries, then you can do this by enabling ExpressRoute Premium.

---

5   ExpressRoute partners and peering locations: https://bit.ly/365gOw3

However, the peering location itself is still a single point of failure, so to provide a fully redundant connection between your on-premises network and Azure it is essential to connect from two different on-premises locations to two different peering locations, as shown in *Figure 2-2*:

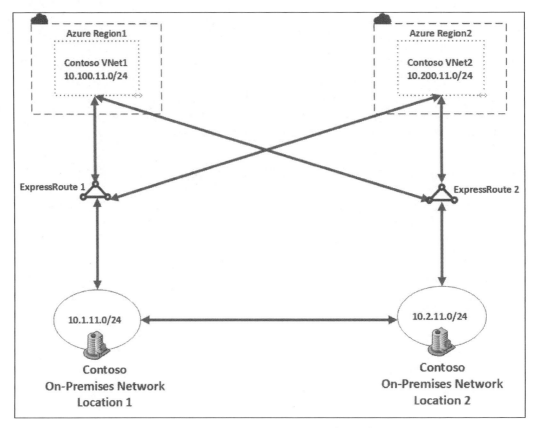

Figure 2-2: ExpressRoute Disaster Tolerance[6]

Now if the peering location for ExpressRoute 1 is unavailable then traffic can be routed by ExpressRoute 2.

---

6   Designing for disaster recovery with ExpressRoute private peering: `https://bit.ly/2PmDlh9`

Management groups, subscriptions, and resource groups

With your Azure landing zone in place, the hub VNet created, and network connectivity established between your on-premises data center and Azure, you can now start to plan how you will organize your resources in Azure. This is important to how you manage security and cost management in Azure. It is a good idea to start by reading the Azure Governance Documentation[7].

Figure 2-3 shows the available levels of management control:

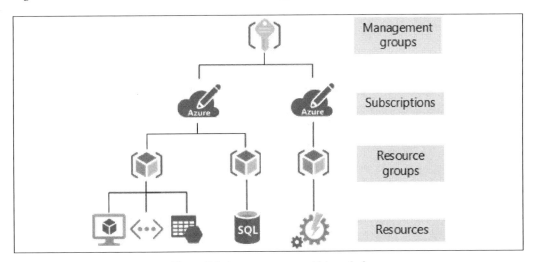

Figure 2-3: Azure management hierarchy[8]

Strictly, there is no right or wrong way to use subscriptions to manage SAP workloads in Azure, but in planning your hierarchy you may want to consider the following:

- Creating a management group for all your SAP subscriptions may be desirable so that you can manage some aspects of access, policy, and compliance in a consistent way across all of them.
- In general, try not to over-complicate the subscription model; if there is no good reason to separate resources into separate subscriptions, don't do it just for the sake of it.

---

7   Azure governance documentation: https://docs.microsoft.com/en-us/azure/governance/
8   Organize your Azure resources: https://bit.ly/2RtvbGj

- Using separate subscriptions for production and non-production workloads is generally a good idea, as access and security will generally be different across the two.
- Having multiple subscriptions for non-production may make sense if there is a specific requirement to provide different controls in the different environments: development, QA/test, pre-production, and so on. In many cases, however, a single subscription for all non-production may be adequate.
- You need to be conscious that there are certain Azure subscription limits, and where you need to exceed those limits you will need to split resources into multiple subscriptions.

Sizing

One of the important differences between sizing for Azure and sizing for on-premises is that you have much greater flexibility to scale up and scale down your **Virtual Machines (VMs)** as required. Historically when purchasing hardware for SAP, you had to try and predict not only what you need today but also what you might need in the future. If you typically depreciate hardware over 3 to 5 years, then you want to know that the hardware you purchase today will meet your needs for the next 3 to 5 years. While it is relatively easy to add an additional application server to an existing landscape, if the database server needs to be expanded then that is more difficult. If you are lucky, you bought a server with some expansion room – that is, bought an 8-processor capable server, but only purchased 4 processors – in which case you can add more processors, assuming they are still available to purchase. If not, then you may have to purchase a whole new server – so now you are depreciating two servers.

In Azure, the correct approach is to size for what you need today, and then scale up or down as the business actually requires, and we call this *right sizing*. This way you only pay for what you need today, rather than pay more than you need just in case your business grows in the future. Resizing a VM in Azure generally requires little more than to shut down the VM, change the VM type, and then restart the VM, and can be accomplished in a matter of minutes. Of course, if this is a VM running a production database, then even a few minutes downtime will require careful planning, so you need to ensure that you size the VMs to provide the capacity required until the next scheduled downtime window.

We can take this a stage further with *tight sizing*: looking for opportunities to further fine-tune the sizing. For example, in retail there is typically much higher activity on SAP systems between October and January, which is peak buying time in many countries. During this period, you may need twice or three times the application server processing power that you need for the rest of the year.

You can simply create the extra application servers that you need for this peak in October, and then shut down and delete them again in January. That way, you only pay for the extra capacity while you need it.

One of the objections to tight sizing can be that it is potentially cheaper to purchase the additional VMs as reserved instances than to pay for them for three or four months each year on pay as you go. However, there are ways to get around this. Azure VM reservations allow lots of flexibility; you don't reserve an individual VM as such, but you reserve capacity within a VM family. In many cases you will have a change freeze during this peak period, so many of your non-production VMs can be reduced in size, freeing up VM reservations that can then be used by the additional production VMs. This does take some thought and planning, but many of the savings from moving workloads to the cloud can only be realized by thinking and behaving differently.

There are even more opportunities to right size and tight size non-production environments. Many of you will have a non-production environment, possibly pre-production or quality assurance, which is sized and architected identically to production. This allows you to perform full volume performance tests, but in reality, how often do you do that? Because you can resize VMs in minutes, and add additional VMs in a few tens of minutes, why not keep this environment as small as possible until needed, and scale it up when you actually need to perform a volume performance test. Here is an example:

	Production	Pre-Prod Steady State	Pre-Prod Volume Test
DBMS VM	1 x E64sv3	1 x E16sv3	Resize to E64sv3
App Server VMs	8 x E8sv3	2 x E8sv3	Add 6 x E8sv3
Total Esv3 vCPU	128	32	

You may think that this seems like a lot of effort, but using automation, the creation of the additional application servers can be fully or mostly automated. During daily operation you reduce your vCPU count by 75%, saving 75% of the VM costs. You only pay for the extra VMs when you actually need them. There will be additional costs for the extra capacity consumed during the volume testing period, but again, if you have other VMs that you have reserved and can shut down during this time, then you may be able to run the volume test environment at no additional cost.

Rehosting and replatforming

This section mostly focuses on sizing as you migrate existing SAP estates into Azure. We use the term *rehosting* when the current **operating system (OS)** and **database management system (DBMS)** that are being used on-premises can be migrated to Azure without the need to change either.

However, if the current OS is not supported in Azure – normally this will be one of the Unix versions such as AIX, HP-UX, or Solaris, but could also be IBM i/OS or z/OS – then you will need to change the OS. We call this *replatforming*. You may choose to change the DBMS as part of the migration, in which case this is also classed as replatforming.

In these cases, you know the capacity that you have deployed, you can measure its current utilization (both average and peaks), and as part of the migration to Azure you can optimize the sizing. If you are planning a new implementation of SAP, then you will be reliant on tools such as SAP Quick Sizer and the SAP Sizing Guidelines to provide an estimate of your likely capacity requirements. I will come back to how best to handle this later in the section, while for now I will focus on migrating existing SAP workloads to Azure.

We have already discussed right sizing and tight sizing, and when you are rehosting or replatforming SAP to Azure it is relatively easy to right size; you have existing systems that are running your business and from which you can obtain real utilization data. Particularly when migrating from an already virtualized SAP platform, for example running on VMware on x86 servers, it can be very tempting to simply provision new VMs on Azure to be the same size as the existing on-premises physical or virtual servers. But when you look at the current utilization, using either SAP EarlyWatch Alert reports or other tools, it is often the case that peak CPU and memory utilization is much lower than the size of the current machines. The general guidance from SAP for many years has been for peak CPU utilization to not exceed around 67%, so if your current server never exceeds 30% utilization, it is massively oversized. This aspect of right sizing is not actually specific to Azure, as this has been good practice whenever replatforming SAP, even in the on-premises world, and is a way to reduce the over-provision caused by trying to guess what you would need in 3 to 5 years' time.

Tight sizing will depend to some extent on the nature of your business and how your SAP systems are used. Once again, the great benefit when rehosting or replatforming is that you can obtain useful information as to how your current systems are utilized. While in some cases there may be limited scope for tight sizing in production, most customers with large multi-tiered SAP landscapes can find ways to save cost by tight sizing non-production. In general, there is more scope for tight sizing the more complex the SAP landscape; where you have sandbox systems, multiple development and test systems (separate ones for BAU support and project support), pre-production, training, and so on. In Azure, rather than size each of these for its peak workload, you can simply scale up the VM when required and scale it back down again when the workload reduces.

New installations

For new installations, you will mainly rely on SAP Quick Sizer and SAP Sizing Guidelines to estimate your sizing. In general, SAP takes a very cautious approach to sizing, meaning that they will err toward oversizing rather than under sizing because that is the safer option. In particular, user-based sizing (Concurrent Users) in Quick Sizer produces notoriously oversized results, while Transaction (Throughput) based sizing is generally more realistic, but often the transaction data is not available.

In the case of new installations, the benefits of deploying on Azure are even greater. Historically you had little choice other than to take the sizing estimates, provision servers to meet that sizing, and accept that in 95% of cases you have probably oversized; better that than being the 5% who are undersized and have to find budget to expand their servers. Normally, you will still need to undertake this sizing exercise in order to calculate a budgetary cost for Azure, but you don't need to provision resources and start spending until you are ready to use them.

For non-production, you can simply start small and grow as you need. You can resize a VM in a matter of minutes, and scheduling a short outage at a lunch break or overnight will not generally be a problem. Better to be undersized and have to resize, than be oversized and pay twice or more for months "just in case." If you want some way to make an initial estimate of the size of these non-production VMs, then here are some tips:

- Assume each user requires ~ 50 SAPS. People developing and testing on SAP are not your average users, and they will typically use many more SAPS. So, once you know the size of the team working on each component, then you can estimate the size of the VMs.
- If you plan to run these systems 2-tier, that is, run the application and DBMS on the same VM, then best to use VMs with more memory per vCPU, such as the Ev3 series. SAP likes memory and can always make use of more, and in real terms there is only a small difference in cost between Dv3 series (4 GB RAM per vCPU) and Ev3 series (8 GB RAM per vCPU).
- For some of the larger instances, you may want to run 3-tier, with separate application server(s) and a database server, and in this case database servers are generally less memory hungry than application servers, so may suit Dv3 series, while the application servers still use more memory and therefore suit Ev3 series.
- Once the systems are in use, you can quickly resize based on real need; this just provides a starting point.

For new projects, sizing should always be an iterative process, so as the blueprinting and realization progress, and as the business processes, transaction volumes, and the number of users become clearer, you can review the production sizing.

Other sizing considerations

Having looked at the main items relating to sizing, let's now look at some other minor areas that are related to sizing. There are many ways in which running SAP in Azure provides opportunities and benefits not available in the on-premises world.

In many projects, there may be times when it would be highly desirable to have additional systems in the landscape, for example, to allow more parallel testing, or to provide dedicated training systems. In the on-premises world, it is not practical to provision additional hardware for a few months to support these activities, so the project team has to work around the capacity and systems that are available. In Azure, you can simply create additional systems as required, and only pay for them while you need them. This opens up new possibilities, and is something you should factor into your design.

With Azure you can move towards just in time provisioning. In a traditional on-premises environment it is common for the project to size all the required hardware and then order and provision all the hardware at the start of the project. In SAP projects, it is common for it to take between 12 and 18 months from standing up the first sandbox or development systems to finally going live in production. As you only have to pay for what you use when you use it, in Azure it is better to provision what you need just ahead of time. This also fits better with the sizing process, as during the project you will be able to continually refine the sizing.

If as part of your move to Azure you are also planning a migration to a SAP HANA database or to S/4HANA, this might be a good time to consider how you manage the refresh of non-production environments using production data. For traditional disk-based databases, taking full copies of data from production into non-production may use a lot of disk space, but is relatively cheap. When moving to a SAP HANA database, all that data needs to be loaded into memory, and having more data than really required for testing can get very expensive. If you assume that storing 1 TB of data in memory in SAP HANA is approximately 10 times more expensive than storing the same data on disk in a disk-based DBMS, then you begin to understand why it is not a good idea to keep multiple copies of production data. There are a number of data slicing tools available, from SAP TDMS to third-party tools, and in most cases the cost of the tool and the services to implement it will be quickly recouped where HANA is the target database.

Virtual machines and storage

Once you have your sizing, you will need to translate this into Azure Virtual Machines and determine the correct storage for each VM. As you will see, these two areas are closely connected – which is why we will look at them together.

Virtual machine size

When it comes to mapping the compute requirements for SAP applications, the two components are CPU and Memory. For SAP systems, SAP devised a standardized benchmark to measure the performance of different CPU types to allow for easy comparison. This is the SAP Application Performance Standard, or SAPS for short. Whether this is a new implementation and you are working from the SAP Quick Sizer and SAP Sizing Guidelines, or you are looking to rehost an existing SAP landscape in Azure, you will use SAPS as a measure of CPU performance. Memory is rather more simple, as this is simply specified in **Giga Bytes** (**GB**).

There are a wide range of SAP-certified Azure VM onto which you can map your requirements. The full list of SAP-certified VMs is contained in SAP Note 1928533, and details of the most common VMs used for SAP are shown in following *Table 2-1*. As well as the details from the SAP Note, the table includes other parameters for each VM taken from Azure documentation[9]:

VM Type	VM vCPU	VM Memory (GiB)	Temp SSD (GB)	SAPS	Max data disks	Max IOPS (cached)	Max Disk Bandwidth (cached) (Mbps)	Max NICs	Max Network Bandwidth (Mbps)
D2s_v3	2	8	16	2,177	4	4,000	32	2	1,000
D4s_v3	4	16	32	4,355	8	8,000	64	2	2,000
D8s_v3	8	32	64	8,710	16	16,000	128	4	4,000
D16s_v3	16	64	128	17,420	32	32,000	256	8	8,000
D32s_v3	32	128	256	34,840	32	64,000	512	8	16,000
D64s_v3	64	256	512	69,680	32	128,000	1,024	8	30,000
E2s_v3	2	16	32	2,189	4	4,000	32	2	1,000
E4s_v3	4	32	64	4,378	8	8,000	64	2	2,000
E8s_v3	8	64	128	8,756	16	16,000	128	4	4,000

---

9   Sizes for Linux virtual machines in Azure: `https://bit.ly/2OYI35P`

Architect SAP on Azure

VM Type	VM vCPU	VM Memory (GiB)	Temp SSD (GB)	SAPS	Max data disks	Max IOPS (cached)	Max Disk Bandwidth (cached) (Mbps)	Max NICs	Max Network Bandwidth (Mbps)
E16s_v3	16	128	256	17,513	32	32,000	256	8	8,000
E20s_v3	20	160	320	21,775	32	40,000	320	8	10,000
E32s_v3	32	256	512	35,025	32	64,000	512	8	16,000
E64s_v3	32	432	864	70,050	32	128,000	1,024	8	30,000
M32ts	32	192	1,024	33,670	32	40,000	400	8	8,000
M32ls	32	256	1,024	33,300	32	40,000	400	8	8,000
M64ls	64	512	2,048	66,600	64	80,000	800	8	16,000
M64s	64	1,024	2,048	67,315	64	80,000	800	8	16,000
M64ms	64	1,792	2,048	68,930	64	80,000	800	8	16,000
M128s	128	2,048	4,096	134,630	64	160,000	1,600	8	32,000
M128ms	128	3,892	4,096	134,630	64	160,000	1,600	8	32,000
M208s	208	2,850	4,096	259,950	64	80,000	800	8	16,000
M208ms	208	5,700	4,096	259,950	64	80,000	800	8	16,000
M416s	416	5,700	8,192	488,230	64	250,000	1,600	8	32,000
M416ms	416	11,400	8,192	488,230	64	250,000	1,600	8	32,000

Table 2-1: Common SAP-Certified Virtual Machines

It is important to always check SAP Note 1928533 for the latest information when starting any new project. For production SAP environments, Microsoft recommends that Accelerate Networking is enabled on each virtual machine. Accelerated Networking is supported on all M-series and Mv2-series VMs, and also on Dv3-series and Ev3-series with 4 vCPU or more. This means that D2s_v3 and E2s_v3 are not recommended for production VMs, although they may be suitable for some non-production environments, and also for use as utility servers providing some supporting capabilities.

Virtual machine storage

As detailed in *Table 2-1* every VM comes with an allocation of temporary disk storage, and it is easy to assume that this will be your OS disk. But the clue is in the name. The temporary storage is a disk attached to the VM that uses the local storage of the physical server.

When you shut down the VM and it is deallocated, then the temporary storage is lost as the next time the VM is started it may well be on a different physical host. The main use case for temporary storage is as an area for Linux swap or Windows page files, as these are by their nature volatile and not required after a VM reboot. They can also be used for the temporary storage of files such as installation media; just remember they will be lost when the VM is deallocated.

Azure VMs use Page Blobs[10] to store the operating system, SAP, and DBMS executables, DBMS data and log files, and any other storage requirements. For SAP, you should always use Azure Managed Disks[11], which provide maximum availability and durability, and fully support VM Availability Sets and Availability Zones. Every Azure Managed Disk provides three replicas of your data, so there is no need to consider disk mirroring or **Redundant Array of Independent Disks (RAID)** – this is already provided by Azure.

Azure Managed Disks come in four disk types[12]:

- **Ultra SSD**: These are the newest addition and offer the lowest latency and highest IOPS and throughput, with the ability to adjust the IOPS and throughput independent of the capacity. They are currently only supported as data disks, and there are a number of limitations that may be removed in the future.
- **Premium SSD**: These are the mainstay storage for SAP on Azure VMs. Until the arrival of Ultra SSD, these disks offered the highest performance in Azure. Also, if you want to benefit from the Azure single VM SLA (see section on *Resilience*), then you have to use premium SSD storage.
- **Standard SSD**: These are an entry point to SSD storage in Azure, and while they can be used in some non-production environments, they lack the IOPS and throughput to support most production databases. Where cost is a concern, and you are prepared to lose the single VM SLA, then they can be an alternative for non-production.
- **Standard HDD**: In general, these are not suited to SAP workloads due to their high latency even compared with Standard SSD. While they are cheaper than standard SSDs, they are generally best avoided in SAP environments.

---

10   About Page Blobs: https://bit.ly/2PnZ5ci
11   Introduction to Azure managed disks: https://bit.ly/2rZkjp6
12   What disk types are available in Azure?: https://bit.ly/364k1vC

All data stored in Azure Storage is automatically replicated for resilience:

- **Locally redundant storage (LRS)**: Provides at least 99.999999999% (11 nines) durability of objects over a given year. It's a default replication for objects stored in Azure Storage. Three copies of your data are kept in a single Azure region.
- **Zone-redundant storage (ZRS)**: Data is replicated synchronously to three storage clusters in a single region. Each cluster is physically separated and located in its own availability zone. ZRS offers durability for storage objects of at least 99.9999999999% (12 nines) over a given year.
- **Geo-redundant storage (GRS)**: Designed to provide at least 99.99999999999999% (16 nines) durability of objects over a given year. The data is replicated to another Azure region, which is hundreds of miles from the primary region. Azure stores in total six copies of the data – three in the primary region and another three in the secondary region. Data replication between region is asynchronous, which means it's firstly saved to LRS storage and then distributed.
- **Read-access geo-redundant storage (RA-GRS)**: This is the same as GRS but provides read-access to the data in the secondary region as required. Read access to standard GRS storage is only available when a region outage is declared by Microsoft.
- **Geo-zone-redundant storage (GZRS)**: This is a geo-redundant version of ZRS where data is replicated synchronously to three storage clusters in the primary region and replicated asynchronously to three storage clusters in the secondary region.
- **Read-access geo-zone-redundant storage (RA-GZRS)**: This is the same as GZRS but provides read-access to the data in the secondary region as required. Read access to standard GRS storage is only available when a region outage is declared by Microsoft.

However, it is important to realize that Microsoft recommends using **Azure managed disks**[13] for SAP and that Azure managed disks only support LRS. So, replicating data to another Zone or Region must be done in another way, rather than using storage replication.

In addition, every VM has a parameter called *max data disks*, which is the maximum number of disks that can be attached to that VM. The larger the VM, the greater the number of disks that can be attached. Typically, an application server will only need one or two disks for the operating system and SAP executables, and hence any size of VM will support sufficient disks.

---

13   Introduction to Azure managed disks: `https://bit.ly/2rbr5rQ`

However, a database server will need many more disks for the data and log files. The max data disks parameter leads to a number of implications:

1. For database VMs, in order to achieve the required IOPS for data and log files, you may need to use multiple disks, and this is where you need to ensure you don't exceed the max data disks for your chosen VM. If you genuinely need more IOPS, then you may have to use a larger VM.

2. You also need to think about the whether you may want to be able to scale down the VM. If you allocated more disks than are genuinely needed, then you may limit your ability to scale down the VM, as the smaller VM may not be able to attach all the disks. If you use one disk for the operating system, one for software executables, two for database logs, and five for database data, then you will have a total of nine disks. The smallest VM that supports nine disks is D/E8_v3, which means you cannot scale down to a D/E4_v3 if you don't require all the CPU/memory. If instead you reduce the data disks from five to four, then you only have eight disks in total, and now have the option to scale down to a D/E4_v3. These sorts of details are easily overlooked when planning your SAP on Azure solution, but it is essential that you consider this during your design.

When using Premium SSD, the best ratio of IOPS to capacity is provided by the P30 disk, which is why it is often favored for DBMS data disks, while the best ratio of throughput to capacity is provided by the P20 disk, which is why it is often favored for DBMS log files. It can be tempting just to create a single volume using multiples of these two disk types to meet all your data and log needs, to provide optimum performance, but this is where you need to keep in mind the VM max data disk limit, and not try and provision more disks than the VM can support.

While on the subject of IOPS, you also should note that every VM also has a max throughput, in terms of both IOPS and **Megabytes per second** (**Mbps**). In fact, there are two sets of values, one with caching enabled and one without. As a rule, it is recommended[14] that you enable read caching on data files and no caching on log files, so your maximum IOPS will be somewhere in between the two values.

For disk storage, it is recommended that for SAP on Azure you use Premium SSD or Ultra SSD Managed Disks, at least in production.

For VMs destined to run SAP HANA, then, as part of the certification, Microsoft uses a storage configuration that is known to pass the SAP HANA **Hardware Configuration Check Tool** (**HWCCT**) for SAP HANA Platform 1.0 and SAP HANA Hardware and Cloud Measurement Tools for SAP HANA Platform 2.0 or newer.

---

14   Caching for VMs and data disks: `https://bit.ly/2YoFdd6`

Based on testing, Microsoft publishes two sets of recommendations:

- Production storage solution with Azure Write Accelerator for Azure M-series virtual machines[15]
- Cost-conscious Azure storage configuration[16]

For production HANA instances and production-like systems such as **Disaster Recovery (DR)**, and potentially pre-production, then you should always use the validated production storage solution. For non-production environments, it depends on whether you insist on using a certified configuration or whether you would rather save cost by following the cost-conscious storage configuration. In the early days of SAP HANA, when the software was only supported when running on a certified appliance, then these appliances would be used across all tiers of the landscape. With the release of the SAP HANA **Tailored Data center Integration (TDI)** option, support for on-premises virtualization, and more recently public cloud such as Azure, it has become more common for people to use non-certified solutions for non-production.

A recent addition to the available storage types in Azure is **Azure NetApp Files (ANF)**. ANF storage is already supported for certain SAP use cases and will be supported for more use cases in the future. ANF is a fully managed and integrated cloud service in Azure, which brings all the features of the NetApp ONTAP storage OS into Azure. Unlike NetApp Cloud Volumes ONTAP, which uses Azure VMs and storage, ANF uses dedicated NetApp storage hardware deployed inside Azure data centers.

ANF is very different to other Azure storage, and is organized in the following hierarchy:

- **Azure NetApp Account**: An administrative grouping of capacity pools.
- **Azure NetApp Capacity Pool**: The provisioned amount of storage for use by volumes. The minimal amount you can provision is 4 TiB. A capacity pool can only have one service level.
- **Azure NetApp Volume**: The logical data container that contains the filesystems that you can mount to a VM.

---

15   Production storage solution with Azure Write Accelerator for Azure M-series virtual machines: https://bit.ly/2LtYEfx
16   Cost conscious Azure storage configuration: https://bit.ly/38b3Yhr

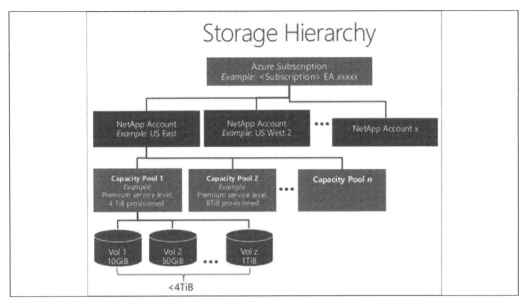

Figure 2-4: Azure NetApp files storage hierarchy

Depending on the ANF volume size, you can determine the performance. Azure NetApp Files offers three performance tiers:

1. **Standard**: 16 MiB/s of throughput per 1 TiB of volume quota
2. **Premium**: 64 MiB/s of throughput per 1 TiB of volume quota
3. **Ultra**: 128 MiB/s of throughput per 1 TiB of volume quota

If you need 256 MiB of throughput, it means the minimal volume would be 4 TiB for the Premium performance tier, or 2 TiB for the Ultra, even if you do not require this amount of data capacity. It is common practice to over-provision storage capacity to achieve the required performance. As the price difference between the tiers is low, in general it is better if you always choose the Ultra tier in production landscapes.

At the time of writing, ANF can be used for the following use cases with SAP:

- To provide the shared storage for SAP Central Services Clusters using SMB for Windows Server[17] and NFS v3.0/4.1 for Linux[18].
- For VMs running the SAP HANA database, ANF can be used to store `/hana/data` and `/hana/log` using NFS v4.1, and for `/hana/shared` using NFS v3 or v4.1[19]. You must not mix the use of ANF for these three directories with Azure Premium or Ultra SSD, although Azure Premium and Ultra SSD should be used for the OS and Exe disks.

For the shared filesystems required for a Central Services cluster, ANF brings the simplicity of a fully managed NFS service. This is much simpler to manage than either a Windows SOFS cluster or a Linux HA-NFS cluster.

ANF for SAP HANA VMs has three main benefits:

- ANF supports the online resizing of the underlying storage volumes should you need to scale up the size of your HANA VM, without the need to unmount the volumes, stop the VM, or stop HANA.
- ANF allows SAP HANA scale-out to be supported on Azure VMs with a standby node[20].
- ANF snapshots can be used for backup and the fast recovery of your SAP HANA database.

While ANF brings a number of new capabilities to Azure, it is important to know that at the time of writing ANF is only available in a limited number of Azure regions, starting with those regions where M/Mv2-series VMs are deployed. Also, ANF is not currently Zone-aware, and in most regions is currently only available in a single Zone, so if you are thinking of using a Zone-based deployment for HA, do not use ANF at this time.

---

17   High availability for SAP NetWeaver on Azure VMs on Windows with Azure NetApp Files(SMB) for SAP applications: `https://bit.ly/2OYK7e5`
18   High availability for SAP NetWeaver on Azure VMs on SUSE Linux Enterprise Server with Azure NetApp Files for SAP applications: `https://bit.ly/340Txdm`
19   NFS v4.1 volumes on Azure NetApp Files: `https://bit.ly/2DPKNfj`
20   Deploy a SAP HANA scale-out system with a standby node on Azure VMs by using Azure NetApp Files on SUSE Linux Enterprise Server: `https://bit.ly/33TgHlF`

Currently, ANF is not supported for the data or log files for databases other than SAP HANA. While technically ANF might work, it has not been tested by Microsoft and is therefore not supported.

Cost considerations

While the main focus of this book are the technical considerations in moving SAP to Azure, how the solution is architected will have an impact on cost. In an ideal world, the technical architects would design the perfect solution, and then simply build that in Azure. In the real world, however, you cannot ignore costs; you have to consider budgets, **total cost of ownership** (**TCO**), and **return on investment** (**ROI**) – otherwise, the project will not proceed. As a technical architect, you always have to have one eye on costs in order to maintain a project that is grounded in reality.

If you happen to be one of the minority of customers still running SAP on physical servers with no virtualization, then just virtualizing SAP in Azure will probably save you money. However, the majority have already heavily virtualized their on-premises SAP environment, and simply performing a like-for-like migration to Azure will probably not save you any money, but maybe even cost you more. To gain the benefits of moving to the cloud, you need to adopt a cloud mentality, follow the best practices advice on sizing and only provision and run what you actually need today, and generally leverage the capabilities that the cloud can offer.

One area for potential savings is shutting down VMs when not in use, sometimes referred to as *snoozing*. When you shut down a VM in Azure, and – importantly – the VM is deallocated, then you stop paying for the VM. You still pay for the storage, but for a typical SAP VM billed on **pay as you go** (**PAYG**) pricing you will save 60-70% of the cost through snoozing. You can create the rules to stop the system automatically, but the start process is usually much harder to achieve, as each component has to be started in the correct order. Additional configuration may be required at the operating system level.

There are two ways you can use snoozing:

- **Non-production systems that are only occasionally required**: There are often systems that you want to keep, but only use occasionally. These may be sandbox systems, training systems, or additional test systems, and you can save money by snoozing them when not required.
- **Production systems used for peak workloads**: This has already been mentioned, but if you have irregular workloads with peaks significantly higher than average workload levels, where there is a significant extra capacity required at certain times of the week, month, or year, then consider having application servers that are only started up when needed, and shut down when no longer required.

Snoozing non-production systems requires a change of culture, and some organizations are reluctant to change. The normal starting point is that the development and test users are used to having the systems available 24×7 and won't accept anything less. In the on-premises world, shutting down systems would only save a small amount of the overall cost in power and cooling, but the majority of the costs are fixed. In Azure, you can save a lot more – and your users need to understand that.

In order to persuade these development and test users of the benefits of snoozing, you can use Azure Cost Management to show how much these non-production systems are costing, known as *showback*. You can then show the cost savings if these systems are shut down when not needed, and how these savings can be used to create additional VMs for extra testing, training, and other purposes. This creates a potential win-win situation providing the development and test users a more flexible environment whilst at the same time saving cost. Ultimately, these users could be empowered to manage their own budget within Azure.

In production, starting an additional application server is relatively easy, but to shut it down again is more difficult. To shut down an application server, first you need to remove it from the login group, then wait for all the users to log off, and only then are you able to shut it down. There are a couple of good uses cases for this. Firstly, if you have large batch workloads, then you can start up the VMs before the batch processing starts, then shut them down when the batches are complete and there are no issues with users being logged in. Secondly, if the extra capacity is required for a sustained period – for example, for a week at the end of every month, or, as in the retail case described earlier, for several weeks around the Christmas peak trading period – then this works well. Trying to spin up an extra application server to cover a peak hour every day probably won't work so well, as once users are logged in, at least some of them won't log out until the end of the day, meaning that you have to leave the VM running for the rest of the day at least, thus negating any potential savings.

Snoozing is just one of the ways to reduce your VM costs in Azure. For those VMs that need to be running all or most of the time, then you also need to think about Azure Reserved Instances. There are a number of Azure services that support reserved instances, but for SAP the only ones currently relevant are Reserved Virtual Machine Instances[21]. For the VMs used by Azure, you can typically save 40-45% of costs by reserving a VM for 1 year, and 60-65% of costs by reserving for 3 years[22]. For any VM that you plan to run 24×7, these savings are very significant and need to be factored into your thinking: which VMs should be reserved for 3 years, which for 1 year, and which should be consumed on a pay as you go model?

The typical break-even point between pay as you go and 3-year reserved instances is that any VM required for more than 12 hours per day, five days per week, is likely to be cheaper on a 3 year reserved instance. This is important to understand because, while snoozing VMs that are on a pay as you go plan will save cost, in many cases, changing to a reserved instance may save more.

In Azure, there is significant flexibility within VM reserved instances, which is not the case in all public clouds. Azure provides:

- **Instance size flexibility**: You can use the reserved instance for any VMs within the same series. If you reserved a D64_v3 then that reservation could be used for 1 × D64_v3, 2 × D32_v3, 1 × D32_v3 + 2 × D16_v3, 4 × D16_v3, and so on.
- **Exchange**[23]: Where you have reserved too much capacity, then you can exchange the capacity no longer required for VMs from another series, providing the purchase total is greater than the return total.
- **Refund**[24]: If you have simply reserved too much capacity, and you have no other use for it, you can obtain a refund, although there is an early termination fee.

---

21 Azure Reserved VM Instances (RIs): https://azure.microsoft.com/en-gb/pricing/reserved-vm-instances/
22 Savings vary greatly depending on the VM series and whether or not the OS subscription is included.
23 Exchange an existing reserved instance: https://bit.ly/2Ppvqjg
24 Cancel, exchange, and refund policies: https://bit.ly/34ROTzo

Reservations can be scoped to a single resource group, to a single subscription, or shared across all eligible subscriptions within a single billing context[25]. If you plan to use VM reservations, and you want to maximize the flexibility while at the same time keeping those reservations just for use by SAP, then you may need to factor this into your design.

Resilience

Planned and unplanned downtime

There are two types of events that can cause downtime when running SAP in Azure:

- **Planned maintenance**: Such as periodic platform updates
- **Unplanned maintenance**: Occurs due to hardware or software failure

It's important to plan your landscape to meet the availability that your business requires, but that does not mean that full application level high availability is always the best solution. While you may traditionally have used clustering to protect your SAP workloads when running on physical servers, if you have already migrated your SAP workloads to a virtual platform such as VMware vSphere, then you may already have gone through the process of deciding whether to retain clusters or simply rely on VMware HA to automatically restart your VMs in the event of a VM or host failure.

Azure provides a **Service Level Agreement (SLA)** of 99.9% for a single VM, providing you use premium managed disks, which is financially backed by service credits should the SLA not be achieved. Azure has the means to detect the health of VMs and will perform auto-recovery of VMs should they ever fail; a process referred to as Service Healing.

In addition, since early 2018, Microsoft has been using live migration[26] where possible to avoid unplanned downtime. By using **Machine Learning (ML)**, Azure can predict disk and system failures and live migrate VMs before the failure occurs. While this capability was initially restricted to a small number of VM series, live migration is now available on all VM series except G, M, N, and H series[27].

---

25   Scope reservations: `https://bit.ly/2Rn4fYR`
26   Improving Azure Virtual Machine resiliency with predictive ML and live migration: `https://bit.ly/2RpFdZ3`
27   Live migration: `https://bit.ly/2Plh0jU`

If you deploy a highly available cluster across two VMs in an availability set, then the SLA increases to 99.95%, while if you deploy the cluster into Availability Zones, then the SLA increases further to 99.99%. To translate those SLAs into something easier to understand:

SLA	Monthly downtime	Yearly downtime
99.9%	43m 49.7s	8h 45m 57.0s
99.95%	21m 54.9s	4h 22m 58.5s
99.99%	4m 23.0s	52m 35.7s

Table 2-2: SLA downtime/unavailability (Source: uptime.is)

It is important to understand that these are infrastructure SLAs, not application level SLAs, and that the application level SLA will always be lower; if the infrastructure availability is 99.99%, the application level availability is likely to be closer to 99.95%.

Whether you require application-level high availability with clustering will depend on the level of criticality of SAP to your organization. For industries such as manufacturing, any downtime for SAP may result in production lines having to be halted. If you are a multi-national company running a single global instance of SAP, then the cost of downtime may be measured in millions of dollars per hour. On the other hand, if you are a people-centric services business where SAP is primarily used as a back-office financial system, then your business may be able to operate for hours or even days without SAP; you can continue providing the services, but you may not be able to order goods or invoice your customers.

Ultimately, there is no universal right or wrong solution; it is a case of investigating the costs versus benefits. To move from a single VM model relying on Azure VM auto-restart, to a clustered solution using either Availability Sets or Availability Zones, will typically double the cost of your production VMs. If you are investing in clusters in production, then you should strongly consider having a cluster in one of the non-production environments so that you have somewhere to test patches and updates prior to rolling them into production. Not only do clusters increase the infrastructure cost, they will also increase services costs, both in initial deployment and ongoing management and administration, as they add significant complexity to the environment.

That said, clusters do not only protect against unplanned downtime, but can also be used to avoid planned downtime. In an environment where all single points of failure are clustered, then it is possible to perform "rolling upgrades". In general terms, you remove the standby VM from the cluster, patch that VM, integrate it back into the cluster, and, once fully resynchronized, failover the service onto the patch VM.

You can now take the other VM out of the cluster, patch that VM, and, finally, reintroduce it into the cluster. If you plan to perform these type of service activities, then having a cluster in your non-production environment is essential.

SAP NetWeaver high availability

In order to make a SAP NetWeaver system highly available we need to eliminate all single points of failure, which are:

1. Application Servers
2. SAP Central Services Instance
3. The database

High availability requires each of above components to be redundant. It's important to remember that even if your system is configured to run in high availability mode, you may still encounter downtime due to a failure of other, non-SAP related components. Therefore, it is important that the entire infrastructure – like routers or internet connection – between end user and the system are also made highly available.

Application server high availability

Redundancy of the SAP application server is easy to achieve, as all that is required is to deploy multiple instances and connect them to the Central Services Instance. If an application server fails, all users connected to that application server will lose their session and any incomplete transactions, but that is a limitation of the SAP software. The application servers should be provisioned in a single Azure availability set to ensure that they are in separate fault and update domains to minimize the probability of multiple application servers being affected by a physical failure in Azure, or from an enforced Azure update.

If there is a failure, the application server VMs will be automatically restarted by Azure. The application servers do not need to run in a cluster, and therefore they don't need a load balancer in front. In production at least, it is normally good practice to have a minimum of two application servers, a **Primary Application Server** (**PAS**) and an **Additional Application Server** (**AAS**), and to minimize the impact of a VM failure having more smaller application servers can be preferable to having fewer larger ones. If you have four application servers and one fails, only 25% of your users will be affected:

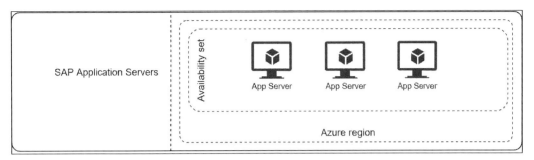

Figure 2-5: SAP application servers in an availability set

Application servers are not the only component that affects the system availability. To ensure users can log in and access the data we need to protect the SAP Central Services instance as well.

SAP Central Services Instance High Availability

The SAP Central Services Instance is a key component of an SAP system. It contains three main elements:

1. The /sapmnt directory
2. Message Server
3. Enqueue server

Each of these components must be protected against failure.

The /sapmnt directory should be hosted using a highly available shared storage solution or file share. For Linux-based systems you can use an HA NFS service built on Azure VMs or **Azure NetApp Files (ANF)** using NFS, while for Windows Server-based systems, you can use a Scale-Out File Server cluster with **Storage Spaces Direct (S2D)** or ANF using SMB. Azure Files is not currently supported for hosting the /sapmnt directory due to lack of POSIX permissions. Keeping the /sapmnt on the file share instead of shared disk has been available SAP NetWeaver 7.40 with SAP Kernel release 7.49. Customers who are on lower release have to use third-party software like SIOS Data Keeper to replicate the disk at the byte level and simulate the cluster shared disk.

The message server can be protected using an operating system failover cluster. When the primary node fails, the service on the secondary node is started and operations resume.

The enqueue server stores information about all locks in a memory resident lock table. If the lock table is lost it may cause application inconsistencies as users or system process could update entries that are being edited by others. The enqueue server lock table can be protected by creating an **Enqueue Replication Server** (ERS) on a second node, and all locks will then be replicated to the ERS replica table.

Using an operating system cluster, if the enqueue server fails then the cluster will restart the enqueue server on the ERS node where it will create a new enqueue table from the ERS replica table. In this way, the locks would not be lost. However, the cluster framework then must restart the ERS either on another node within the cluster or on the node that previously ran the enqueue server, when that becomes available again. During this time there is no ERS and no replica table, and locks could be lost.

Since **NetWeaver Application Server for ABAP (NW AS ABAP)** 7.51, a new standalone **enqueue server 2 (ENQ2)** became available that provides improved scalability. With NW AS ABAP 7.2, a new **enqueue replicator 2 (ER2)** has been introduced that provides an improved failover process. With this new enqueue server 2 solution, if the enqueue server fails, then the HA framework restarts it on a completely different host, where it generates a new lock table by retrieving data from the enqueue replicator 2. If the enqueue replicator 2 fails, then the HA framework restarts the enqueue replicator on a different host, and the replicator retrieves data from the enqueue server to recreate the replica table. In this way, the time without a replicated lock table is minimized.

This ENQ2/ER2 solution is optimized to work with multi-node clusters with more than two nodes, so there is always a third (or fourth) node on which to restart the failed service. Because neither Red Hat nor SUSE Linux Pacemaker clusters currently support multi-SID "stacking", while this offers an enhanced availability solution, it will increase still further the number of VMs required to support a highly available central services from two to three nodes.

However, it does offer the potential of a cheaper non-clustered solution to central services availability, if you are prepared to wait for the ENQ2 to auto-restart. If the ENQ2 VM fails, then the replicator table is still maintained by ER2, and when the EMQ2 VM restarts, it will be able to create its lock table from the replica table. This does not require any cluster software, but it could be minutes (or hours) before the ENQ2 VM restarts.

In Linux environments, the landscape will require up to eight servers for the Central Services cluster, which would include:

- Two node failover cluster hosting ASCS and ERS instances
- Two or three node NFS cluster

- Three SBD devices (shared between NFS cluster and ASCS cluster)

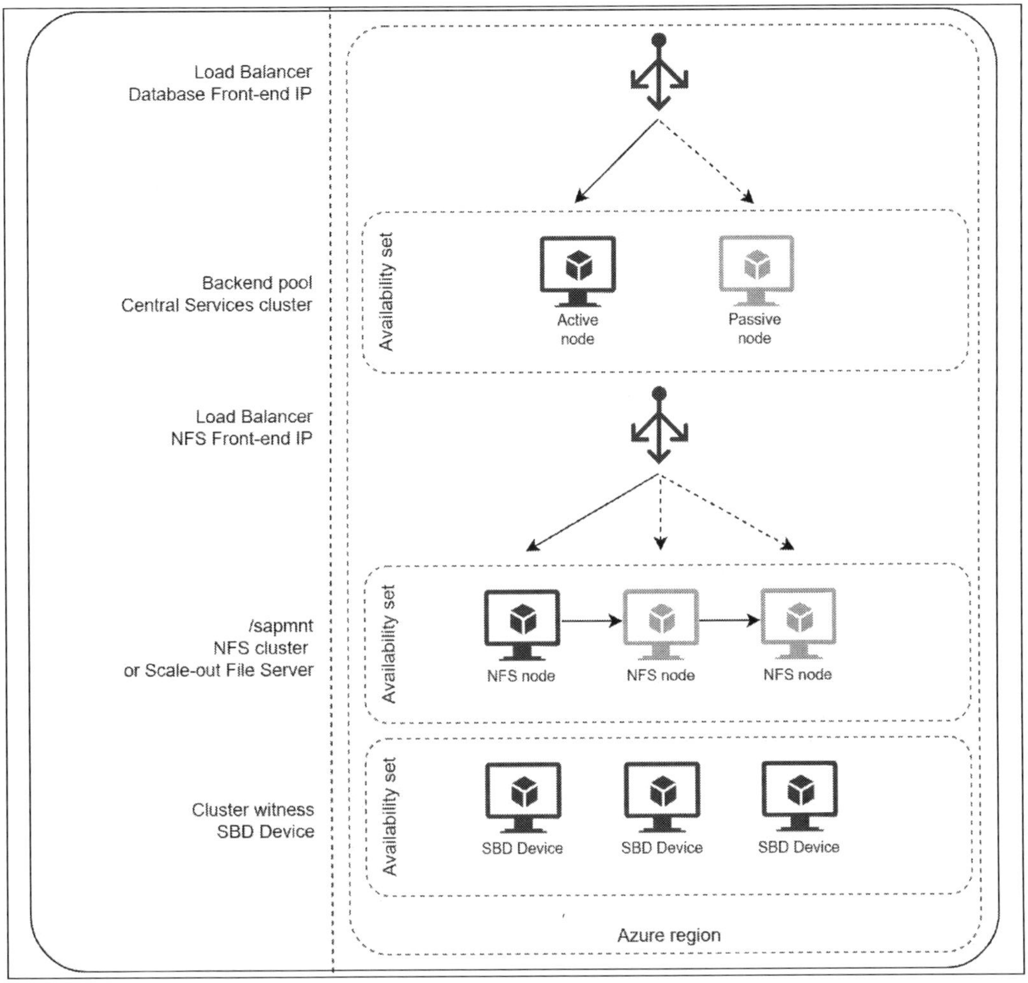

Figure 2-6: Linux Central Services cluster using the NFS cluster and SBD

If you are using the Azure Fencing Agent rather than SBD devices, then clearly this removes three of the VMs. At the time of writing, the Azure Fencing Agent is supported by RHEL but not by SLES, so for SLES you currently have to use SBD devices, but this is due to be fixed in a future update to SLES. Also, it is important to note that both the NFS cluster and the cluster witness SBD devices can be shared across multiple SAP systems, which reduces the total number of VMs required. Typically, the NFS cluster would be shared between five or six SAP systems, while the SBD devices can be shared across all the systems in a production landscape. If you are building clusters in non-production for testing purposes, and that is highly recommended, then these should use a separate NFS and SBD cluster.

In Microsoft Windows, the network share can be created using the **Storage Spaces Direct (S2D)** together with SOFS. Starting with the SAP Kernel 7.49, SAP supports the use of SOFS/S2D to host the `/sapmnt` directory between two ASCS/ERS nodes. Please note that older SAP Kernel releases such as 7.22 do not support this feature. Installation using file share is supported starting with SAP Software Provisioning Manager 1.0 SP 25. Older releases require a cluster-shared disk.

In a Windows Server environment, the landscape will require less servers when using Azure Storage Account as a cloud witness:

- Two node failover cluster hosting ASCS instance
- Three node Scale-Out File Server

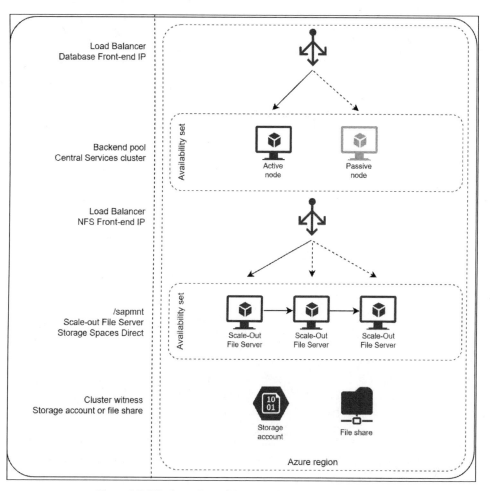

Figure 2-7: Windows Central Services cluster using SOFS/S2D

Storage Spaces Direct allows you to build a highly available storage solution where data is distributed and replicated across multiple nodes. In combination with the Scale-Out File Server feature it is possible to build highly available file shares. The minimum number of servers is two; however, it is highly recommended to use at least three VMs. The Azure Marketplace includes a preconfigured image that can be used for the Storage Spaces Direct.

As with the Linux solution above, the SOFS/S2D cluster can be shared across multiple SAP systems, which reduces the total number of VMs required. Where you have a large number of production SAP systems, it is better to add more nodes to a single SOFS/S2D cluster than to add additional separate clusters. Once again, if you are building clusters in non-production for testing purposes – and that is highly recommended – then these should use a separate SOFS/S2D cluster:

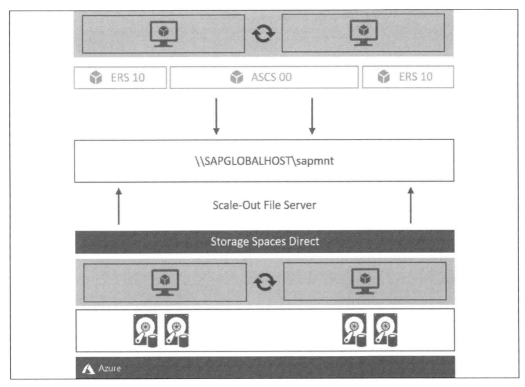

Figure 2-8: Windows scale-out file server using storage spaces direct

A new option that has become available is ANF to provide the shared storage for /sapmnt. The Central Services instance can be directly pointed to the ANF storage pool for its shared files.

As Fencing Agent or Cloud Witness could be used as the cluster witness, the requirement for SBD devices is eliminated and the cluster set-up is simplified.

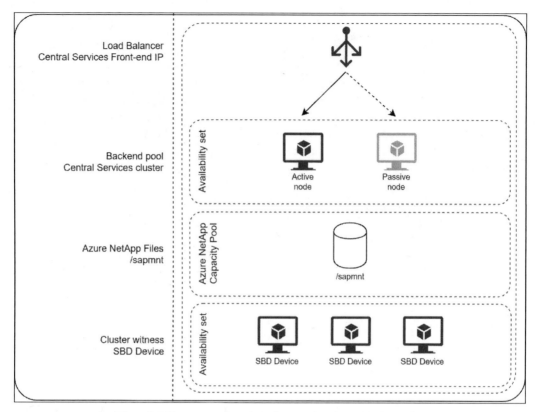

Figure 2-9: Linux central services cluster using Azure NetApp Files

Database high availability

There are two common scenarios in which to deploy a highly available database:

1. **Using shared storage**: The underlying database volumes are shared between the two hosts, with one host active and one in standby mode. If the active node fails, the cluster framework will failover the shared disks to the standby node and then restart and recover the database.

2. **Using replication**: Each database has its own storage, and the data is replicated between the databases by the DBMS software. If the active node fails, the cluster framework will simply promote the standby node to become the active node.

Chapter 2

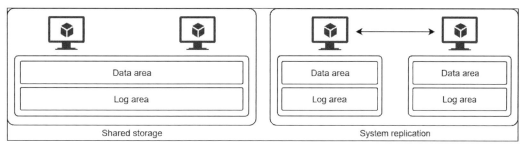

Figure 2-10: Database High Availability options

All the major DBMS that work with SAP NetWeaver support both technologies. Currently shared storage for database workloads is not available in Azure, although it may be made available for some DBMS in the future, and therefore the only option is to use DBMS replication.

It is possible to build three or even four node clusters and combine High Availability with Disaster Recovery. There are two main replication methods available:

1. **Synchronous replication**: This provides greater protection as the database commit is only considered successful when the log entry has been written to the log storage on the secondary node. The disadvantage is that this can impact system performance and is only suitable for high availability where the two databases are located relatively close to each other. It is usually used to provide high availability where you want to avoid any data loss. It provides a **recovery point objective (RPO)** of zero, or last committed transaction.

2. **Asynchronous replication**: This provides a slightly lower level of protection, as the database commit is successful when the log entry is written to the primary node only and then sent to the secondary node. The primary does not wait for the secondary to acknowledge receipt of the log. If a failure occurs before the data is written to the secondary node, a data loss will occur. It provides an RPO of between a few seconds and several minutes, depending on the commit rate, network latency, and network throughput, which is an acceptable value for DR scenarios. It is generally assumed that an RPO of approximately 15 minutes is achievable, although you may be lucky and see much less data loss.

The supported DBMS replication technologies to provide high availability for SAP on Azure are:

- **SAP HANA**: HANA System Replication in synchronous mode.
- **Oracle Database**: Oracle Data Guard running in Maximum Availability mode. Currently, **Oracle Real Application Clusters (RAC)** is not supported in Azure – either for high availability in a two-node cluster, or for scalability and availability in a multi-node cluster.

- **Microsoft SQL Server**: SQL Server Always On Availability Groups in synchronous-commit mode.
- **IBM Db2**: Db2 HADR in SYNC or NEARSYNC mode. In SYNC mode, the logs need to be written to disk on the standby node, while with NEARSYNC they only need to be written to memory on the standby node. With NEARSYNC there is risk of data loss if both nodes fail at the same time.
- **SAP Adaptive Server Enterprise (ASE)**: ASE Always-On HADR in synchronous mode.
- **SAP MaxDB**: Only basic log shipping is supported by MaxDB, so it is not suitable for an HA solution. To enable high availability of a MaxDB database in Azure it is necessary to use a third-party product such as SIOS DataKeeper[28], as the log replication doesn't support automatic failover. It is important to realize that this is a third-party solution that runs in Azure but is supported by SIOS and not Microsoft.

All database VMs that belong to a cluster should be part of an availability set or availability zone. Because Azure does not support the concept of floating IP addresses, where the IP address of a specific service can be migrated between VMs in a cluster, then an Azure load balancer must be deployed in front of the cluster, which provides the frontend IP address used by applications to connect to the database service. The Load Balancer constantly monitors the health of the backend database VMs using a health probe and routes inbound traffic to the correct node.

The cluster framework requires a quorum device to provide a fencing mechanism to ensure that only one node is active at a time. There are different solutions depending on your operating system:

- For Windows Server, you can use either a file share witness or a cloud witness.
- For Red Hat Linux, the only option is to use the Azure Fencing Agent. The original fencing agent could be very slow to failover, because it tried to initiate an orderly shutdown of the failed VM, but the fencing agent was enhanced in 2019 to provide faster failover, by essentially killing the failed VM. The new fast fencing agent is supported in RHEL 7.4 or later using the Azure Shared Image Gallery.

---

28   How to cluster MaxDB on Windows in the Cloud: `https://bit.ly/2PhiCv7`

- For SUSE Linux as well as the Azure Fencing Agent, you can use a **STONITH Block Device (SBD)**. Using an SBD has been preferable to the fencing agent because it supports fast failover, but at the expense of having to deploy another three VMs to act as the SBD device. SUSE will support the new fast fencing agent, although it is not supported at the time of writing:

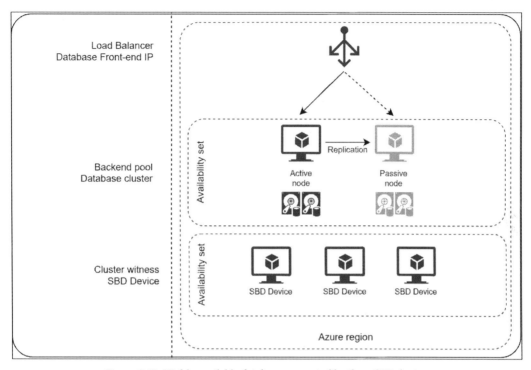

Figure 2-11: Highly available database supported by three SBD devices

The high availability ensures that the system is accessible even in case of a local hardware issue. But what happens if there is a wider technical outage that affects the entire datacenter or even the entire region? The business continuity is provided by a disaster recovery strategy that involves data replication to another data center located further away.

Disaster recovery

DR protects the system in case of the failure of a whole Azure region. In the on-premises world it is normal to have the disaster recovery site a significant distance from the primary site, to ensure that the two sites will not be affected by any single event. The distance will depend to some extent on local geography, with the distance needing to be greater in areas subject to earthquakes, hurricanes, and other severe natural events.

Microsoft takes the same approach to building Azure regions, building regions in pairs, and ensuring there is sufficient separation to provide proper DR. It aims to offer a minimum of two regions per geopolitical area to meet the needs of customers with stringent data sovereignty requirements. Microsoft prefers at least 300 miles (480 km) of separation between data centers in a regional pair, although this is not possible in all geographies. In this way you can build DR solutions in Azure that meet the same standards as you have in the on-premises world.

In general, it is best to use the regions that are officially paired by Microsoft[29]. This is because certain services automatically replicate between the regions in a pair, and you cannot control this; for example, Azure Backup. GRS is often used as a backup target for third-party tools. There are other benefits of using paired regions, such as updates being applied sequentially across the two regions in a pair, and in the event of a wider outage one data center in each pair will be prioritized for recovery. However, in some geopolitical regions not all VM series are available in both regions within a pair, and in this case you will be forced to implement DR across non-paired regions. From a SAP perspective this mostly applies to M series, Mv2 series, and S series (HANA Large Instances).

While Azure is a hyperscale cloud, it does not have limitless resources. You need to be aware of the statement in the Microsoft documentation regarding cross-region activities[30], where it states:

- **Azure Compute (IaaS)**: You must provision additional compute resources in advance to ensure resources are available in another region during a disaster.

This needs to be factored into how you architect for DR. The simplest (and costliest) solution is simply to pre-provision the resources you require in the secondary region and leave them ready for when a disaster occurs. Alternatively, there are potential options to use at least some of the resources to support some non-production workloads, reserving the required capacity but also making use of it. We will explore these options later.

You may wonder whether you could simply use Azure Availability Zones to provide DR. Microsoft is very clear that it does not consider Availability Zones as a DR solution; they exist to provide enhanced high availability. This is because, in general, the separation between the zones within a region does not guarantee that a single event could not impact all the zones, and therefore it does not constitute a DR solution.

---

29   Business continuity and disaster recovery (BCDR): Azure Paired Regions: `https://bit.ly/2DSz2EQ`
30   Cross-region activities: `https://bit.ly/33RkQ9H`

To provide disaster recovery, the main principles are the same as for high availability:

1. The database must be replicated to the secondary region
2. The central services instance and application servers have to be available in the secondary region
3. The contents of the `/sapmnt` directory must be replicated to the secondary region

The main difference compared with the high availability scenario is that in a disaster the failover will be triggered manually, all user sessions will be lost, there will normally be a level of data loss, and the recovery time will be significantly longer. Manual intervention is important, because in most cases you will want to assess the cause and likely duration of the outage before initiating failover to the secondary region. If your business continuity plan states a recovery time objective of four hours, then you may be better off waiting for the primary region to recover, rather than having failover to the secondary region with the resultant data loss. This is the same decision process as in the on-premises world.

Landing zone

One of the prerequisites when implementing DR in Azure is that you must have a landing zone in place in a second Azure region. This provides the core services that are required to access and operate resources in the DR region.

As described earlier in the section on Network Connectivity, you need to ensure that you have resilient connectivity between your on-premises network and Azure. A single ExpressRoute will connect you via an ExpressRoute peering partner and provide access to all the regions within a geopolitical region, so you can access both your primary and secondary region. However, in terms of DR planning, this makes the peering location a single point of failure, so it is recommended that you connect from two on-premises locations to two peering locations.

Azure Site Recovery

Azure provides several technologies that protect workloads in case of regional failure. The **Azure Site Recovery** (**ASR**) service is one technology that can be used to replicate the VM disks on a regular basis to a secondary region.

Architect SAP on Azure

In the case of failover then, ASR will create new resource groups and VNets in the secondary region, before recreating the VMs based on the replicated disks:

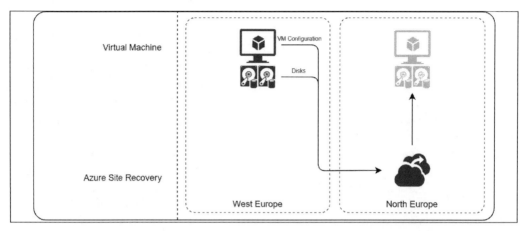

Figure 2-12: ASR creates new resource groups and VNets in a secondary region if the primary region fails

ASR supported platforms are as follows:

- Windows Server 2008 R2 SP1 – 2019
- RedHat Enterprise Linux 6.7 – 7.6
- SUSE Linux 11 SP4 – 12 (all SPs)

Not all Linux Kernels are currently supported on ASR – please check the documentation for details. Windows Servers may require updates to be installed prior to enabling the ASR.

Not all SAP workloads can be protected with ASR:

1. **Database**: Not supported
2. **SAP Application Server**: Supported
3. **SAP Central Services instance**: Supported, but if the Central Services are clustered, then manual post-processing is required to adjust the IP addresses
4. **NFS cluster**: Not supported
5. **Storage Spaces Direct**: Supported for crash-consistent recovery points
6. **Scale-Out File Server**: Supported for crash-consistent recovery points

While the SAP workloads that can be protected with ASR are quite limited, ASR can be used to automate the complete failover process using customized recovery plans, custom scripts and potentially a few manual operations. In this way, ASR can be used to orchestrate most or all of the failover process.

There are two recovery point types available:

- **Crash-consistent recovery point**: A crash-consistent recovery point represents the on-disk data as if the VM crashed or the power cord was pulled from the server at the time the snapshot was taken. It doesn't include anything that was in memory when the snapshot was taken.
- **Application-consistent recovery point**: Application-consistent recovery points are created from application-consistent snapshots. Application-consistent recovery points capture the same data as crash-consistent snapshots, with the addition of all data in memory and all transactions in process. Because of their extra content, application-consistent snapshots are the most involved and take the longest to perform.

The frequency of crash-consistent recovery points is customizable. Azure supports replication every 15 minutes, 5 minutes, or 30 seconds. Application-consistent recovery points are created every hour.

Unlike with high availability, in the disaster recovery scenario failover is usually not automatic but manual and executed only after it is confirmed the primary region will not be able to resume operations. The failover is also usually only triggered for the entire landscape, not for the failure of a single VM, which will be restarted by Azure automatically.

Application Server Disaster Recovery

The SAP Application Servers including the SAP Central Services contain mostly static files, and the ASR is mostly supported. The underlaying VM disks are replicated by ASR, and ASR will build new VMs when the failover occurs:

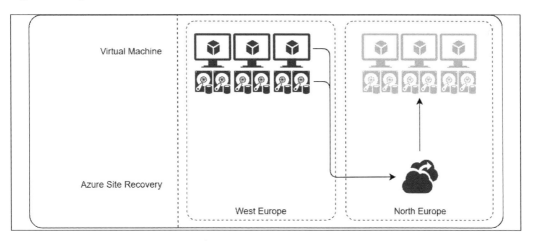

Figure 2-13: Application Server Disaster Recovery using ASR

Database server disaster recovery

As already mentioned, ASR cannot be used to replicate VMs running a database. This is because ASR does not guarantee that the replication across all disks attached to a single VM is fully synchronized, which is a problem when using striped disks for database data and log files. The database disks on the secondary region may not be consistent, the database may not be able to be restarted. The only exception is when you only want to replicate the database binaries, and you plan to restore the database from backup. A further restriction with ASR is that it only supports limited data change rates[31], and on many SAP production database VMs, the change rate will exceed that which is supported by ASR.

As ASR is not a supported solution for SAP databases, you need to choose between one of two options depending on your recovery point and recover time objectives:

1. Using DBMS replication similar to that used for high availability, but in asynchronous mode. Asynchronous mode must be used as otherwise the impact on database performance would be unacceptable. This will provide the lowest RPO and RTO.
2. Backup and restore, where SAP is less critical to your business and you can afford a high RPO and RTO.

Using DBMS replication is the most reliable solution and it is Microsoft's recommendation for protecting SAP workload in Azure. Certainly, if SAP is considered business critical then this is the only solution likely to be able to deliver the recovery point and recovery time objectives that your business requires. The database is continuously replicated from the primary region to a secondary region using the same technologies as for high availability but operating in asynchronous mode. It is also the most expensive solution as the database VMs on the secondary site must be constantly running:

---

31   ASR limits and data change rates: https://bit.ly/2RplpVJ

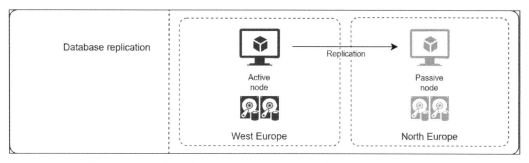

Figure 2-14: Database disaster recovery using asynchronous DBMS replication

Where SAP is less critical to the operation of your business, and you are prepared to accept greater data loss and a longer time to recover, then a cheaper option is to use a backup and restore approach. The database backup is written to Azure Blob storage, which is geo-replicated to a second region. In the event of the loss of the primary region, the database can be restored from the backup copy. Unfortunately, depending on the backup frequency, the amount of data lost is much higher than when using DBMS replication. The time required to restore the database is also much higher as the DBMS VM must be started, the database backup copied from the Blob storage and the database recovered.

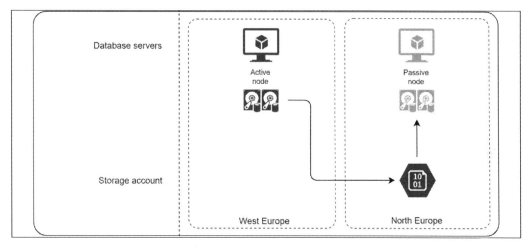

Figure 2-15: Database Disaster Recovery using backup and restore

With the application servers and the database server protected, the final element that requires protection is the SAP Central Services.

Central services disaster recovery

When the SAP Central Services is just a standalone VM, then it can be protected by ASR in the same way as the application servers, as described previously in this chapter. ASR will replicate the central services VM disks and the target VM configuration will be an exact replica of the source.

However, where the Central Services in the primary region runs in a highly available cluster, then a different solution is required. The solution will also depend on whether the target environment is also to be made highly available.

Central services target is not highly available

As well as having a highly available database server cluster on the primary site, it is normal to have a highly available SAP central services cluster, and in both cases to have only a single node (non-clustered) deployment on the recovery site. In theory you could use ASR to replicate one node of the SAP central services cluster. However, if the source VM is part of a cluster, then the target VM will also expect to be, and when the VM is recreated by ASR it will not be part of a cluster and the SAP central services will fail to start.

Currently, the recommended solution is to manually create the SAP central services VM when the solution is being deployed. This VM can be kept shut down until there is a failover. The VM will need to be started from time to time to apply patches, updates, and configuration changes to the SAP software and the operating system, but mostly you will just pay the cost of the underlying disk storage, which is the same as when using ASR. This solution is illustrated in *Figure 2-16*:

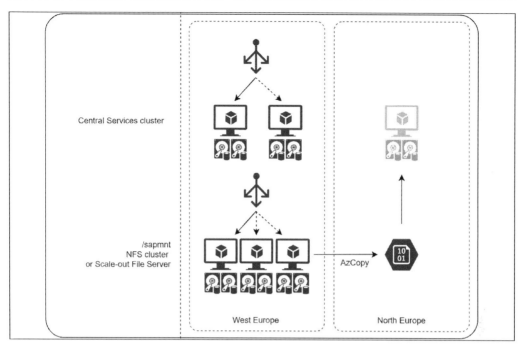

Figure 2-16: SAP central services DR with clustered primary and standalone DR

The `/sapmnt` directory stills needs to be replicated.

An additional layer of protection can be added by running the DR environment also in a highly available mode.

Central services target is highly available

To provide the highest levels of availability, even following a disaster, you may want the SAP central services to be clustered in the target environment. Again, in theory you could use ASR to replicate both virtual machines, and, when ASR recreates the VMs, they will still be part of a cluster and consistent. However, additional post-failover processing is required to configure cluster IPs as the target virtual network IP range should not overlap and cluster IPs are static. The load balancers could be provisioned upfront, however in such cases they would incur additional cost. An alternative is to create a script that deploys the load balancer during failover and orchestrate it using an ASR recovery plan.

Once again, the current recommended solution is to manually create both SAP central services VMs when the solution is being deployed. These VM can be kept shut down until there is a failover. Both VMs will need to be started from time to time to apply patches, updates, and configuration changes to the SAP software and the operating system, but mostly you will just pay the cost of the underlying disk storage, which is the same as when using ASR.

The content of the /sapmnt directory has to be replicated as well; see below for options:

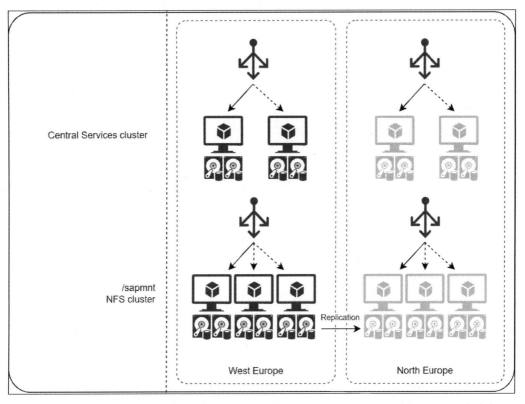

Figure 2-17: The replicated VMs and /sapmnt cluster should be prepared and kept up to date in case of a failover

The central services instance requires the /sapmnt directory, which should also be replicated to the target DR environment.

Handling the /sapmnt directory

If the primary system is part of a failover cluster, then the /sapmnt directory is kept separately from the Central Services instance on shared storage, which could be an NFS cluster for Linux VMs, a **scale-out file server (SOFS)** for Windows VMs, or ANF for both.

For both Linux NFS cluster and Windows Scale-Out File Server, the generally recommended solution from Microsoft has been to use a scripted file copy of the /sapmnt directory using rsync or robocopy, respectively. However, ASR does now support replication of Windows Scale-Out File Server and this could be an option going forward. Data stored on Azure NetApp files currently has to be replicated to the secondary region using external copy tools (rsync for NFS and robocopy for SMB) or a NetApp Cloud SYNC service. In the longer-term native NetApp storage replication may be supported.

Backup

The entire SAP landscape should be regularly backed up to ensure business continuity in case of data loss or corruption. There are different strategies to protect different parts of the SAP workload. The most important component is the database, which holds all business-related data. In case of a database corruption, all stored information may be irreversibly lost. However, data stored on application servers is also important. A good backup solution should enable you to recover the system from the corrupted state.

Disaster recovery versus backup

Both disaster recovery and backup are connected to each other, but there are slight differences in their purpose and execution method. While disaster recovery is focused mainly on how to continue the business operations after infrastructure failure, the backup protects the logical structure of the data to ensure recoverability in case of partial data loss.

Many people think that if they have a synchronous database replica for high availability, and a second asynchronous replica in a second region, then why do they need to worry about backup? However, if an employee accidently deletes a set of important data, then the deletion will be replicated to the local high availability copy and to the remote disaster recovery copy. As the underlaying infrastructure is still working fine, there is no point in failing over to the second region, and if you did, the data in the disaster recovery database will also have been deleted. Backup gives the opportunity to "travel in time" and restore the database to just before the issue occurred.

Filesystem backup

The simplest way to implement a backup is to copy the files stored on a server to an external, safe location – for example, Azure Blob storage. In case of failure, the files can be used to re-create the environment. But while copying files is in fact easy, it may be difficult to automate the process and make it reliable.

It works well in cases where a single configuration file needs to be recovered, but when the entire server is down due to a disk failure it may be required to reinstall all the software.

Using Azure Blob storage is a common solution to protect all types of data including database backups; every time a database backup file is created on primary storage, it can then be copied to Azure Blob storage, and then deleted from the primary storage.

Disk snapshot

A more advanced approach is to take the filesystem backup as a snapshot. In virtual environments such as Azure, where the disks are basically stored as files, it is possible to create an image of the current state of the storage. It contains all the data, but if the virtual machine is running it doesn't guarantee application-level consistency, it only provides a crash consistent image. To achieve application-level consistency requires additional pre- and post-processing steps to ensure that a database can be recovered. Customers using Microsoft SQL Server benefit from the integration with **Volume Shadow Copy Service (VSS)** functionality in Windows Server to ensure the database snapshot backup is recoverable; however, for other database management systems and Linux operating systems, a solution needs to be scripted.

A big advantage of creating disk snapshots is the speed, both when creating the snapshot but also should you need to restore a VM, particularly when compared with copying files to Azure Blob storage. It is a good solution to create a recovery point before executing complex administrative tasks such as a kernel update. However, you do need to be careful when taking a snapshot of a VM with multiple disks, particularly one running a DBMS, as Azure disk snapshots only provide a crash-consistent copy. It is recommended that you script a solution to quiesce the database, ensure all data is flushed to disk, and then take the disk snapshot.

Currently you cannot specify retention policies and storage tiers for storage snapshots, although you can decide whether the store is locally-redundant or zone-redundant. This means that you have to put in place processes to manage the snapshots and to delete them when no longer required – there is no automated process for this. The price is calculated based on the actual storage consumption – even if the disk size is 100 GB you pay only for the used space, which may be lower.

Database backup

In most databases, copying the underlying files doesn't guarantee the recoverability of the system. All databases have implemented a functionality to dump all stored information to a disk, which can be later secured using a filesystem backup and sent to Azure Blob storage. Taking a backup of the transaction logs allows you to recover the database to a particular point in time.

If a user accidentally deletes important data, this approach allows the database to be restored to a moment before the deletion happened. The data loss is minimized relative to a full backup.

The database backup heavily relies on the storage performance. If the target storage doesn't offer a high throughput, the process can take a lot of time. Therefore, most databases offer functionality to dump only data that has changed since the last backup. Incremental and differential backups are much smaller, but require a full backup to recover the database. A common approach is to take a weekly full backup, at a time when the database is at its least active, and then take daily incremental or differential backups.

For SAP HANA databases, Microsoft published a sample storage layout that includes a volume to keep database backup. It's possible to include additional disks to increase the throughput and therefore decrease the backup and restore time.

VM storage throttling needs to be taken into account. During the backup and restore process the database reads and writes data at the same time. The virtual machine size should reflect the additional storage performance requirements to avoid hitting the throughput limit, otherwise the backup process may affect the overall performance of the system. A good practice is to use the temporary disk available in Azure during the recovery process to avoid virtual machine throttling, as the operations against the temporary disk does not count against the virtual machine limits.

Database snapshot

A database snapshot works in a way analogous to a storage snapshot. It creates an image of the current state of the database, including all existing data. It's very quick as it doesn't involve any data dumps, but it's important to understand that the snapshot itself is not a backup. To ensure you can recover the system, the snapshot has to be copied to an external location like Azure Blob storage; otherwise, when the snapshot is confirmed, the snapshot is merged with the database and can't be used any longer as a recovery point.

In Microsoft Azure you can combine the database and filesystem snapshot to create a consistent recovery point. For the SAP HANA database the process looks as follows:

1. Execute SAP HANA snapshot prepare
2. Freeze the filesystem
3. Create disk snapshot in Azure
4. Unfreeze the filesystem
5. Confirm SAP HANA snapshot

If the data area is distributed across multiple disks, it's required to create a snapshot of each disk that creates the volume.

Database snapshots are suitable for executing very fast backups and recoveries of large data volumes, with a minor impact on SAP HANA performance in environments with a low Recovery Time Objective.

As there is no consistency check performed during the database snapshot, the traditional backup should also be included in the backup strategy.

Database streaming backup

Some databases provide an interface for third-party backup solutions. Instead of writing the data to a disk, a streaming backup sends them over the network to an external system. It eliminates the need for an additional disk attached to the VM and reduces the storage cost.

Where the primary backups are taken using snapshots, it is good practice to run a weekly streaming backup to allow data verification. Most third-party backup tools have a capability to verify that the backup files are not corrupted and can be used for recovery purposes. With snapshots alone, silent corruption could be happening and remain undetected.

Azure Backup

Azure Backup is part of the Azure Recovery Services that allows you to create a recovery point for a workload running in the Azure cloud. It can also be used to back up on-premises workloads, where it integrates well with Hyper-V and VMware, and can also be used to protect physical servers, but that is beyond the scope of this book and we'll not go into further detail on that.

The native backup solution allows users to create policies that schedule the backup and configure the retention policies to drop obsolete data. The full virtual machine backup cannot be scheduled more often than once a day. The same limitation applies to database workloads; however, the log backups can be taken every 15 minutes. Different retention policies can be scheduled for daily, weekly, monthly, and yearly backups. You can choose the storage replication option (GRS and LRS are available), but you can't influence the storage tier.

Azure Backup for virtual machines

During the first execution Azure Recovery Services installs a backup extension to the virtual machine agent. For Windows VMs that are running, Backup coordinates with the Windows VSS to take an application-consistent snapshot of the VM. If Backup is unable to take an application-consistent snapshot, then it takes a file-consistent snapshot.

For virtual machines running Linux by default, a file-consistent backup is taken. However, it is possible to extend this functionality using custom scripts and create application-consistent backups.

SAP application servers can be protected using Azure Backup. For the database servers you can use Azure Backup to back up all the disks other than those used for data and logs. Because Azure Backup does not guarantee application-level consistency a separate database backup is required.

During a recovery process, you can decide to restore an entire virtual machine or selected disks or even individual files.

Azure Backup for databases

Microsoft SQL Server and SAP HANA databases can be protected using Azure Backup. It works without any agent installed on the server, but the VM must communicate with a set of public IP addresses that belong to Azure Backup service. The backup is streamed from the database to the cloud service and no data is written to the VM disk. Azure Backup uses the database functionalities to stream the backup directly to the Recovery Services vault and it doesn't require backup data to be stored on a filesystem.

Azure Backup for SAP HANA is currently in private preview and has a number of limitations:

- Only selected operating systems are supported
- The backup works only for a single instance of SAP HANA (no scale-out deployments)
- Multiple SAP HANA instances on the same VM are not supported

Third-party backup solutions

As well as using native Azure capabilities for backup, you can also use third-party backup tools. They are separate products and, in most cases, will require an additional license. It is likely you will be using a third-party backup tool already on-premises and in many cases the same tool can be used in Azure, but you will need to check with the backup tool vendor.

Enterprise-ready backup products can have additional capabilities when compared with native Azure Backup. A list of advantages includes:

1. Support for various databases, including SAP HANA scale-out
2. Support for SAP HANA snapshot backups

3. Data reduction through advanced compression and deduplication that decrease backup storage costs
4. Customizable backup policies
5. Advanced retention policies

It may be necessary to provision additional infrastructure to run the third-party backup solutions. Normally there is a management component, where backup policies are configured, which also controls the backup process, and one or more data movers that manage the physical transfer of data. These will normally run in VMs in Azure. In some cases a single management component can be used to manage both on-premises and Azure backups, useful when running in a hybrid cloud environment, but the data movers for workloads running in Azure and being backed up to storage in Azure should always also run in Azure.

Azure Blob Storage for backup

Whether using Azure native backup tools or third-party tools for backup, for long term retention the data will be stored in Azure Blob storage. All data in Azure is automatically replicated for local durability, and there are multiple redundancy options as described earlier in this chapter. When choosing the right storage for your backups you need to consider the following:

- **Locally redundant storage**: Only stores backups in a single region, so in the event of a region becoming unavailable, you will have no access to your backups.

- **Zone-redundant storage**: Only stores backups in a single region, but there will be one copy in each of the three zones. If a zone is lost then a copy of the backup will be available in the remaining zones, but in the event of a region becoming unavailable, you will have no access to your backups.

- **Geo-redundant storage**: Stores copies of your backups in a primary and secondary region. In the event of one region becoming unavailable, you will have access to your backups in the other region. This is the minimum sensible resilience for backups, which provides an "off-site" copy.

- **Read-access geo-redundant storage**: If you will want read access to your backups in the secondary region, for example, to use them to restore and refresh another system, then you should choose RA-GRS.

- **Geo-zone-redundant storage**: If you are using a region that supports Availability Zones, then this is the recommended option to ensure you have both local copies in all three zones within the primary region, and also have copies in a secondary region.

- **Read-access geo-zone-redundant storage**: If you are planning to use GZRS but will want read access to your backups in the secondary region, for example, to use them to restore and refresh another system, then you should choose RA-GZRS.

As well as the different redundancy options, Azure Blob storage also offers three storage tiers that reflect how often the data is accessed. It has a direct influence on the cost of data storage and data retrieval:

- **Hot**: For files that are accessed frequently. It offers the highest storage price, but the access and transaction costs are the lowest.
- **Cool**: For files that are accessed infrequently and stored for at least 30 days. It offers lower storage price, but the access and transaction cost is higher.
- **Archive**: For files that are accessed very rarely and stored for at least 180 days. It offers the lowest storage price, but the access and transaction cost is the highest.

Data in the archive tier is kept offline and it may take a few hours before it is available to the user.

Files that are transferred to cool and archive tiers are a subject to early deletion fees if they are kept for a shorter period of time.

Azure offers storage life cycle management that can automatically transition the storage tier based on the customizable policies. You can create rules that transition the Blobs between tiers to optimize the performance and cost.

Monitoring

Each SAP system requires constant monitoring to ensure all processes are running correctly with no disruptions. Many organizations rely on the availability of the SAP system and even a short unplanned downtime could lead to temporary company shutdown. Without the SAP system being available customers cannot place orders, factories cannot produce goods, and goods cannot be picked and shipped. Even a small disruption can lead to significant financial loss.

Microsoft Azure has a set of features that constantly monitor all services and provide recommendations. Customers can use the metrics collected to ensure that their system is running with the best performance and also to optimize the cost of running SAP in Azure. Having full visibility helps to track the health of the system and makes it easier to perform a root cause analysis in case of any failure.

Architect SAP on Azure

By default, each VM built using an Azure Marketplace image has a preinstalled Linux Agent that orchestrates the interactions between a virtual machine and the Azure Fabric Controller. Using additional extensions, it is possible to enhance the basic monitoring capabilities.

Azure Diagnostics extension

Using the Diagnostic Extension Azure can collect performance metrics from the virtual machine and store them in a storage account. In addition, it retrieves the operating system and application logs and makes them available through the Azure portal. The exact list of available metrics and logs may vary depending on the operating system and is available in Azure documentation.

Azure Enhanced Monitoring Extension for SAP

There is a dedicated monitoring extension for virtual machines running SAP.
It consumes the diagnostic data collected by the Diagnostic Extension and transforms it into an aggregated dataset appropriate for the SAP Host Control process to consume.

Both extensions are mandatory for VMs running SAP workloads.

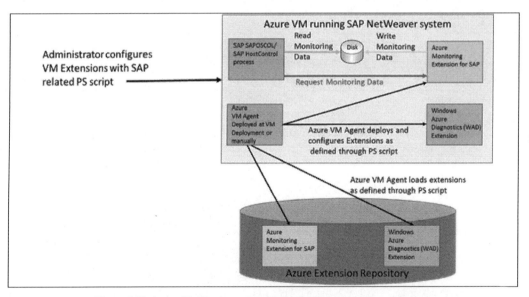

Figure 2-18: Azure Monitoring extension for SAP (source: Microsoft.com)

By using this extension, additional information about the hardware and architecture becomes visible in the system, for example, the operating system monitor in the SAP system (ST06) will correctly report Microsoft Azure as the hyperscalar.

Azure Monitor

Azure Monitor is the central framework for service monitoring in the Azure platform. All telemetry data and application logs are stored in Azure Monitor and are available to the system administrator. There are two basic types of collected information: metrics and logs.

Metrics are numerical values that represent a state of a service at a point in time. It could be CPU utilization or disk write speed. The logs contain unstructured data such as events or traces that come from the operating system or supported application. Both are valuable inputs during monitoring and troubleshooting of a SAP environment.

External applications can send custom logs using the Data Collector API. This allows you to create custom monitoring scenarios and extend monitoring to resources that don't expose telemetry through other sources.

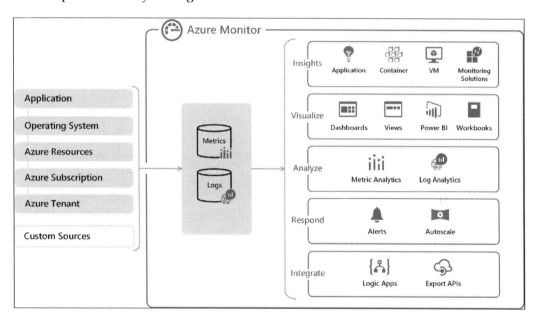

Figure 2-19: Azure Monitor overview (source: Microsoft.com)

Azure Monitor is commonly used to track virtual machine utilization. It cannot collect the SAP system or HANA database logs, which should be analyzed using SAP-dedicated tools.

Activity Logs

Activity Logs collect events that occurred in the Azure platform. It describes anything that happened to the resources in a subscription. When a VM is deployed, started, or deleted, it will be captured by the Activity Log and the information is available to system administrators:

Figure 2-20: Azure activity log (source: Microsoft)

You can use the Activity Log to track why the server was rebooted or who changed the size of the VM, and when.

Alerts

Based on the telemetry data, Azure Monitor issues alerts that inform system administrators when a service reaches a defined threshold, for example, the CPU utilization is high or there is low memory available. System administrators can create alert rules that trigger an action type such as Email/SMS, Logic App, Webhook, or Automation Runbook:

Figure 2-21: Example alerts page (source: Microsoft.com)

Dashboards

Collected telemetry and log data can be visualized in Azure Dashboards using charts and graphs to create a central monitoring space for administrators:

Figure 2-22: Example dashboard (source: Microsoft.com)

A dashboard lets you build a centralized space to monitor Azure resources and simplify the daily tasks. Instead of looking for values in many places, you can combine them all into a single view.

Azure Advisor

Based on the collected telemetry data, the Azure Advisor service proactively recommends solutions that optimize the environment. There are four best practice categories:

1. **High availability**: Improve the business continuity of the service
2. **Security**: Detect threats and vulnerabilities
3. **Performance**: Improve the speed of applications
4. **Cost**: Optimize and reduce cost

The following screenshot displays the Azure Advisor Dashboard:

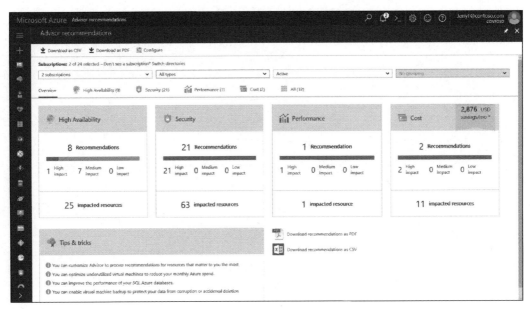

Figure 2-23: Azure Advisor dashboard (source: Microsoft.com)

You should always review the recommendations on a regular basis, as they will provide you with initial ideas on how to optimize the landscape. If a VM is under-utilized, why not consider changing its size?

Microsoft Azure provides various tools to run the SAP system in an efficient and cost-optimized manner. In the past, you'd require additional tools to monitor the entire hardware infrastructure. In Azure, all data is captured by default, which gives you the potential to obtain deeper insights.

SAP NetWeaver-based systems

In this section, we will look in more detail at specifics relating to architecting SAP NetWeaver-based systems that run on a non-HANA database, generally now referred to by SAP as AnyDB. These SAP applications use one of the SAP-supported DBMS: IBM Db2, Microsoft SQL Server, Oracle Database, SAP ASE, or SAP MaxDB. With the exception of the details of how each DBMS handles high availability and disaster recovery, all other aspects of the architecture are similar.

Supported platforms

The first thing you need to check when planning a migration of SAP to Microsoft Azure is whether the system is fully supported in Microsoft Azure, or if an upgrade is required as a prerequisite.

The *SAP Note 1928533 - SAP Applications on Azure: Supported Products and Azure VM types* lists the SAP software versions supported to run in Azure. You should always check the latest version of this SAP note to get the most up-to-date information, as it changes regularly. As an example, version 100 of the note, from August 2019, lists the following products as supported in Azure:

Supported operating systems and products:

- Microsoft Windows Server 2008 R2, 2012 (R2), 2016, and 2019
- **SUSE Linux Enterprise Server (SLES)** 12 and higher
- SLES 12 for SAP Applications and higher
- **Red Hat Enterprise Linux 7 (RHEL7)** and higher
- Red Hat Enterprise Linux 7 for SAP and higher
- Red Hat Enterprise Linux 7 for SAP HANA and higher
- **Oracle Linux 7 (OL7)**

Supported SAP NetWeaver releases:

- Applications running on the Application Server ABAP as part of SAP NetWeaver 7.0X:
    - SAP Kernel 7.21 EXT (min. PL #622)
    - SAP Kernel 7.22 EXT (min. PL #112)
    - Higher SAP Kernel versions
- Applications running on the Application Server ABAP and/ or Java as part of SAP NetWeaver 7.1 or higher:
    - SAP Kernel 7.21 EXT (min. PL #622)
    - SAP Kernel 7.22 EXT (min. PL #112)
- Applications running on the Application Servers ABAP and/ or Java as part of SAP NetWeaver 7.4 or higher:
    - SAP Kernel 7.45 (min. PL #111)
    - Higher SAP Kernel versions

Supported databases running on Windows:

- Microsoft SQL Server 2008 R2 or higher
- SAP ASE 16.0 SP02 or higher
- IBM Db2 for Linux, Unix, and Windows 10.5 or higher (see SAP Note 2233094)
- Oracle database; for versions and restrictions, see SAP Note 2039619
- SAP MaxDB version 7.9
- SAP liveCache as part of SAP SCM 7.0 EhP2 (or higher): Minimal version for SAP liveCache: SAP LC/LCAPPS 10.0 SP 27 including liveCache 7.9.08.32 and LCA-Build 27, released for EhP 2 for SAP SCM 7.0 and higher

Note:

SAP liveCache based on SAP MaxDB technology has to run on an Azure VM solely dedicated to SAP liveCache (that is, without any other application software running on this VM).

Supported databases running on Linux:

- SAP HANA 1.0 SP12 and higher, SAP HANA 2.0:
    - On Microsoft Azure Large Instances
    - On Microsoft Azure Infrastructure as a Service IaaS (Azure Virtual Machines)
- SAP ASE 16.0 SP02 or higher
- IBM Db2 for Linux, UNIX, and Windows 10.5 or higher
- SAP MaxDB version 7.9.09.05 or higher
- Oracle Database – only on Oracle Linux
- SAP liveCache as part of SAP SCM 7.0 EhP4 (or higher): Minimal version for SAP liveCache: SAP LC/LCAPPS 10.0 SP 34 including liveCache 7.9.09.05 and LCA-Build 34, released for EhP 4 for SAP SCM 7.0 and higher.

Note:

SAP liveCache based on SAP MaxDB technology has to run on an Azure VM **solely dedicated to SAP liveCache** (that is, without any other application software running on this VM).

Due to Oracle licensing, deployment of the Oracle database or its components is supported only by a Windows Server or Oracle Linux. As the SAP application servers use Oracle Client to connect to the database, they are supported only when deployed to Windows Server or Oracle Linux.

Sizing SAP systems

General guidance on sizing has already been provided earlier in this chapter. In this section we will focus on specific considerations for SAP NetWeaver-based systems.

CPU and memory

For new SAP deployments, there is no difference in sizing for on-premises or in Azure. As described before you will use a combination of SAP Quick Sizer and SAP Sizing Guidelines to estimate the required CPU and memory based on the number of users and/or transaction volumes. These will provide the CPU requirements in terms of SAPS and you can then compare the sizing with the SAPS values published in *SAP Note 1928533 – SAP Applications on Azure: Supported Products and Azure VM types*. You may still want to follow the earlier guidance, and initially tight size the VMs so as to reduce cost, and then scale-up the VM if actually required.

When migrating an existing workload from on-premises to Azure, it is recommended to use reference sizing, using the capacity and utilization of the existing installed hardware to calculate the required resources in Azure. Just because the current server has 128 GB of RAM does not mean it is the appropriate amount of RAM; it is quite possible that this amount was overallocated and the system has never used all this memory. In such a case, if you simply use the current allocated memory, then you may choose a larger VM than required, which will cost more despite the fact that there is no additional benefit in terms of application performance. Similarly, for the CPU, if the average utilization is low, most probably you can assign a smaller VM type. Usually the peak CPU utilization should not exceed 65%.

Assuming you have access to the current Azure environment, you can collect performance metrics such as CPU and memory usage, and you can then correlate the actual usage data with Azure VMs and create appropriately-sized configurations, rather than simply provisioning on a like-for-like basis, based on current provisioned capacity.

Again, Azure gives you the opportunity to quickly scale-up and scale-down VMs, so if you discover that the VM requires more or less resources, then you can quickly change the VM size.

Ideally for replatforming you will want the following performance metrics:

1. CPU:
    1. Make and model of processor
    2. Number of cores
    3. Processor speed
    4. Average utilization
    5. Maximum utilization
2. Memory:
    1. Total available memory
    2. Average memory consumed
    3. Maximum memory consumed

As well as the average utilization of the compute resources, you should also look at the peak utilizations. There may be background jobs that are scheduled to run at night or during weekends that require more CPU resources, and during the hours they are running, the CPU utilization may be much higher.

In a few cases, you may find that the existing server is in fact undersized, and that the CPU utilization is regularly much higher than 65%, or that nearly all the memory is being used. In this case you should look to size a larger VM that will bring the CPU utilization back to the target of 65%.

To calculate the required SAPS the following formula can be used:

$$[Required\ SAPS] = [Provisioned\ SAPS] * \frac{[Peak\ Utilization\%]}{65\%}$$

When sizing the application tier, it is also possible to combine multiple application servers into a smaller number that fit more closely to the available VM sizes in Azure. It is likely that your environment has grown over time, and that the number of servers has grown with it. You may have started with two application servers but, after a year, there was a requirement to deploy an extra one. Moving to Azure is a good opportunity to redesign this outdated landscape.

Instead of provisioning a large number of application servers where all have to be updated and managed, you can easily decrease the number of servers, making each one larger, and assign more work processes. You benefit from the lower administration cost while the performance is still the same.

The following table shows how you can model the Azure resources based on the existing platform data. You should always take into account the current hardware utilization, as very often the infrastructure is oversized and doesn't reflect the possibilities that comes with the cloud:

On-premise workload					Microsoft Azure			
Qty	vCPU	CPU Utilization	RAM	RAM usage	Qty	VM Type	vCPU	RAM
1	4	65%	16 GB	80%	1	D4s_v3	4	16 GB
1	16	20%	64 GB	70%	1	E8s_v3	8	64 GB
1	8	40%	64 GB	80%	1	E16s_v3	16	128GB
1	8	50%	64 GB	60%				
3	12	50%	96 GB	60%	2	E16s_v3	16	128 GB

Table 2-3: Mapping existing servers to Azure VM

A full list of SAP-certified Azure VMs is available in *SAP Note SAP Note 1928533 - SAP Applications on Azure: Supported Products and Azure VM types*. An extract of that list, is included earlier in this chapter.

Storage sizing

Together with the basic compute resources like vCPU and memory, you should have a look at the storage layout. In the on-premises environments the storage is considered as an amount of space available for application and as one of the performance factors – faster disks process more information at the same time. In the cloud, the disk also influences the availability of the VMs. Next, you'll find information on how to correctly plan the storage for application servers and databases.

Application servers

SAP application servers do not require high performance disk storage as they do not require a large number of IOPS or high throughput, and therefore assigning a disk that supports a large number of IOPS or high throughput is unnecessary. However, application servers with premium SSD managed disks will benefit from higher availability. The 99.9% SLA of a single VM is only valid when the VM uses premium managed disks.

For VMs that are equipped with standard storage, either standard HDD or standard SSD, Microsoft does not offer any availability guarantee. For cost-saving, standard SSD disks could be used for non-production workloads, while for production the recommendation is to always use premium managed SSD disks.

It's recommended that each application server VM has one disk for the operating system and a second disk for the SAP executables, rather than install the executables on the OS disk. For a Windows VM the storage layout may look like this:

Drive letter	C:	D:	E:
Type	OS Disk	Temporary disk – page file	SAP Binaries
Disk size	P10	n/a	P6

The temporary disk is the recommended place to host the Windows page or Linux swap files. If you use an Azure gallery image to deploy Windows, then the page files will be automatically deployed on the temporary disk, but for Linux images the swap file will not automatically re-deployed on the temporary disk; this needs to be configured manually.

The caching of the SAP Application Server should be set to read-only.

Database servers

The database performance is usually highly dependent on the underlying storage. For new workloads on Azure, the number of IOPS and throughput should come from the sizing estimates. In migrations, the storage performance requirement can be obtained either from the underlying storage platform, whether it has performance monitoring tools available, or from the database itself.

To achieve a higher performance, multiple disks can be combined into logical volumes. The volume performance is then a sum of IOPS and throughput of particular disks. By combining three P30 disks as in the example below, you create a single volume that offers 15,000 IOPS and 600 Mbps throughput:

Azure Disk	IOPS	Throughput	Logical volume	IOPS	Throughput
P30	5000	200 Mbps			
P30	5000	200 Mbps	LV	15,000	600 Mbps
P30	5000	200 Mbps			

The caching should be set to read-only for the data disks and operating system disk. No caching should be used for the log disks.

For DBMS other than HANA, Microsoft only provides high-level guidance on storage layouts and sizing the storage layer. The final solution will depend on the choice of DBMS and the size and throughput of the database, and this will vary for each SAP application and database size. To achieve the best performance, the data volume should be built from at least three P20 disks and the log area from two P20 disks.

The table below shows a sample storage layout for database workloads. The database executables are stored on a single P6 disk to avoid installing software on the operating system drive. The data volume is built based on three P20 disks that together offer 1.5 TB of space and high throughput. In addition, the performance benefits from the data caching, which is not allowed for the log area. Therefore, it requires a separate volume built from the disk with caching disabled:

	Disk type	Caching	Volume
OS disk	P10	Read/Write	C:
Temp disk	n/a	n/a	D:
Exe disk	P6	Read-only	E:
Data disk	P30	Read-only	F:
Data disk	P30	Read-only	
Data disk	P30	Read-only	
Log disk	P20	No caching	G:
Log disk	P20	No caching	

For sizing storage for SAP HANA databases, please refer to the section *SAP HANA sizing*.

Network sizing

The network can be described using two main metrics:

1. **Throughput**: Represents the amount of bits transferred over a specified time. For example, the network throughput of 1 Mbps means you can transfer one megabit of information during every second.

2. **Latency**: Represents how much time it takes to transfer the data to the destination. In SAP, we always look at the round-trip, which means the latency is the time required to transfer the data and receive acknowledgment it was received.

The network throughput inside a virtual network is always limited by the virtual machine size. Larger VMs support a higher network throughput.

The latency is more complex to estimate. During the deployment of virtual machines, you cannot control on which physical host they will be provisioned. It can be the case that two VMs in a virtual network are placed at opposite ends of a data hall. As each network packet would be routed by many network switches, the latency could be longer. You should always use the NIPING tool to measure the latency between servers, as the ping won't return correct results when accelerated networking is enabled.

The placement of VMs can be partially controlled using **Proximity Placement Groups (PPGs)**. When VMs are deployed into a PPG then Azure attempts to locate them as close to each other as possible and limit the number of network hops during communication. PPGs should generally be used per SAP system, rather than deploy multiple SAP systems within a single PPG, although if the two SAP systems are closely coupled, with a high level of real-time interaction, then it may be desirable to place them within the same PPG.

When using PPG, always deploy the scarcest resource first, and then add the other VMs after. As an example, in most Azure regions, M-series VMs, and now Mv2-series, will be the scarcest resource, and may only exist in one data hall, or within one Availability Zone in a region that supports Availability Zones. By creating the M/Mv2-series VM first, that will pin the PPG to a specific data hall, and the more common VMs types can then be provisioned in the same data hall. If you don't need an M/Mv2-series VM today, but expect to need to upsize to one later, then deploy a temporary M/Mv2-series VM first, then deploy some other VMs, and finally delete the M/Mv2-series VM. Your Proximity Placement Group will now be pinned to the data hall where the M/Mv2-series VMs exist.

Latency is particularly important in internal communication between the database and application server, where *SAP Note 1100926 – FAQ: Network performance* recommends the following:

- **Good value**: Roundtrip time <= 0.3 ms
- **Moderate value**: 0.3 ms < roundtrip time <= 0.7 ms
- **Below average value**: Roundtrip time > 0.7 ms

The goal should be to achieve a roundtrip time below 0.7ms.

Another latency optimization can be achieved by using the Azure Accelerated Networking, which is a mandatory setting for all SAP workloads in Azure. When using Accelerated Networking, the VM communicates directly with the network and bypasses the virtual switch in the hypervisor, which results in a much lower latency between hosts:

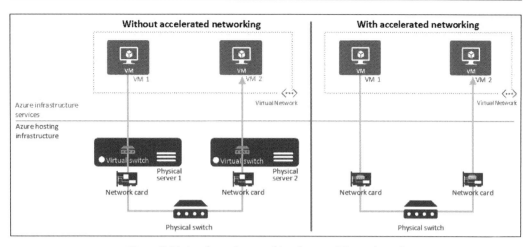

Figure 2-24: Accelerated networking (source: Microsoft.com)

It's also important to correctly size the network between the on-premises data center and the Azure data center. In most cases you will not move all your workloads from on-premises to Azure in a single "big bang" migration, but will migrate workloads one or a few at a time. Even when just migrating SAP to Azure, it is common to migrate a few SAP applications at a time, creating move groups of logically connected applications. Therefore, in sizing the network between on-premises and Azure you will need to consider:

- User traffic between your users and workloads that have been migrated to Azure. The number of concurrent users and the protocol used are both factors that should be considered when planning the network.
- Application traffic between applications still running on-premises and applications already migrated to Azure.

Each SAP application has certain requirements towards network bandwidth and latency. You should always refer to SAP Notes and plan the network segments to fulfil these requirements. The system access method is also important. SAP Fiori communication, which is based on the HTTP protocol, requires much more throughput per user than access using SAP GUI.

System deployment

When deploying a SAP NetWeaver-based system in Azure, you have the same options as on-premises:

1. A standalone installation, where the database, central services instance, and the dialog instance are kept on the same host

2. A distributed installation, where each component is installed on separate VMs
3. A highly available installation, which prevents unplanned downtime due to redundancy of components

The deployment method influences the performance, availability, and cost of running SAP in Azure.

Standalone installation

Keeping all SAP components on a single VM is the easiest way to install the SAP system. The database, central services instance, and the dialog instance are deployed to a single VM. Such deployment is often called two-tier. While the installation process is simplified, such systems are difficult to scale. All components share the virtual machine resources, and the server has to be capable to process database and application server workloads. It may cause problems with tuning the database and application servers as memory is shared between two components.

The maximum performance of a two-tier system is limited by a single virtual machine size. It's good for smaller installations, but not recommended in the case of large systems.

The standalone installation can be expanded by deploying an additional application server to another VM:

Figure 2-25: Standalone installation

The standalone system shares the virtual machine resources for all components. The system availability is limited by a single VM SLA.

Distributed installation

It is possible to separate each SAP NetWeaver component and distribute the workload to multiple VMs. The installation process is more complex, as each component has to be individually provisioned. Internal communication within the SAP NetWeaver becomes an important factor. The ports between the application server, the database, and the central services instance must be open and network performance sized accordingly.

It's possible to stack components with each other. The Central Services instance doesn't consume much in the way of resources, and it's therefore a common practice to deploy it together with either the database or primary application server.

As specified in *SAP Note 2731110 – Support of Network Virtual Appliances (NVA) for SAP on Azure*, you must not deploy a **network virtual appliance** (**NVA**) in the communication path between the SAP Application Server and the database server. This restriction does not apply to **Azure Security Group** (**ASG**) and **Network Security Group** (**NSG**) rules as long they allow a direct communication.

Figure 2-26 shows the database, central services, and primary application server distributed across three virtual machines.

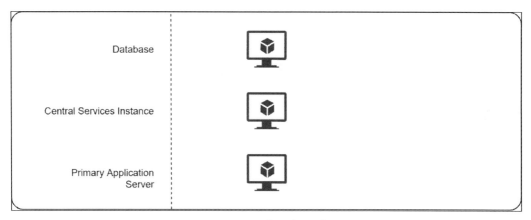

Figure 2-26: Distributed installation

If you want to make your SAP systems highly available, then you need to use a distributed installation, and we will now look at this in more detail.

Highly available installation

When you cannot afford any unplanned downtime, it is possible to make each component redundant in order to prevent system unavailability. The database server replicates the data to another VM, the central services instance runs in a failover cluster, and the application workload is distributed to at least two servers.

These highly available systems are more difficult to provision and maintain. Administrators should have prior experience in working with such environments, as the wrong configuration can undermine efforts to increase system availability, potentially even leading to a loss in system availability:

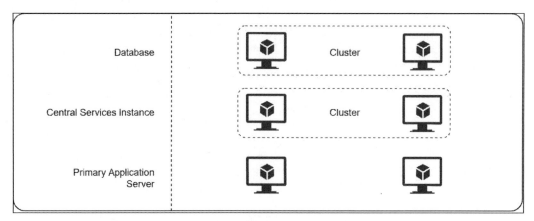

Figure 2-27: Highly Available Installation

On the Linux operating system, high availability can be enabled by configuring the Pacemaker HA extension, and in Windows Server it is possible to install the Failover Cluster feature. However, not all Linux distributions include the required packages, in particular Oracle Linux does not come with built-in Pacemaker and in this case third-party software such as SIOS Protection Suite for Linux can be used instead. With Red Hat and SUSE, the HA extensions are available as an add-on, but are generally bundled as part of the RHEL for SAP and SLES for SAP subscriptions.

Stacking multiple components on a single VM is generally not supported in Azure, particularly on Linux. While customers have tried this, it has generally proved to be unreliable, although there are a few scenarios where it does seem to work and these are detailed later. Therefore, a minimal install would consist of at least six VMs, and once again NVAs should not be placed in the communication between nodes of Pacemaker cluster or SBD devices as they can easily double the latency.

Multiple SAP databases running on one server

In large environments, it may be desirable to stack multiple databases on a single server in order to minimize the number of required VMs. Such configuration is supported by SAP. However, additional attention is required as it is not always easy to implement. There are two variants of stacking the database, Multiple Components on One System and Multiple Components on One Database. We'll look at these individually.

Multiple components on one system (MCOS)

Instead of hosting a separate server for each database instance, with MCOS, multiple separate databases can be deployed together on a single server. In theory it could simplify the administration, but in real life additional effort is required to manage the performance. The database components may interfere with each other and could require special configuration of the operating system, especially if the database release is not exactly the same.

It is not recommended for production workloads, however it may be an optimization technique for non-production environments such as development and test. It can also be used to combine a Disaster Recovery system with a non-production workload.

Multiple components on one database (MCOD)

An alternative method of hosting multiple databases on one server is to use MCOD and create separate schemas for each SAP NetWeaver system in a single database instance. In such deployments, all databases are on the same release and share the libraries.

Such deployment is even more difficult to maintain, as the level of integration is higher. A restart of a single database requires a downtime for all of them. It's also not possible to upgrade the DBMS software for only one database – they all must be upgraded at the same time.

Like MCOS, this scenario should only be considered for non-production workloads but is probably best avoided. While MCOD has been officially supported by SAP for many years, it has very rarely been used by customers:

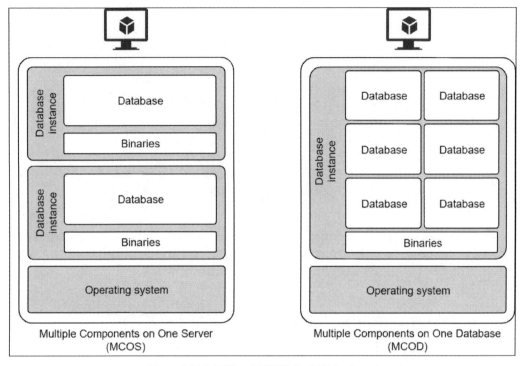

Figure 2-28: MCOS and MCOD for SAP databases

Figure 2-28 shows the difference between MCOS and MCOD. With MCOS whilst the OS is shared, each database runs in its own database instance with its own DBMS binaries. Each database can be managed independently, starting, stopping, and even patching the binaries. With MCOD, the OS and the DBMS binaries are shared, and all the databases run within a single database instance. Shutting down the database instance will shut down the entire database, and any patch to the DBMS binaries will affect all the databases.

Central services instance stacking

The Central Services Instances do not require significant resource and for this reason you may want to stack multiple instances on a single VM; this is sometimes referred to as a multi-SID configuration. This is not a problem when using standalone VMs, but you do need to be careful when using clustered VMs.

A highly available multi-SID configuration is supported on Azure when using Microsoft Windows Server and **Windows Server Failover Clustering (WSFC)**. However, it is not supported to create a multi-SID central services cluster on Linux when using Pacemaker for the clustering. Pacemaker is not designed to cluster multiple services in this way, and the failover of a single service is likely to cause the failover of multiple instances.

Oracle Linux does not include Pacemaker, and the recommended cluster solution is to use SIOS Protection Suite for Linux instead, and this does support multi-SID configurations. Interestingly, SAP supports the use of SIOS Protection Suite for Linux[32] on Azure for SUSE, and Red Hat as well as Oracle Linux, so this may provide an option for multi-SID clusters; however at the time of writing this has not been tested:

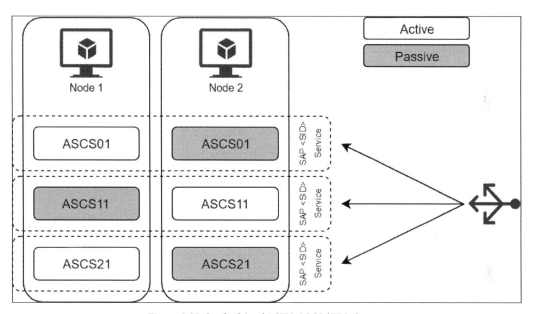

Figure 2-29: Stacked (multi-SID) ASCS/ERS clusters

As shown in *Figure 2-29* a pair of VMs is used to host multiple ASCS, reducing the total number of VMs and associated OS costs. The load balancer that is deployed in front of the clustered services and acts as an entry point to the system constantly monitors which node hosts the active service and redirects the traffic accordingly.

---

32 SAP Note 1662610 – Support details for SIOS Protection Suite for Linux

Additional considerations

SAP NetWeaver is a technology foundation for a set of business solutions. Depending on the workload, additional considerations may need to be taken into account.

SAP Business Suite

SAP Business Suite is the most common SAP workload. The SAP Business Suite applications are very often tightly integrated with one another. For example, very often, data residing in the ERP system is accessed by the SRM system or extracted from the SAP Business Warehouse. The network bandwidth and latency can impact system performance in cross-system communication. Very often, the communication is synchronous and the source system making the request will pause until it receives a response from the target system. A background job that requires data from an external system can trigger a lot of requests, and in such a case, even a small increase in network latency can cause a significant delay in job execution.

The network latency will be high especially when the connection is established between an on-premises environment and Azure, or in multi-cloud scenarios between Azure and other clouds. If two systems are highly dependent on one another, with a lot of communication, then it is important that they are both located within close proximity. This means that when it comes to migration planning, they should be migrated simultaneously.

SAP S/4HANA and SAP Fiori

SAP S/4HANA is the new business solution and a direct successor of SAP ERP, also known as SAP **ERP Central Component** (**ECC**). The business processes have been redesigned and the business model has been simplified, but there is an additional important change. The recommended user interface is changed from SAP GUI to SAP Fiori, which means the system should be accessed through a web browser instead of a dedicated client. The SAP GUI can still be used with S/4HANA, and if you are planning a conversion (technical upgrade) of an existing ECC system to S/4 and you want to minimize user impact, then this is a valid solution.

While such change may not appear very significant, it has a major impact on the overall system architecture. SAP Fiori may be combined with SAP S/4HANA, which is called an embedded deployment and it is the recommended scenario from SAP when it will be used exclusively with S/4HANA. However, SAP Fiori can also be deployed as a completely separate system, with its own application servers and database. This is referred to as a hub deployment and is mostly used when a single SAP Fiori will provide access to multiple back-end SAP systems.

SAP Fiori is, in fact, an application based on NetWeaver AS ABAP and a database, and if it is deployed as a separate system, it has to follow all the recommendations as per normal SAP NetWeaver-based systems, including sizing and resilience. If high availability is planned for the backend system, it must also be considered for the front-end. Otherwise, in the event of an unexpected downtime of Fiori, users will not be able to access the back-end application even if it is still up and running.

The separate SAP Fiori system usually does not store a lot of data in the database and acts as a proxy between the user and back-end system. Therefore, to optimize the solution, its database can be stacked together with the back-end system database. Such optimization is especially useful when SAP HANA is the database. The certified hardware for SAP HANA is expensive, so stacking the databases together using SAP HANA **Multitenant Database Containers** (**MDCs**) will decrease the cost of hosting Fiori.

While it is technically possible to use another DBMS for SAP Fiori, since SAP intends to end support for other DBMSes except SAP HANA as of 2025, this is only a short-term solution, and within a few years, the Fiori system will have to be migrated to HANA.

SAP Fiori is accessed through the HTTP protocol and it is good practice to add an extra security layer. SAP Web Dispatcher is a reverse-proxy that can be placed between a user and the system. It can accept or reject a user connection and load balance traffic between multiple application servers. SAP recommend using the Web Dispatcher in front of the Fiori system.

The SAP Web Dispatcher should be deployed in the DMZ area of the network. The VM hosting the reverse proxy should have two network adapters – one for user connections and the second for communications with the SAP Fiori server. Each area of the network is associated with Network Security Groups that filter the unwanted or dangerous traffic and provide an additional security layer:

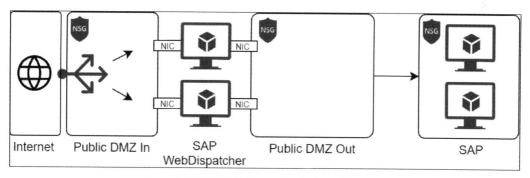

Figure 2-30: SAP Web Dispatcher deployed in a DMZ

The availability requirements should be also considered for the SAP Web Dispatcher. A highly available SAP landscape should include a highly available SAP Web Dispatcher that runs on two VMs with load balancer in front of it.

The Azure Load Balancer works in layer 4 of the TCP/IP stack, and provides only basic capabilities of routing the request to a VM. A good alternative is to use the Azure Application Gateway solution, which works on the application layer and therefore provides additional network capabilities.

Both SAP Web Dispatcher and Application Gateway solutions work as a reverse proxy, and therefore it would be tempting to use only the Application Gateway. The Web Dispatcher, however, contains unique features to understand the SAP landscape and therefore the load balancing works better than Application Gateway. On the other hand, the Application Gateway offers advanced threat detection and web application firewall, which significantly increase the security of the entire landscape, especially if the system is exposed to the internet. Combining both solutions gives the best results.

SAProuter and SAP Cloud Connector

SAProuter and the SAP Cloud Connector are proxy applications that allow connection between on-premise landscapes and the SAP backbone.

The SAProuter is currently used most often to download SAP notes or establish a support connection, but it can also be used as a proxy for user connection using SAP GUI. It should follow the SAP Web Dispatcher recommendations and be placed in the DMZ area of the network. When it's used as a proxy for SAP GUI, then it should also follow the availability requirements of SAP Web Dispatcher.

The SAP Cloud Connector is software that allows connection with the SAP Cloud Platform without the need to expose the SAP NetWeaver system to the internet. It is used by developers to deploy enhancements or completely new SAP Fiori applications, and it's a mandatory component for SAP S/4HANA deployments. Usually, it is less critical than other components, which means it's usually deployed as a single node, but the highly available mode is also possible. The deployment should follow the SAP Web Dispatcher recommendations.

Having considered the requirements for running SAP applications using AnyDB (IBM DB2, Microsoft SQL Server, Oracle Database, SAP ASE, and SAP MaxDB) let us now look at running SAP applications on SAP HANA. While there are some differences, in many ways SAP HANA is just another database and a lot of what we have already discussed is not changed by using SAP HANA as the database.

SAP HANA

SAP released its new SAP HANA in-memory database in 2010. It was initially supported for use with SAP BW as an additional DBMS alongside the existing supported AnyDB, and over the years support has been extended to most SAP Business Suite applications. In 2015 SAP announced its next generation ERP system called SAP S/4HANA, which only supports the SAP HANA database as the data storage and processing layer, and for which some of the code has been reimplemented to take maximum benefit from SAP HANA's in-memory capabilities. To ensure the best performance, SAP works with hyperscalers to provide certified reference architectures that should be adjusted and implemented by customers. In the next section you'll understand the best practices to deploy SAP HANA on Azure.

Supported platforms

SAP HANA is a certified workload in Microsoft Azure and runs on virtual machines or on bare-metal Azure **HANA Large Instance (HLI)** servers, which are designed for the largest HANA deployments that require massive amounts of memory; up to 24 TB scale-up, and 60 TB scale-out.

All database revisions starting from SAP HANA 1.0 SP12 are supported, including all releases of SAP HANA 2.0. Customers can choose to use either Red Hat Enterprise Linux or SUSE Linux Enterprise Server operating systems. Both vendors publish OS images for SAP in the Azure Marketplace.

SAP HANA can be used as a standalone database but is more usually deployed to support existing SAP Business Suite applications – ECC, BW, CRM, and SRM – or be used with the latest generation applications such as SAP S/4HANA and SAP BW/4HANA.

SAP HANA is generally deployed as a single-node scale-up solution for OLTP applications, while for OLAP applications such as SAP BW or SAP BW/4HANA, it can be deployed as a scale-out solution. SAP HANA scale-out solutions can be deployed on both HLI and VMs.

Why SAP HANA certified platforms?

SAP HANA database performance is highly dependent on the underlying hardware. SAP publishes a long list of hardware and network requirements that ensure that the database can efficiently process massive amounts of data. SAP provides the SAP HANA **Hardware and Cloud Measurement Tools (HCMTs)** that vendors must use to validate that their platform meets the required **key performance indicators (KPIs)**.

Microsoft is one of the hyperscale cloud vendors that has successfully certified a wide range of virtual machines and bare-metal servers to run SAP HANA. It ensures all hardware components are compatible and offer the required performance.

However, the requirements to achieve certification are very stringent – some might say onerous – and for non-production environments, it may not always be necessary to choose a fully certified platform. You may require one non-production environment to be fully certified, to allow problem investigation away from production, but for other environments you may wish to choose a more cost-conscious solution. There are two main ways to reduce costs when running HANA on Azure:

- **Use non-certified VMs**: There are a range of Ev3 series VMs that are adequate to run HANA, are available in smaller sizes than the M series (64 GiB, 128 GiB), and where they offer similar memory to the M series, they are generally cheaper.
- **Cost-conscious storage configuration**[33]: Microsoft has published suggested storage configurations that will provide adequate performance for non-production HANA, but are known not to pass the HCMT KPIs.

If you are currently running SAP HANA on VMware in your on-premises environment, then it is highly likely are you already running cost-conscious solutions in non-production.

SAP HANA sizing

SAP HANA has some very specific requirements regarding CPU, memory, networking, and storage. The rules for these are defined by SAP in order to ensure that a HANA database will achieve its optimum performance. As we will see later, while this is critical for production HANA databases, you may want to consider more cost-optimized solutions for at least some of your non-production environments.

CPU and memory requirements

SAP HANA database sizing is primarily focused on the amount of memory required. Originally, there was no CPU sizing (SAPS) as such as SAP simply use a fixed CPU to memory ratio for HANA, or more accurately two ratios.

---

33   Cost-conscious Azure Storage configuration: https://bit.ly/2RqRuwc

One ratio for OLTP systems and a second for OLAP systems, with the OLTP systems allowed twice the memory per CPU when compared with the OLAP systems. This was based on the logic that in general OLAP systems use more CPU power to process their work for a given volume of data.

As with sizing SAP NetWeaver systems, sizing SAP HANA based systems depends on whether this is a new installation or a migration of an existing application to SAP HANA. For new installations, you can use SAP Quick Sizer and SAP Sizing Guidelines, the same as for SAP NetWeaver-based systems. When using SAP Quick Sizer, it is worth noting that there are two versions, one Classic for sizing traditional NetWeaver applications on AnyDB, and a new HANA version, for sizing applications on HANA.

Where you are running existing SAP NetWeaver-based systems and want to migrate them to HANA, then SAP provides two sizing reports that you can run to get an estimate of the HANA database sizing. These sizing reports are published via SAP notes as follows:

- 2610534 – HANA BW Sizing Report (/SDF/HANA_BW_SIZING)
- 1872170 – ABAP on HANA sizing report (S/4HANA, Suite on HANA)

Each of these reports will provide a detailed estimate of the sizing of your existing SAP database when migrated to HANA. It is important to note that these reports do not provide any sizing for the application tier, and in general the starting point for this is to perform a reference sizing for the application tier based on the existing deployed application servers, as described in the general sizing section earlier.

To obtain a rough order of magnitude sizing without running these reports, or where you are currently not in a position to run the reports, it is possible to manually estimate the sizing as well. Assuming that the system is well maintained, and the current database is not compressed, then the recommendation from *SAP Note 1793345 Sizing for SAP Suite on HANA* can be used. These state that you should:

- Take half of size of your disk-based database
- Add a safety buffer of 20%
- Add 50 GB fixed size for code, stack, and other services

This means that if the database is currently approximately 2000 GB in size (tables plus indexes), the maximum memory consumption will be 1250 GB (2000 GB/2 * 1.2 + 50 GB).

Based on the required memory, customers can choose a certified platform to run the database workload in Azure. Currently, Microsoft offers 12 VM sizes and 12 bare-metal servers that are sized to cover memory requirements of small or medium companies or large enterprises. An up-to-date list is available on the SAP-Certified and Supported SAP HANA Hardware Directory[34]:

VM Size	Memory	Scale-Out (Clustering)	Certified workload
DS14v2	112 GiB	No	SAP Business One
E64sv3	432 GiB	No	OLTP / OLAP
M32ts	192 GiB	No	OLTP / OLAP SAP Business One
M32ls	256 GiB	No	OLTP / OLAP SAP Business One
M64ls	512 GiB	No	OLTP / OLAP SAP Business One
M64s	1000 GiB	No	OLTP / OLAP SAP Business One
M64ms	1792 GiB	No	OLTP / OLAP
M128s	2000 GiB	Yes	OLTP / OLAP
M128ms	3800 GiB	No	OLTP / OLAP
M208s_v2	2850 GiB	No	OLTP / OLAP
M208ms_v2	5700 GiB	No	OLTP / OLAP
M416s_v2	5700 GiB	No	OLTP / OLAP
M416ms_v2	11400 GiB	No	OLTP / OLAP

Table 2-4: SAP HANA certified Azure VMs

HLI Size	Memory	Scale-Out (Clustering)	Certified workload
S144	1.5 TiB	Yes	OLTP / OLAP
S144m	3 TiB	No	OLTP / OLAP
S192	2 TiB	Yes	OLTP / OLAP
S192m	4 TiB	No	OLTP
S384	4 TiB	Yes	OLTP / OLAP

---

34   SAP-Certified and Supported SAP HANA Hardware Directory: https://bit.ly/34Wt1TE

HLI Size	Memory	Scale-Out (Clustering)	Certified workload
S384m	6 TiB	No	OLTP
S384xm	8 TiB	Yes	OLTP / OLAP
S576m	12 TiB	Yes	OLTP
S72	768 GiB	No	OLTP / OLAP
S72m	1.5 TiB	No	OLTP
S768m	16 TiB	No	OLTP
S960m	20 TiB	No	OLTP

Table 2-5: SAP-certified Azure HANA large instances

Scale-out deployment is only allowed for OLAP workloads. Scale-out for S/4HANA is technically supported by SAP, but not currently supported on Azure.

During the annual SAP SAPPHIRE NOW conference in May 2019, Microsoft announced two new innovations for SAP HANA:

- Availability of VMs with up to 6 TB of memory imminently, and availability of VMs with 12 TB of memory in Q3 CY2019.
- A plan to launch large bare-metal Azure HANA Large instances using Intel Optane memory, including a 4-socket 9 TB instance and an 8-socket 18 TB instance. These instances will enable customers to benefit from faster load times for SAP HANA data in case of a restart and a reduced TCO when compared with current HANA instances that use only **Dynamic Random Access Memory (DRAM)**.

Network requirements

In the SAP HANA Network Requirements document SAP distinguish three network zones:

1. **Client Zone**: Client applications that connects to database and execute SQL or MDX queries. In addition, it includes the HTTP communication when using the SAP HANA XS engine.
2. **Internal Zone**: Internal communication between SAP HANA instances, for example in a System Replication scenario or in Scale-Out deployment.
3. **Storage Zone**: For accessing data and log files that are stored on SAN or NAS.

SAP NetWeaver-based systems are latency sensitive. Following the *SAP Note 2543171 – Latency issue between application server and Database* the response time between application server and the database should be lower than 0.7 ms. As described earlier this can be achieved in Azure by using PPG.

Storage requirements

For HANA VMs, you must build the SAP HANA storage configuration manually based on the four disk types available in Azure:

- **Standard HDD**: A storage solution based on HDD disks, should not be used with SAP HANA.
- **Standard SSD**: A storage solution based on SSD disks, offers similar throughput as the Standard HDD storage, but improves the data access latency. Not used for production HANA instances but can be used as part of cost-conscious storage configuration for non-production environments if you are not concerned about having a certified configuration.
- **Premium SSD**: A solution based on high performance SSD, and the recommended storage for M series and Mv2 series VMs when used for SAP HANA and combined with the Write Accelerator.
- **Ultra SSD**: A solution based on ultra performance SSD, the only supported storage for Ev3 series VMs, and gradually being supported on M series and Mv2 series.

Azure will fulfil the SAP storage performance, throughput, and latency requirements when you follow the recommended storage configuration, based on Premium SSD disks and the Write Accelerator[35] – a feature of M series and Mv2 series virtual machines that significantly reduces the latency when writing to the HANA log files. It is essential to realize that the Write Accelerator is not automatically enabled, and you need to ensure that this is enabled manually. One of the most common faults found during pre-GoLive checks for SAP HANA on Azure is that the Write Accelerator has not been enabled.

The table below presents a verified storage layout optimized to run SAP HANA on Azure VMs using premium disks:

---

35   Production storage solution with Azure Write Accelerator for Azure M-series virtual machines: `https://bit.ly/34VvhKX`

VM SKU	RAM (GiB)	Max. VM I/O Through-put (Mbps)	/hana /data	/hana /log	/hana /shared	/root volume	/usr /sap	/hana /backup
M32ts	192	500	3 x P20	2 x P20	1 x P20	1 x P6	1 x P6	1 x P20
M32ls	256	500	3 x P20	2 x P20	1 x P20	1 x P6	1 x P6	1 x P20
M64ls	512	1000	3 x P20	2 x P20	1 x P20	1 x P6	1 x P6	1 x P30
M64s	1000	1000	4 x P20	2 x P20	1 x P30	1 x P6	1 x P6	2 x P30
M64ms	1750	1000	3 x P30	2 x P20	1 x P30	1 x P6	1 x P6	3 x P30
M128s	2000	2000	3 x P30	2 x P20	1 x P30	1 x P10	1 x P6	2 x P40
M128ms	3800	2000	5 x P30	2 x P20	1 x P30	1 x P10	1 x P6	4 x P40
M208s_v2	2850	1000	4 x P30	2 x P20	1 x P30	1 x P10	1 x P6	3 x P40
M208ms_v2	5700	1000	4 x P40	2 x P20	1 x P30	1 x P10	1 x P6	3 x P50
M416s_v2	5700	2000	4 x P40	2 x P20	1 x P30	1 x P10	1 x P6	3 x P50
M416ms_v2	11400	2000	8 x P40	2 x P20	1 x P30	1 x P10	1 x P6	4 x P50

Table 2-6: SAP HANA VM storage layouts using Azure premium SSD

Customers can also implement the recently released Ultra SSD disk, which is already certified for SAP HANA on E64s_v3 and will be certified in the future for further VMs. Certification of the Ev3 series was not possible before as the Write Accelerator feature was only available for M series VMs, as it required a specific hardware feature. Ultra SSDs are not yet available in all Azure regions.

Ultra SSD performance can be customized based on throughput and IOPS requirement. The table below summarize the storage layout for virtual machines using Ultra SSDs:

VM SKU	RAM (GiB)	Max. VM I/O Throughput (Mbps)	/hana /data volume (GB)	/hana /data throughput (Mbps)	/hana /data IOPS	/hana /log volume (GB)	/hana /log throughput (Mbps)	/hana /log IOPS
E64s_v3	432	1200	600	700	7500	512	500	2000
M32ts	192	500	250	500	7500	256	500	2000
M32ls	256	500	300	500	7500	256	500	2000
M64ls	512	1000	600	500	7500	512	500	2000
M64s	1000	1000	1200	500	7500	512	500	2000
M64ms	1750	1000	2100	500	7500	512	500	2000
M128s	2000	2000	2400	1200	9000	512	800	2000
M128ms	3800	2000	4800	1200	9000	512	800	2000
M208s_v2	2850	1000	3500	1000	9000	512	500	2000
M208ms_v2	5700	1000	7200	1000	9000	512	500	2000
M416s_v2	5700	2000	7200	1500	9000	512	800	2000
M416ms_v2	11400	2000	14400	1500	9000	512	800	2000

Table 2-7: SAP HANA VM storage layouts using Azure ultra SSD

Since November 2019, ANF is also now certified as a storage option for SAP HANA running on Azure VMs. In order to use ANF for SAP HANA storage, you need to be aware of the per node throughput requirements:

- Enable read/write on /hana/log of a 250 Mbps with 1 MB I/O sizes
- Enable read activity of at least 400 Mbps for /hana/data for 16 MB and 64 MB I/O sizes
- Enable write activity of at least 250 Mbps for /hana/data with 16 MB and 64 MB I/O sizes

The ANF throughput limits per 1 TiB of volume quota are:

- Premium Storage Tier = 64 MiB/s
- Ultra Storage Tier = 128 MiB/s

To fulfil the SAP HANA requirements the minimal volume should be:

Volume	Size Premium Storage tier	Size Ultra Storage tier	Supported NFS Protocol
/hana/log/	4 TiB	2 TiB	v4.1
/hana/data	6.3 TiB	3.2 TiB	v4.1
/hana/shared	Max (512 GB, 1xRAM) per 4 worker nodes	Max (512 GB, 1xRAM) per 4 worker nodes	v3 or v4.1

Please note that these are the minimal requirements. The recommended values depend on the number of hosts and their sizes. For a landscape with one master node, two workers, and one standby deployed on the M128s VM (with 2 TB of memory), you should consider at least:

Volume	Size Premium Storage Tier	Size Ultra Storage Tier
/hana/log	12 TiB	6 TiB
/hana/data	18.9 TiB	9.6 TiB
/hana/shared	2 TiB	2 TiB

The preceding configurations are the minimum storage configurations required to run SAP HANA on these VMs, and in most cases will be sufficient. However, should you enable some of the data tiering capabilities that SAP are starting to roll out, which do not preload all data into memory, then over time the size of the database on disk may continue to grow, without the need for more memory. In this case, for example, you could require more capacity for /hana/data because the size on disk is continuing to grow.

In order to decrease the cost of storage, customers may wish to adjust the storage configuration for non-production environments. While these storage configurations will not meet all the storage KPIs required to pass the HCMT tests published by SAP, and won't be officially supported, they still perform well and will save costs for non-production workloads. Microsoft has published these cost-conscious storage requirements that provide a sensible balance between performance and cost, by using a mix of Premium and Standard SSD disks.

While they do reduce the cost, because they introduce Standard SSD disk, the VM will not benefit from the Single VM SLA, which is only valid when Premium SSD disks are used. *Table 2-8* shows the suggested storage layouts:

VM SKU	RAM (GiB)	Max. VM I/O Throughput (Mbps)	/hana/data and /hana/log striped with LVM or MDADM	/hana /shared	/root volume	/usr /sap	Hana /backup
DS14v2	112	768	3 x P20	1 x E20	1 x E6	1 x E6	1 x E15
E16v3	128	384	3 x P20	1 x E20	1 x E6	1 x E6	1 x E15
E32v3	256	768	3 x P20	1 x E20	1 x E6	1 x E6	1 x E20
E64v3	432	1200	3 x P20	1 x E20	1 x E6	1 x E6	1 x E30
GS5	448	2000	3 x P20	1 x E20	1 x E6	1 x E6	1 x E30
M32ts	192	500	3 x P20	1 x E20	1 x E6	1 x E6	1 x E20
M32ls	256	500	3 x P20	1 x E20	1 x E6	1 x E6	1 x E20
M64ls	512	1000	3 x P20	1 x E20	1 x E6	1 x E6	1 x E30
M64s	1000	1000	2 x P30	1 x E30	1 x E6	1 x E6	2 x E30
M64ms	1750	1000	3 x P30	1 x E30	1 x E6	1 x E6	3 x E30
M128s	2000	2000	3 x P30	1 x E30	1 x E10	1 x E6	2 x E40
M128ms	3800	2000	5 x P30	1 x E30	1 x E10	1 x E6	2 x E50
M208s_v2	2850	1000	4 x P30	1 x E30	1 x E10	1 x E6	3 x E40
M208ms_v2	5700	1000	4 x P40	1 x E30	1 x E10	1 x E6	4 x E40
M416s_v2	5700	2000	4 x P40	1 x E30	1 x E10	1 x E6	4 x E40
M416ms_v2	11400	2000	8 x P40	1 x E30	1 x E10	1 x E6	4 x E50

Table 2-8: SAP HANA VM cost optimised storage layout

Designing the storage layout for SAP HANA is a much more complex process compared to other databases due to SAP storage throughput and latency requirements. To ensure your workload is supported by Microsoft and SAP, you should always follow the preceding recommendations.

System deployment

There are multiple options for how to design the SAP HANA architecture to run in Azure:

1. Standalone HANA deployment
2. HANA MCOS
3. HANA MDC
4. HANA Scale-Up or Scale-Out

In some cases, these are similar to the options available for deploying AnyDB for SAP NetWeaver systems as already described, but there are also some additional options for SAP HANA. We'll discuss the above options individually in the following sections.

Standalone HANA deployment

A single node installation of the SAP HANA DBMS is the most common scenario. The database is installed on either SUSE Linux Enterprise Server or Red Hat Enterprise Linux. For production workloads, only certified Azure VMs must be used, but for non-production workloads, non-certified VMs can be used, which may offer lower cost and also provide options with less memory; the smallest certified VM is currently 192 GB.

HANA multiple components on one system (MCOS)

Instead of hosting a separate server for each database instance, multiple separate databases can be deployed together on a single server. In theory it could simplify the administration, by reducing the total number of systems that need to be administered, but in real life additional effort is required to manage the system and ensure that the performance of one database is not affected by others. The database components may interfere with each other and could require special configuration of the operating system, especially if the database releases are not all the same.

Keeping multiple database instances on the same virtual machine is not recommended for a production workload; however it may be an optimization technique for development and test environments.

This solution was more common in Azure in the early days of HLI, when less granular sizes were available, but with HANA-certified VMs there is a much wider range of sizes available. Rather than deploy many small independent HLI for non-production workloads, some customers would deploy fewer large HLI and host multiple HANA databases on each. This was also useful where you need to have a large HLI for DR purposes, but under normal operation want to use that HLI to host multiple non-production databases to reduce cost.

HANA multitenant database containers (MDC)

With HANA 1.0 SPS09, SAP introduced the concept of HANA MDC. With HANA 2.0, MDC became the default, although you can deploy a single tenant database. While MDC is superficially similar in concept to MCOD, in detail, it is very different. MDC provides much greater isolation between the individual databases, making it much more secure and robust than MCOD.

MDC is SAP's preferred solution for virtualizing HANA. While they support running HANA on-premises on VMware and in a public cloud such as Azure their preference has generally been to use bare-metal-certified appliances, and then if you have many small HANA databases, to use MDC so they can easily share a single appliance. However, while MDC does allow you to stack multiple databases, all the databases share one set of binaries, so all the databases run on a common release. It is not possible to patch or upgrade the HANA version for a single database container, and if the HANA instance needs to be restarted, it means that all database containers will suffer downtime.

There are a few use cases where MDC makes good sense:

- Where you have many fairly small HANA databases, then MDC can be a cost-efficient way to host them. You might for instance consider using MDC for EP, PI, or Fiori FES and combine them with one of the smaller SAP components such as SRM.
- In certain non-production environments, such as Sandbox and possible Development, then again you may have many small databases and MDC can reduce the hosting costs.
- Where you have a very small landscape and the SAP components are tightly connected with each other. For example, if all you are running is ECC and Portal on HANA, then you might be happy to have them share a common HANA instance and use MDC.

In SAP NetWeaver workloads, such deployment is popular in Disaster Recovery scenarios, where the main use of the of the secondary system is non-production workloads, but in case of the failover it can overtake the production operations.

It decreases the cost of running the disaster recovery systems.

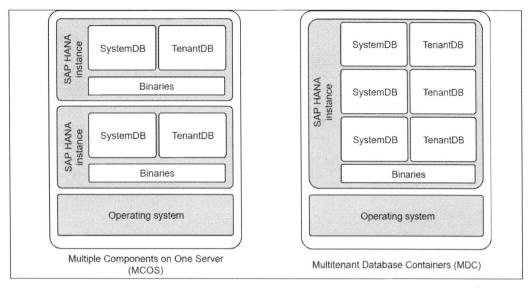

Figure 2-31: Multi components one system versus multitenant database containers

Figure 2-31 represents in a graphical way the difference between MCOS and MDC deployments of SAP HANA. In the example on the left, each tenant database is isolated in a separate SAP HANA instance with its own binaries and system database. It allows independent maintenance of each database including upgrades. The MDC deployments uses the same common binaries for all databases, which simplify the management but doesn't allow independent upgrades.

HANA scale-up and scale-out

HANA supports two main deployment options, Scale-up and Scale-out. With scale-up, the whole HANA instance must fit into a single HANA node, and as the database grows you will need to scale-up the host, be it a VM or a physical bare-metal server. With scale-out, in theory you can scale the size of the HANA instance as the database grows, by adding extra nodes.

While HANA scale-up can be used to support all scenarios, HANA scale-out is only supported in certain scenarios, so will not address all requirements. Supported scenarios for HANA scale-out are:

- SAP BW on HANA, BW4/HANA
- SAP HANA used for OLAP outside SAP applications
- SAP S/4HANA

The basic architecture of SAP HANA scale-out is shown in *Figure 2-32*:

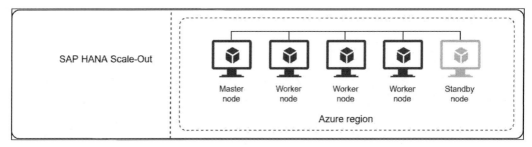

Figure 2-32: SAP HANA scale-out architecture

The architecture comprises:

- A master node.
- One or more worker nodes that hold the majority of the data. As the database grows you can add additional worker nodes to increase the available capacity.
- Optional standby node(s), there can be one or more, which provide a high availability solution. In the event of the failure of the master node or one of the worker nodes, then the standby node can take over its role.

Both scale-up and scale-out are supported in Azure on VMs and also on HLI. Most customers prefer to use VMs, and since the release of ANF, it is now possible to deploy SAP HANA scale-out on VMs with a standby node, which previously was only possible on HLI:

- HLI do still have their place as they address certain requirements that cannot currently be addressed with VMs. The main use case for Azure HLI is where your application requires a single HANA instance of more than 12 TB (11.4 TB); a HLI environment is certified up to 20 TB and can support up to 24 TB under the HANA TDIv5 rules.

SAP HANA resilience

When you are using SAP HANA as the database for SAP applications, then you need to consider high availability and disaster recovery in the same way as for any other database. There are some different options, as SAP HANA has some additional built-in capability, but in many cases the solutions are similar to those we have already examined. In this section, we will look at these topics again, for both SAP HANA running on VMs and for SAP HANA running on Azure HLI.

SAP HANA high availability

There are different solutions for **high availability (HA)** depending on whether you are using HANA scale-up or HANA scale-out, and we will examine these in more detail. As a minimum, when running on VMs, then you can simply rely on Azure VM auto-restart to provide HA for HANA VMs, just as you can for VMs running an other database or the SAP application tier, and this will probably be sufficient for most non-production environments. If you are using HLI there is no auto-restart capability and no spare servers for you to use, so it is even more important that you design for HA. In either case, you need to be aware that the larger the HANA database size, the longer the database will take to start and load its data into memory. For small databases, the restart time may be acceptable, but for larger production databases, the restart time is very unlikely to meet the required SLA. In these situations, HANA-level HA is required.

SAP HANA scale-up HA

To provide HA for SAP HANA scale up, the recommended solution from SAP is to use **HANA System Replication (HSR)** in synchronous mode. This effectively keeps two HANA instances in sync, with updates applied to the primary and the secondary at the same time. This allows rapid failover of the service in the event of a failure of the primary node. This is the solution that is supported in Azure.

This solution is shown in *Figure 2-33*. The SBD devices deployed to an availability set are used as the fencing mechanism for the database.

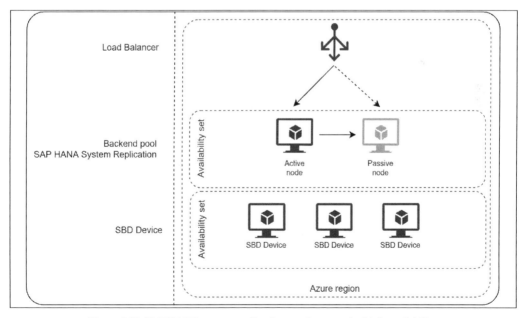

Figure 2-33: SAP HANA system replication synchronous for high availability

You can configure essentially the same solution whether using Azure VMs or HLI.

Failover of the HANA database from primary to secondary is once again handled by Linux Pacemaker. Pacemaker requires a cluster quorum to ensure that both nodes cannot be active at the same time. Currently available options for quorum devices are the Azure Fencing Agent and SBD. Red Hat Enterprise Linux does not support SBD but has implemented the latest Azure Fencing Agent feature that supports fast failover, by forcing the VM shutdown that reduces the time required for failover. For SUSE Enterprise Linux, the SBD device remains the best solution for cluster quorum, but the Azure Fencing Agent fast shutdown option should be supported soon.

You may ask whether it is possible to use the standby node to host another non-production HANA database, but this is not advised in an HA cluster such as this. Using a hot standby node, failover of the HANA instance can happen in seconds. If you use a warm standby where the data is not preloaded into memory, because the memory is being used to host another database, then it will potentially take tens of minutes to load the standby database into memory from disks, too long for HA. If you are running HANA scale-up on VMs, you might as well wait for the failed VM to auto-restart.

While it is technically possible to create a SAP HANA Scale-Out solution with just two nodes, one active and one standby, this is not generally a recommended solution. Once again, the challenge with SAP HANA is that restarting a HANA instance requires that the row store is reloaded into memory, and this can take 5-10 minutes per TB. Using DBMS replication with memory preload means that the standby node is ready to take over processing virtually immediately.

SAP HANA scale-out HA

For HANA Scale-Out, there are two options for HA:

- HANA host auto-failover using a standby node
- HANA System Replication synchronous

In the following sub-sections, we'll describe these options in further detail.

HANA scale-out HA with host auto-failover

HANA host auto-failover has been a native capability of SAP HANA since the early versions, and allows for a standby node to be created that can take over the work of any of the other nodes, either master or workers. This requires shared disk storage as the standby node needs to mount the /hana/data and /hana/log disks from the failed node.

Azure has supported SAP HANA host auto-failover on HLI since the beginning, as HLI uses Azure NetApp storage to provide the required storage for HANA. The NetApp volumes are mounted to the HLI servers using NFS, and the standby node can simply take over the volumes from a failed node.

However, until ANF was certified for use with SAP HANA running on Azure VMs in November 2019 it had not been possible to have a standby node when deploying SAP HANA on Azure VMs. By using ANF storage the same host auto-failover option is now available for VMs as on Azure HLI. This is shown in *Figure 2-34*:

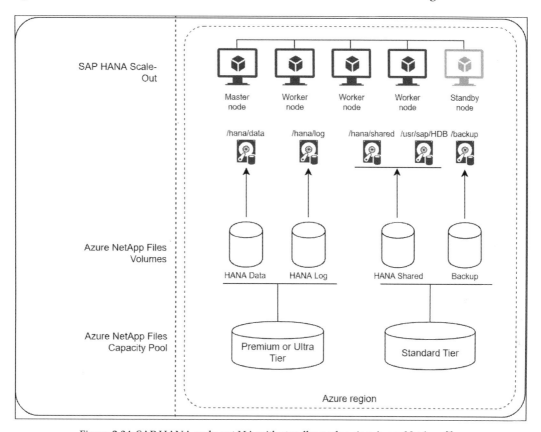

Figure 2-34: SAP HANA scale-out HA with standby node using Azure NetApp files

HANA scale-out HA with HANA system replication

HANA System Replication synchronous (HSR sync) essentially works the same on HANA scale-out as it does with HANA scale-up. This requires you to have two HANA scale-out systems of the same size, and to replicate data synchronously from the primary to the standby. This solution will provide the fastest failover times, as the HANA database is preloaded in memory in the standby instance.

However, it doubles the cost as it requires twice the hardware.

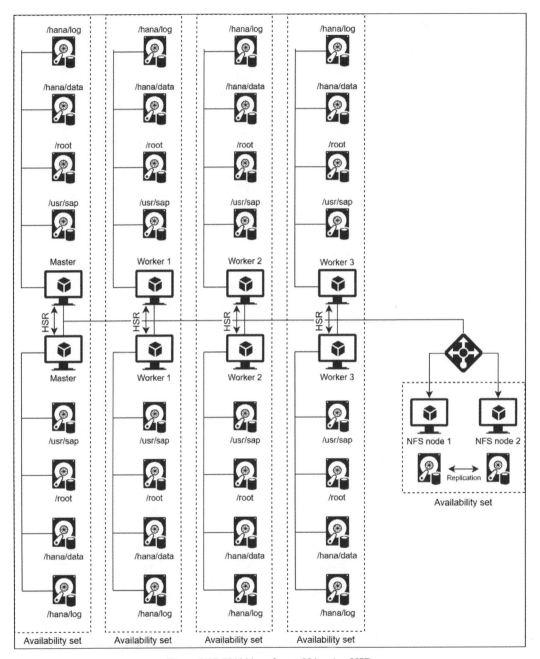

Figure 2-35: HANA scale-out HA using HSR

As shown in *Figure 2-35* each node of the SAP HANA scale-out has its own storage for data and log volumes. To ensure high availability the data is replicated using HSR. A common storage for the /hana/shared is required and, as the high performance is not required for the binaries, it can use a basic NFS cluster deployed on Linux virtual machines.

SAP HANA scale-out HA on VMs

Before the availability of ANF storage, you could still deploy SAP HANA scale-out on Azure VMs but without a standby node. This option is still relevant as you may not always need a standby node, because Azure VM auto-restart will restart a failed node for you. This will not be as fast a recovery as using a standby node but does avoid the additional cost of the standby node.

If you deploy SAP HANA scale-out on Azure VMs using Azure Premium or Ultra SSD storage, then the architecture looks like this:

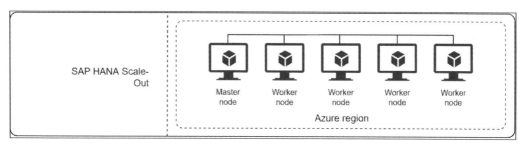

Figure 2-36: SAP HANA scale-out on Azure VMs

Those familiar with SAP HANA scale-out will notice that *Figure 2-36* does not show a standby node. When using Azure Premium or Ultra SSD storage, a standby node cannot be configured as it needs to be able to take over the disks from the failed master or worker node, which is not possible with Azure Premium or Ultra SSD. When running HANA scale-out on Azure VMs without ANF, there are three solutions for HA:

- Rely on the Azure VM auto-restart feature to restart the failed node. This may be adequate for less critical systems, and many BW on HANA or BW/4HANA systems may fall into that category.
- Use HSR in the same way as you would for HANA scale-up as described in *HANA scale-out HA with HANA system replication*.
- Use Azure HLI, shown next.

For some workloads, you may be prepared to rely on the VM auto-restart option and not have a standby node. In this case, you can run HANA scale-out with each database node having its own dedicated storage. To run HANA scale-out in this way, you must set the parameter `basepath_shared = no` in the `global.ini`. In this case, the storage layout is shown in *Figure 2-37*:

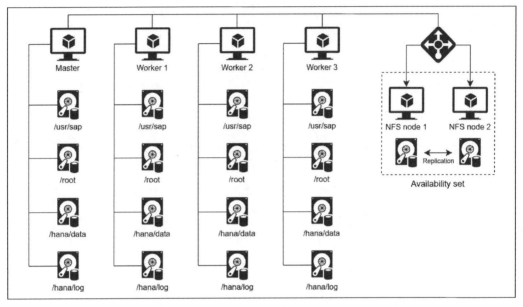

Figure 2-37: HANA scale-out storage on Azure VMs (source: Microsoft.com)

As shown in the preceding figure, a scale-out deployment still requires shared storage for hosting the `/hana/shared` directory. As there is no latency requirement for `/hana/shared`, you can build a custom NFS cluster or use ANF to store the shared filesystem.

The size of the shared filesystem (`/hana/shared`) is determined by how many nodes are to be used. Assuming the usage of m128s (2 TB) virtual machine, the size of the shared filesystem should be:

- One master node and up to four worker nodes; the `/hana/shared` volume would need to be 2 TB in size.
- One master node and five to eight worker nodes; the size of `/hana/shared` should be 4 TB.
- One master node and 9 to 12 worker nodes, a size of 6 TB for `/hana/shared` would be required.
- One master node and using between 12 and 15 worker nodes; you are required to provide a `/hana/shared` volume that is 8 TB in size.

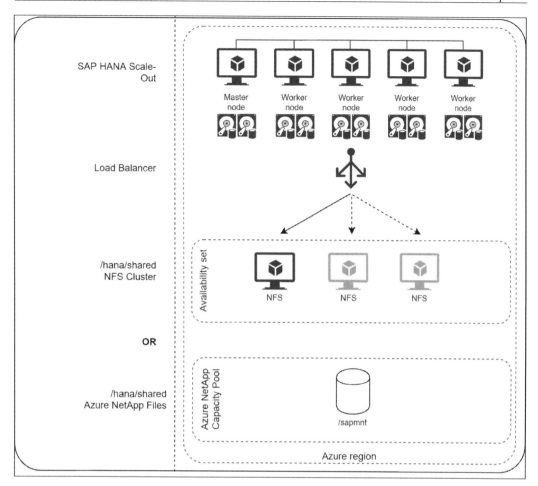

Figure 2-38: HANA scale-out with NFS cluster for /hana/shared

A highly available NFS cluster requires a cluster quorum to perform failover. As described previously, currently available options are the Azure Fencing Agent and SBD. Red Hat Enterprise Linux does not support SBD, but has implemented the latest Azure Fencing Agent feature that supports fast failover by forcing the VM shutdown that reduces the time required for failover. For SUSE Enterprise Linux, the SBD device remains the best solution for a cluster quorum, but the Azure fencing Agent fast shutdown option should be supported soon.

SAP recommend that you separate the client communication from the intranode communication. This can be achieved by creating two subnets and assigning two network interface cards to each virtual machine that is part of the scale-out database. The two network interfaces are then connected to separate subnets and using NSGs it is possible to control the traffic.

This is shown in *Figure 2-39*:

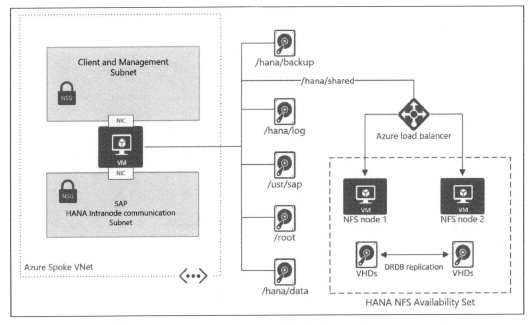

Figure 2-39: Example of one node in a scale-out HANA database (Source: Microsoft.com)

Network traffic between the VMs that form the nodes of the HANA scale-out database, and network traffic between the HANA nodes and the highly available NFS cluster, must not under any circumstances be routed through a **Network Virtual Appliance**[36] (**NVA**) or similar virtual appliances.

It is important to note that SAP HANA scale-out does not run as a failover cluster and therefore does not require load balancers and fencing devices – these are only necessary for the NFS cluster.

HANA disaster recovery

For disaster recovery, the data must be replicated to another Azure region to ensure no data is lost in case of a region-level failure. For SAP HANA, the recommended solution is to have a server provisioned in the secondary region that will be a target for HANA system replication, to ensure the shortest recovery time. Due to the nature of disaster recovery, the failover should be manual, as it is normal to want to determine whether the primary site will be recovered quickly, or an actual failover to DR is required.

---

36   Azure Network Appliances:
https://azure.microsoft.com/en-us/solutions/network-appliances/

Because of this, clustering software is not normally used, and there is no requirement for a fencing solution such as the Azure Fencing Agent or SBD devices.

Following a failover to the secondary Azure region, the IP address of all servers will change. In order for end users to access the systems, it is standard practice to update the DNS records for these systems to resolve the hostname to a different IP:

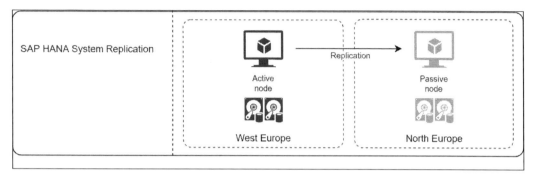

Figure 2-40: Disaster recover for SAP HANA scale-up

When it comes to DR for SAP HANA scale-out systems then you will still use HSR async, but the diagram looks slightly more complex:

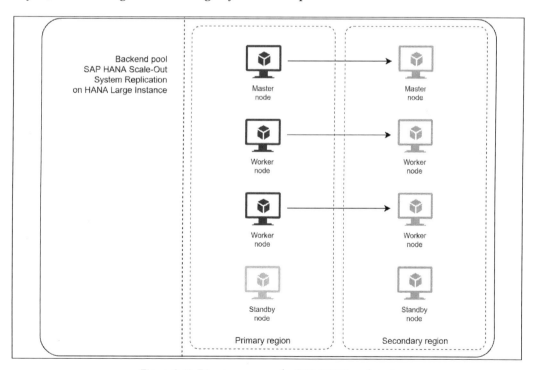

Figure 2-41: Disaster recovery for SAP HANA scale-out

In many cases, you will probably only worry about DR for production, but you may also want to provide some form of DR for non-production as well. Non-production workloads generally have a lower RTO and RPO requirement and therefore it is possible to use other options to protect them. One option is to use ASR with native backup to build a secondary system in case of failure. As ASR does not guarantee that the database data and log files will be synchronized, the replicated database may be inconsistent. As a solution, a database backup including transaction logs should be copied to Azure Blob storage and geo-replicated. During a failover, the backups can be retrieved and restored to a target system. ASR will orchestrate the VM provisioning and configuration, while the database backup from the cloud storage ensures the database consistency:

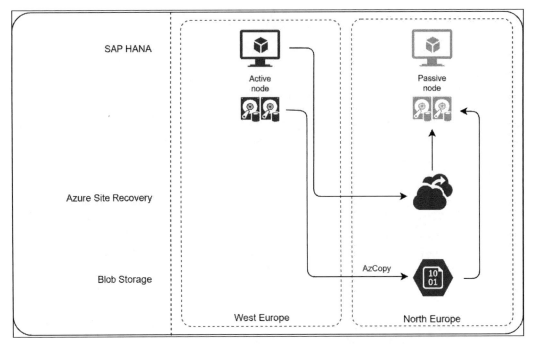

Figure 2-42: DR for non-production using ASR and backup/restore

Having considered the options for SAP HANA disaster recovery, we will now look at the options for SAP HANA backup. Even with local synchronous replication for HA and remote asynchronous replication for DR, it is still essential to implement a separate backup solution, as any logical database corruption is quickly replicated to all copies of the database.

HANA database backup

There are a number of ways to back up a HANA database in Azure, using either Azure native tools or third-party backup products.

HANA backup to a filesystem

The easiest backup solution to implement is to back up the database to a filesystem. This requires additional disks to be attached to the VM to store the database dump. The time required to execute the backup is directly influenced by the disk performance.

Therefore, you can combine multiple disks to create a single logical volume with high throughput. The following table provides a sample configuration depending on the virtual machine size:

VM Size	Memory	Backup Disk configuration	Total storage	Total throughput
M128s	2 TB	2x P40	4 TiB	500 Mbps
M208ms_v2	5.7 TB	3x P40	6 TiB	750 Mbps
M416ms_v2	11.4 TB	4x P50	16 TiB	1 000 Mbps

Table 2-9: Backup disks for performance

Once the backup has been written to the filesystem, it can later be replicated to Azure Blob storage for long-term retention using the AzCopy tool. When the copy is finished, the backup can be removed from the local disk or retained if required for fast restore. To decrease the price of storing the backups in Azure Blob, you can use different storage access tiers:

- **Hot**: For recent filesystem backup
- **Cool**: Optimized for backup from previous days (short term backup)
- **Archive**: Storing the backup for audit purposes

Each access tier is characterized by different pricing policies. The hot storage is the most expensive for keeping backup files; however, the price of accessing the data is low. The cool storage is cheaper, but reading the data is more expensive. Finally, the archive tier offers the cheapest to store the backup files, but accessing them is the most expensive and should be only used for files that are used infrequently (or never). Your auditors may require you to keep an annual full system backup for multiple years, and the archive tier may be a good option as it minimizes the cost, and it is unlikely you will ever access the backups.

The cool and archive storage tiers may have a lower availability in comparison to the hot storage.

The Blob storage also offers keeping copies of the storage:

- **Locally redundant storage**: Provides at least 99.999999999% (11 nines) durability of objects over a given year. It's a default replication for objects stored in the Azure Storage. Three copies of your data are kept in a single Azure region.
- **Zone-redundant storage**: Data is replicated synchronously to three storage clusters in a single region. Each cluster is physically separated and located in its own availability zone. ZRS offers durability for storage objects of at least 99.9999999999% (12 nines) over a given year.
- **Geo-redundant storage**: Designed to provide at least 99.99999999999999% (16 nines) durability of objects over a given year. The data is replicated to another Azure region, which is hundreds of miles from the primary region. Azure stores in total six copies of the data – three in the primary region and another three in the secondary region. Data replication between regions is asynchronous, which means it's first saved to LRS storage and then distributed.

Azure Backup for SAP HANA

Azure Backup is a native backup capability that is built into Azure. Microsoft has developed a SAP HANA backint compatible interface for Azure Backup that allows HANA to backup directly to Azure Backup. This capability is currently in private preview and has some limitations:

- Only selected operating systems are supported
- The backup works only for a single instance SAP HANA (no scale-out deployments)
- Multiple SAP HANA instances on the same VM are not supported
- Full and differential backups are supported, but not incremental

The Azure Backup for SAP HANA connects to the database and streams the data directly to the Azure Backup Vault. There is no need to specify a Storage Account as this is managed internally. You can configure the backup frequency and retention policies.

A further limitation of Azure Backup for SAP HANA is that it does not support HANA multi-streaming data backups, which was introduced with HANA 1.0 SP11. This limits the backup throughput and makes it more appropriate for smaller HANA databases.

HANA backup using filesystem snapshot

The quickest way to backup a HANA database is to perform a filesystem snapshot. It is the best solution for a fast backup of larger database, and also supports fast recovery. However, a snapshot backup cannot guarantee the data consistency, and should only be used in conjunction with a regular full streaming backup that will check the data integrity. Azure Storage does not, by default, guarantee application-level consistency when creating a snapshot. Linux VMs do not support the VSS technology, and therefore additional preparation is required to create an application-consistent snapshot. This is especially important when the SAP HANA files are distributed to multiple disks using LVM.

The overall process is as follows:

1. Execute the SAP HANA snapshot preparation
2. Freeze the filesystem
3. Create a disk snapshot in Azure
4. Unfreeze the filesystem
5. Confirm the SAP HANA snapshot

The snapshot backup can be simplified if the VM can be shut down, and this can be used with non-production systems, particularly where you want to use the snapshot to clone a system. As the HANA database does not perform any disk operations when shutdown, and all data held in memory will have been flushed to disk, then the snapshot will always be consistent and will not require any preparations such as the filesystem freeze.

For more details about the SAP HANA snapshot feature, please refer to the *SAP Note: 2039883 - FAQ: SAP HANA database and storage snapshots*.

HANA Backup using third-party tools

There are a large number of third-party backup tools that integrate with SAP HANA[37], are supported in the Azure environment, and can automate the routine backup tasks. In general, these tools provide centralized control of all your backups, potentially across on-premises as well as in Azure, and offer benefits such as compression, deduplication, and automatic data tiering.

---

37 SAP Note: 2031547 – overview of SAP-certified third-party backup tools and associated support process

At the time of writing, the company that has done the most work to prove its solutions for backing up SAP HANA on Azure is Commvault, who offer a SAP-certified backup solution. The backup is streamed directly to the centralized MediaAgent and stored in Azure Blob storage. The deduplication feature identifies and eliminates redundant data in the backup, thereby reducing not only the volume of data stored in the cloud, but also the bandwidth required for data transfer. A new feature that is due to be released shortly is integration of Commvault Intellisnap with Azure snapshots, which will allow Commvault to also manage the filesystem snapshot process.

The Commvault solution is not limited to HANA Backup. It may also be used to backup the complete SAP landscape, including application servers and all the SAP-supported DBMS types. It can also backup other non-SAP workloads, and therefore can act as the primary backup tool to protect your entire Azure environment. *Table 2-10* summarizes the main advantages and disadvantages of each backup solution.

Backup to filesystem	Azure Backup for SAP HANA	Backup using filesystem snapshot	Third-party tools
+ Easy to implement + Native SAP HANA solution	+ Native Azure solution + Allows you to specify backup and retention policies + Avoids custom scripts	+ The backup and recovery is very fast	+ Solutions certified by SAP + Data deduplication decreases the cost of storage + Allows you to specify backup and retention policies
- Requires storage on the virtual machine - Scripting is required to automate backup and to upload data to Blob storage	- Currently in preview - Doesn't support scale-out systems - Only works for a single HANA instance on a VM	- Complex to execute - Requires scripting to automate	- Requires a separate license - Requires additional Azure infrastructure like VMs for management and data movers

Table 2-10: SAP HANA backup option in Azure

Depending on the architecture of your landscape and its complexity, you can choose the right backup solution. The database backup to filesystem is the easiest to implement, but as it requires additional storage attached to the VM, it increases the total cost. Third-party tools offer the widest capabilities; however, they require an additional license and additional Azure resources.

Monitoring and performance optimization

The SAP HANA database is sized according to its memory requirements. The Azure-certified VMs follow the SAP guidance in terms of core to memory ratios. The HANA workload does not produce consistent and stable CPU utilization, instead it is usual to see the CPU usage as quite low much of the time, with spikes reaching to 80-90% utilization.

An important factor for HANA workloads is the disk write speed, especially on the log volumes. Microsoft Azure provides guidance around the storage layout, which may be further optimized by the customer if required. To fulfill the SAP storage latency requirements when using M series and Mv2 series VMs with Premium SSD, the Write Accelerator should always be enabled on the log volumes. Microsoft is gradually certifying other VM series that do not support the Write Accelerator functionality with Ultra SSD. Check the SAP-certified and Supported Hardware Directory for the latest certifications[38].

In this section, we have reviewed the options for deploying SAP HANA in Azure, using both virtual machines and HANA large instances. We have looked at the options for HA and DR, and finally considered options for backup and monitoring. Microsoft made a commitment in 2016 to make Azure the most scalable and performant platform for running SAP, and since then they have been continuously releasing and enhancing features to extend what can be supported in Azure. In general terms, Azure can now offer similar or better capabilities for SAP HANA as those available on-premises.

SAP Data Hub

With the massive grow in the amount of data that is now being processed and stored, data management is a common and difficult issue. Multiple systems in your IT landscape work in isolation and there are no data governance processes established. If the source information is changed, there is no single place that can answer two basic questions – who changed it and why? In large organizations, the structure of the data is an additional challenge. It is quite likely that you have multiple data marts, or even multiple data lakes, and you are probably also using multiple different analytics and visualization software. Each solution is managed by a different team that uses different toolsets, and getting a holistic view of your data is a big challenge, if not impossible.

---

38   SAP-certified and Supported Hardware Directory: `https://bit.ly/33S2c1C`

The SAP Data Hub, which is one of the newer SAP products, tries to address these issues and provides a common platform for data governance and data orchestration. It implements a data catalogue to keep track of available information sources and allows you to integrate and enrich them using pipeline processes.

Customers that use the Azure data platform capabilities can use SAP Data Hub as a data extraction tool to offload information stored in SAP ERP or SAP S/4HANA to **Azure Data Lake Store (ADLS)**. It opens a world of possibilities – the extracted data can be a source for Machine Learning algorithms or can be blended with information coming from external applications and then analyzed using Power BI.

Modern tools require a modern architecture model that by default implements resilience and simplifies the management of the solution. This is why SAP Data Hub uses Docker and Kubernetes engines as a framework. The core system processes are by default distributed to multiple nodes and this allows them to dynamically scale out. It is possible to run SAP Data Hub on-premises, but the solution fits well in Azure, where it can utilize the native **Azure Kubernetes Service (AKS)**. You only pay for the compute resources used and for the allocated storage. SAP officially supports running Data Hub workloads on AKS. There are five main resources that are required to run Data Hub in Azure:

- **Azure Kubernetes Service**: Orchestrates a cluster of virtual machines and schedules containers to run
- **Azure Container Registry**: Stores the container images
- **Load Balancers**: Exposes the services to the external network
- **Virtual Machines**: Runs the containers
- **Azure Storage**: Stores the data volumes and disks

Each of these resources is required to successfully run SAP Data Hub on Azure and they should be taken into account during landscape planning.

Supported platforms

All SAP Data Hub versions starting from release 2.3 work and are supported in Microsoft Azure. Each version is tested against a certain framework and it is recommended that you follow the requirements detailed in the relevant installation guide.

The current release, (September 2019) SAP Data Hub 2.6, is supported on the Kubernetes 1.11.*–1.13.* releases. AKS allows you to upgrade the deployed Kubernetes engine. If a new SAP Data Hub release requires a higher version of Kubernetes, it is possible to change it without the need to reinstall the entire solution.

System sizing

SAP Data Hub runs in a Kubernetes cluster in Azure. The minimal configuration for production workload suggested by SAP is as follows:

- Four worker nodes, each with:
    - Minimum 64 GB of memory
    - Minimum 8 CPUs
    - Minimum 100 GB of storage

In Azure, you can use the E8s_v3 VM, which fulfils the given requirements.

For non-production environments, the hardware requirements are relaxed:

- Three worker nodes, each with:
    - Minimum 32 GB of memory
    - Minimum 4 CPUs
    - Minimum 100 GB of storage

In Azure you can use the E4s_v3 VM, which fulfils above requirements.

The recommended sizing indicates the minimal requirements to run SAP Data Hub. When running a production workload, the number of concurrently running pipelines and the size of the SAP Vora store are the main drivers to precisely estimate the required hardware.

System deployment

Before running the system installation, you need to correctly configure the Kubernetes environment in Azure. It involves a basic choice such as the VM size, but you also need to consider the networking aspects. As the SAP Data Hub operates in conjunction with other systems in your landscape, you need to ensure there is network connectivity in place.

Azure Kubernetes Service uses a Kubernetes, together with virtual networks already available in the Azure platform. The pods running in the cluster are isolated in the logical network, which should not use address space that is currently deployed in your on-premises or Azure environment. As each pod requires an IP address to communicate with other pods, and there may be tens of pods in a single cluster, using a range that is currently being used would quickly exhaust the available addresses.

In AKS, only cluster nodes receive an IP from the virtual network. **Network address translation (NAT)** is used to enable communication between pods and external systems. Such deployment offers two benefits: it doesn't reduce the number of available IP addresses in the network and it doesn't block connection between SAP Data Hub and other solutions. This is illustrated in *Figure 2-43*:

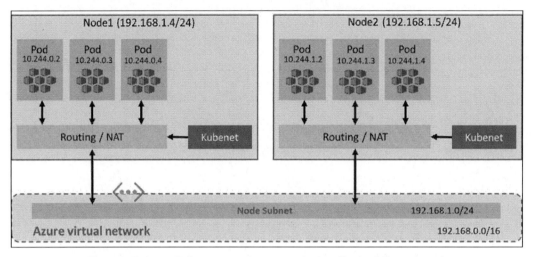

Figure 2-43: Azure Kubernetes service - network view (Source: Microsoft.com)

The next area to consider is how the system will be accessed. It is possible to expose SAP Data Hub Launchpad to the internet, but as the SAP Data Hub connects to other systems in your landscape, in most cases, you will want to secure it inside a virtual network. An internal or public load balancer routes traffic to the correct service within the cluster as shown in *Figure 2-44*:

Chapter 2

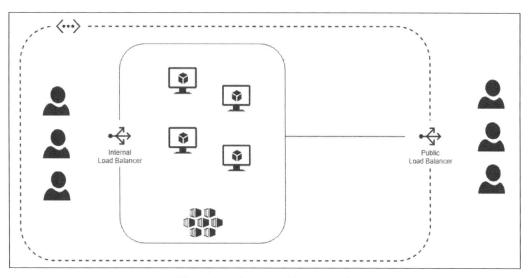

Figure 2-44: Accessing SAP Data Hub

Application deployment in Kubernetes is different to what you will be used to when working with other solutions. This is because it uses Desired State Configuration management. Effectively, you do not install any application; rather, you inform the cluster as to what object you want to run and what its require configuration is. An object is a persistent entity in the cluster – for example, a pod, a service, or a volume. The Kubernetes object is a record of intent – Kubernetes systems will constantly work to ensure that your object exists[39].

System resilience is a built-in capability of the Kubernetes framework. Selected stateless objects are deployed on multiple nodes and the traffic is routed to the active service. In case of a node failure, Kubernetes restarts the affected object by staring another one.

---

39   https://bit.ly/34XDkqj

Architect SAP on Azure

Azure Monitor integrates well with the Azure Kubernetes Engine and provides insights about container performance. You can identify the processor and memory utilization, and similarly to monitoring other resources, you can create a rule to notify someone if the metrics are above a set threshold. SAP Data Hub executes each pipeline as a separate pod and Azure Monitor helps to understand the required capacity and determine the maximum load:

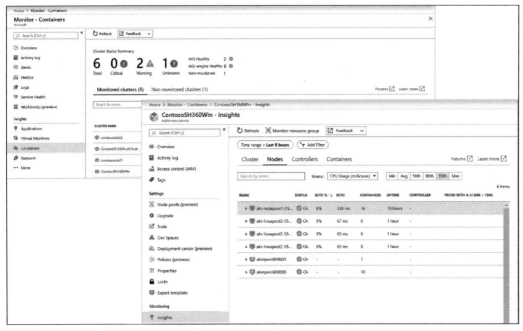

Figure 2-45: Azure Monitor for containers (source: Microsoft.com)

The preceding screenshot shows how Azure Monitor helps to manage the Kubernetes cluster. Information like the status of the node or the number of deployed containers is visible from the Azure portal and it provides a centralized view to a Kubernetes workload.

SAP Hybris commerce

SAP Hybris is now the umbrella name for a number of software solutions, and we don't intend to discuss them all here; our focus is on the SAP Hybris Commerce Platform, which is a leading e-commerce solution. After the acquisition of Hybris in 2013, SAP decided to discontinue their own WebChannel platform and focus on the Hybris Commerce Suite, which is currently known as SAP Commerce. It is an omnichannel sales platform that provides a consistent user experience across every sales channel.

SAP Commerce is not based on the SAP NetWeaver stack, and not written in ABAP. The execution environment for the SAP Hybris Platform is a Java EE Servlet Container. The platform and all extensions to it run within the Spring environment, which allows easy wiring and configuration of each component. It provides generic logic such as security, caching, clustering, and persistence.[40]

SAP Commerce is available in two editions:

- **SAP Commerce**: This is on-premises; running on customer infrastructure or in Public Cloud.
- **SAP Commerce Cloud**: This is a **Software-as-a-Service (SaaS)** offering available from SAP deployed on Microsoft Azure.

The on-premises edition deployment and overall architecture is driven by the implementation partner based on your specific needs. The software can be deployed on VMs, but since release 1811 partners can also deploy the solution on AKS, which is currently the recommended approach. As the SAP Commerce architecture is open, partners choose frameworks and components that complement the solution.

When it comes to the database management system, SAP Hybris actively supports Oracle, MySQL, Percona XtraDB Cluster, SAP HANA DB, or Microsoft SQL Server[41].

---

40   SAP Hybris Commerce Architecture and Technology: `https://bit.ly/2rXlJR0`

41   SAP Hybris Commerce Architecture and Technology: `https://bit.ly/2rlQmzl`

But partners can also influence the deployment model and decide to run the database on VMs, or choose to use native cloud databases such as Azure SQL Database. Similarly, SAP does not provide a strict specification for the reverse proxy engine, which can use Apache server or the Azure Application Gateway:

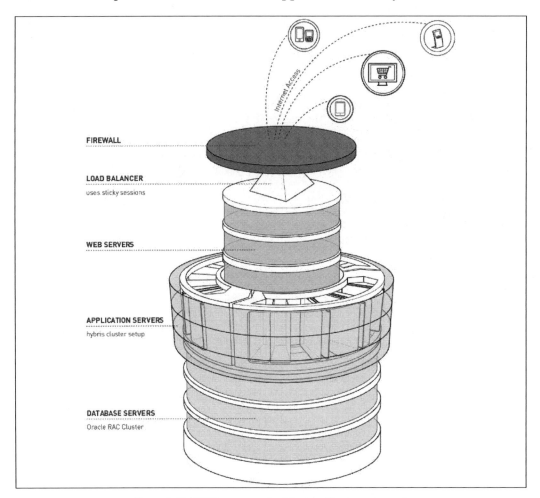

Figure 2-46: SAP Commerce Architecture (Source: sap.com)

The main SAP Commerce components comprise:

- **Reverse proxy**: A web server to route incoming traffic. It can be deployed on virtual machines or on Azure Kubernetes Service. It should reside in a DMZ network where the traffic is filtered using firewalls. A **Web Application Firewall (WAF)**, which is part of Azure Application Gateway, provides an additional layer of security.

- **SAP Commerce**:
    - **Front-end**: Internet-facing storefront.
    - **SAP Commerce Backoffice**: Backend application to manage the SAP Commerce store. Customers do not require access to this application and the traffic can be limited to internal, trusted networks only.
- **Apache Solr**: Provides a search engine and indexing capabilities to optimize solution performance
- **Database**: Stores business data
- **Back-end systems**: ERP systems running in the customer landscape

Figure 2-47 illustrates the distribution of each component in the landscape. The reverse proxy is an entry point for connection from the internet. The main system components are protected by a firewall that filters the traffic:

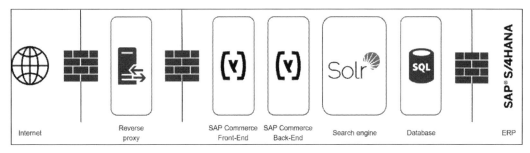

Figure 2-47: SAP commerce components

During the provisioning, by default, SAP Commerce builds a broadcast or a multicast cluster. However, broadcast and multicast network traffic are not allowed on Microsoft Azure and therefore additional configuration is required to change the cluster type to unicast. As a result of this, each application server needs to be manually registered in the database.

The basic implementation of the SAP Commerce solution can be customized and run exclusively on Azure platform services – there is no need to provision VMs. The AKS simplifies the application scaling and reliability. Security of the platform is ensured by using the Azure Application Gateway. Azure Storage hosts images and other objects that are not suitable to keep in the database, and the network latency can be optimized by using Azure **Content Delivery Network (CDN)**. Instead of installing a database platform on VMs, partners will very often decide to choose the fully managed Azure SQL Database that offers up to 99.995% SLA when using geo-replication.

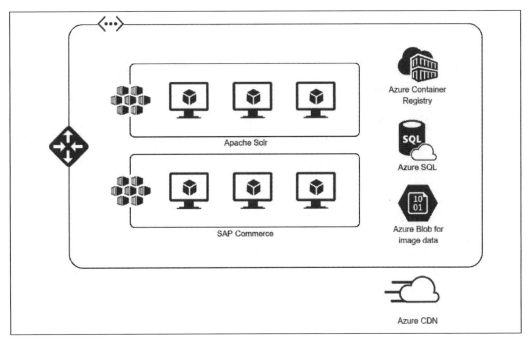

Figure 2-48: A high-level architecture of SAP Commerce on AKS

Many customers license SAP Commerce based on the number of cores used by the software. In such scenarios, the SAP Commerce workload is isolated on a separate set of VMs to save on the licensing cost. Hyper-threading is not supported by the licensing model and therefore customers choose the Dv2-series VMs. Running SAP Commerce on VMs that support hyper-threading like E-series, which is a common choice for SAP NetWeaver workloads, would increase the license cost. Therefore, we recommend that you consider the below D-series VMs for the SAP Commerce workload:

Size	vCPU	Memory	Max data disk	Max uncached disk throughput: IOPS / Mbps	Max NICs / Expected network bandwidth (Mbps)
Standard_DS1_v2	1	3.5	4	3200 / 48	2 / 750
Standard_DS2_v2	2	7	8	6400 / 96	2 / 1500
Standard_DS3_v2	4	14	16	12800 / 192	4 / 3000
Standard_DS4_v2	8	28	32	25600 / 384	8 / 6000
Standard_DS5_v2	16	56	64	51200 / 768	8 / 12000

Table 2-11: SAP Commerce recommended VMs when licensed per core

Azure Monitor Application Insights for Java offers a fully managed, native monitoring capability for Java applications, and it can be used together to monitor SAP Commerce:

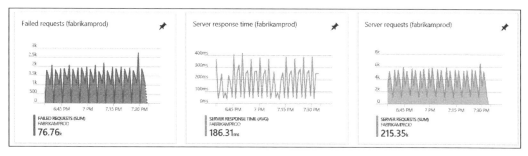

Figure 2-49: Azure Monitor Application Insights for Java (Source: microsoft.com)

You can track performance metrics or access application logs using a common platform – everything you need to monitor the availability, performance, reliability, and usage of your web applications on Azure.

Summary

In this chapter we have looked in detail at hot to architect SAP on Azure. We have considered both traditional SAP applications running on AnyDB (IBM DB2, Microsoft SQL Server, Oracle Database, SAP ASE, and SAP MaxDB) as well as applications running on the SAP HANA database, which can be either the traditional SAP Business Suite applications or the newer SAP S/4HANA and BW/4HANA. We have covered all the key areas of sizing, high availability, disaster recovery, backup, and monitoring. We have also looked into two of the non-SAP NetWeaver-based applications, namely SAP Data Hub and SAP Hybris Commerce. These use totally different architectures to the core SAP applications, and in many ways are more cloud friendly.

Having now learned how to architect for SAP on Azure, in the next chapter, we will look at the options for actually migrating existing SAP workloads to Azure. The solution will depend on both the source platform on which you run SAP today as well as the chosen target platform in Azure. Many organizations will use a migration to Azure as an opportunity to modernize parts of their SAP landscape.

3
Migrate SAP to Microsoft Azure

In the previous chapter we looked at how to architect SAP on Azure to meet your business needs. We covered topics such as sizing and designing the Azure Infrastructure as a Service to meet your business availability requirements. A few of you may be implementing SAP for the first time, in which case this chapter is not relevant, but for the vast majority of you, you will already be running SAP and you will need to migrate some or all of your existing SAP landscape to Azure.

The options for migration depend on the source **operating system (OS)** and **database management system (DBMS)** you are currently running and the target OS and DBMS you plan for Azure. Whatever your intentions, all these migration options use proven techniques and tools that have been in use for many years. Migrating SAP to Azure is no different to migrating SAP to any new data center, and many of you will have experience of this from the past.

Exploring migration

There are typically two main reasons why you may consider migrating SAP to Azure:

- You need to replace the infrastructure that is currently running SAP. This could be because the current hardware is up for renewal, or because an existing data center co-location or managed outsourcing contract is up for renewal.

- You want to migrate SAP to a new database, particularly SAP HANA, or you plan to move to the latest SAP applications such as S/4HANA or BW/4HANA.

Depending on your goal SAP offers different migration paths. You can decide either to migrate the current workload to Azure as-is or to combine it with changing the database and execute both activities as a single step.

In most respects migrating SAP to Azure is no different to any other SAP data center migration, and if you have been running SAP for any significant time it is quite likely that you have already been through one or two migrations during that time. There are four main types of migration:

1. **Lift-and-shift** – where the current choice of OS and DBMS is supported in Azure then the migration becomes a simple homogeneous system copy, a well proven path for replatforming SAP.
2. **Lift-and-migrate** – where the current choice of OS and DBMS is not supported in Azure, then the migration becomes a heterogeneous system copy. This is most commonly used because the current operating system is not supported in Azure, normally because you are currently running on a traditional – dare we say legacy – Unix operating system; HPE HP-UX, IBM AIX, or Oracle Solaris. Of course, while changing the OS, you can always change the DBMS as well.
3. **Lift-and-migrate to HANA** – if you have to undertake a heterogeneous migration then you may want to consider changing from your current DBMS to SAP HANA. From the perspective of the level of effort, changing just the OS or changing the OS and DBMS does not result in significant additional effort. In terms of timescales, complexity, and testing, they are very similar, where changing both OS and DBMS at the same time may increase effort is in debugging problems.
4. **Lift-and-transform to S/4HANA** – if you are having to migrate anyway, and have considered migrating the DBMS to SAP HANA, could this also be the time to switch to S/4HANA? The S/4HANA conversion process (technical upgrade) has continued to be refined, making this a possible option, and of course future-proofing your SAP investment.

Ultimately, the level of complexity will depend on where you are starting from and where you want to finish. There are two technical approaches to SAP migration classified based on OS or DBMS change.

A homogenous migration is an option when the operating system and the database does not change; that is, this is a lift-and-shift migration. You can also perform a homogeneous migration between different releases of the same OS and DBMS, which means that you can, for example, migrate systems from Windows 2008 to Windows 2016 or from Oracle 11 to Oracle 12 using a homogenous migration. As there is no data conversion taking place, the migration is easier and quicker to execute.

The homogenous migration most commonly uses the database tools to export the data (database backup) and then import to the target machine (database restore), but you could achieve similar results just by copying the underlaying disks and attaching them to a virtual machine running in Azure. In general, the second approach is not preferred as it provides no option to perform even the smallest improvement, such as updating the operating system, but there are cases where it may be used.

When the underlying OS or DBMS is changed, then you have to perform a SAP heterogenous migration, which is what you will use for lift-and-migrate. In its simplest form, all data residing in the database is exported to flat files and then imported into the target system, although there are some more exotic solutions available, mainly aimed at minimizing downtime. A heterogenous migration is more complex to execute and requires additional testing to achieve good performance and reliability, especially when working with large databases. However, it does have one advantage; the exported flat files are much smaller than the source database – indexes are not copied, but recreated – which means it reduces the data to be copied to Azure, which can be useful when network bandwidth is limited.

Examples of instances of homogeneous or heterogeneous migration are shown in *Table 3-1*:

Source system	Target system	Copy mode	Explanation
OS: Windows 2016 **DB: SQL Server 2016**	OS: Windows 2016 DB: SQL Server 2016	Homogenous migration	The system platform doesn't change
OS: Windows 2008 **DB: Oracle 11g**	OS: Windows 2016 DB: Oracle 12c	Homogenous migration	The system platform doesn't change – only software release is different
OS: Windows 2008 **DB: Oracle 11g**	OS: Windows 2016 DB: SQL Server 2016	Heterogenous migration	The database software is different
OS: SLES 12 **DB: DB2**	OS: SLES 12 DB: SAP HANA	Heterogenous migration	The database software is different
OS: HP-UX **DB: Oracle 11g**	OS: Oracle Linux DB: Oracle 12h	Heterogenous migration	The hardware architecture is changed – HP-UX system uses the big endian and Oracle Linux uses little endian

Table 3-1: Examples of SAP homogeneous and heterogeneous migrations

Sometimes people will talk about one-step, two-step, or three-step migrations when discussing migrating SAP to Azure. Depending where you start, migrating your SAP estate may require a number of activities to be performed. In almost all situations, where the target is not just a simple lift-and-shift of the current landscape, multiple steps will be required:

- Changing the DBMS
- Upgrading the SAP solution
- Unicode conversion

Depending on the source and target environment, migrating to SAP HANA running in Azure may require three steps:

- Firstly, to fulfil the minimum requirements for SAP HANA you may need to upgrade SAP NetWeaver to at least release 7.40.
- Then you need to migrate from the current DBMS to HANA.
- Finally, you need to migrate the data to Azure.

If you implement these activities separately, then you will need three projects, three test plans and three sets of downtime. While it is difficult to find a good reason to split the migration to HANA from the migration to Azure, you may decide to upgrade your systems to the required release levels in advance of performing the migration (two-step). However, SAP now provides the possibility to combine all three actions and execute them as part of a single process (one-step) with the **Software Update Manager (SUM)** and **Downtime Minimized Option (DMO)**, therefore reducing the testing requirements and minimizing the number of downtimes.

Planning

Planning is an essential part of any migration project, and you should not underestimate the importance of this phase. The systems included in your landscape and the target goal of migration, whether it is just a lift-and-shift or complex system transformation and innovation, will dictate the migration strategy approach. During the planning phase, you define what resources you require and what is the order of task execution. You should ensure that all areas of SAP migration are covered in detail, otherwise you may encounter unexpected surprises. For example, if the current network bandwidth does not allow you to copy your SAP system to Azure in an acceptable time, then you need to either temporarily upgrade your ExpressRoute connection or potentially set up additional **site-to-site (S2S)** VPN connections.

While in theory you could use an offline transfer solution such as Azure Data Box to migrate your data, in practice the current time for this service to get data into Azure will in most cases be slower than using network transfers. However, Azure Data Box can still be useful for transferring large volumes of SAP data to Azure for proofs of concept.

In the following sections, we'll cover the key considerations for planning any SAP to Azure migration and highlight the most important areas that need to be considered.

Interfaces

One of the most important tasks when planning any SAP migration is to ensure that all the interfaces are documented. As you move workloads into Azure you will need to ensure that all the interfaces are re-pointed correctly. One unavoidable fact is that IP addresses will change as each workload is moved into Azure, so any interface that uses a hard-coded IP address will need changing. Where hostnames have been used, then changing the DNS entry should be all that is required.

In most cases, the move to Azure will not happen as a single event but will take place in phases. Each phase will require another set of interfaces to be re-pointed. This all needs to be planned in advance, and test plans developed to ensure that you can adequately test each interface. Where the interfaces are to external organizations then particular attention is required, as generally it is more difficult to test these interfaces. You may have to work with your trading partners and plan a test window during which you create and send test data from the migrated system. You may have to work with these organizations to find ways to create dummy transactions.

Move groups

Once you have a full understanding of all the interfaces, then you can start to plan the move groups. It is likely that your SAP landscape is too complex to allow for all workloads to be migrated simultaneously. Instead, they will likely require several phases of migration. Therefore, move groups are necessary to assist the transition over to Azure. Move groups are sets of workloads that can be moved together within a given phase. As a general rule, applications that are closely coupled will need to be moved together as a single move group, to ensure that network latency does not impact performance. This does not just apply to SAP applications themselves, but also to third-party applications that are an integral part of the SAP landscape and are tightly coupled.

Once the basic move groups have been identified then you can start to plan the order in which to move these groups. In general, it is better to start with the smaller and less critical systems so that you can prove the migration strategy in a way that minimizes disruption to the business.

As an example, a SAP Portal that is used for employee self-service applications is unlikely to be critical to the business, other than possibly at certain times of the month, quarter, or year, and may be a good candidate for an early migration. By contrast, if your core ECC system is required 24x7, and you can afford only one 12 hour downtime in a year, then you want to be as sure as possible that the migration has been fully tested, and any problems ironed out, before you start the work.

Preparing the environment in Azure

In general, when migrating SAP to Azure, you need to build a new environment in Azure, and then migrate only the data from on-premises to Azure. You will create new **virtual machines** (**VMs**) from scratch and reinstall the SAP and DBMS software.

Once again, this is no different to what you would normally do in any other data center move. In fact, it has several advantages:

- In most cases you will want to develop a new governance model for Azure, including new naming conventions, security models, and so on. Freshly creating the VMs in Azure may prove to be easier than moving them and applying the new governance model.
- You can leverage Azure automation to ensure all VMs are built to a consistent standard and avoid the configuration drift that often happens in the on-premises world.
- You can use standard Azure gallery images for the operating systems, or create your own custom images, and again ensure all VMs are built to a consistent standard.
- You can then reinstall the SAP and DBMS software. This process can be semi-automated in Azure, but unless you plan to regularly reinstall software, there is less benefit to automating this part of the process.

Clearly this work can be completed well in advance of any migration and will need to be in place for the migration testing. Once the VMs are created, if they are not required for testing, then they can be shut down and deallocated to avoid any costs for the VMs; the allocated storage will still be charged.

Housekeeping and archiving

It is always advisable to complete basic housekeeping and archiving prior to a migration. Anything that reduces the size of the databases to be migrated will reduce the potential downtime required and, in some cases, may make one of the simpler and cheaper migration solutions possible, whereas the current database size may preclude this and require a more complex and costly approach.

While housekeeping should be possible in most projects, typically, archiving projects takes much longer and may not be possible in the timescales available, depending on what is driving the move to Azure. It is still worth looking at which are the biggest tables in your databases, and see if archiving is possible. Unless data retention policies are already in place, however, it is likely that any archiving will require the approval of the business owners for that data.

As mentioned elsewhere, the flexibility of Azure means that you can potentially migrate first, and archive once in Azure, and then reduce the size of the VMs in Azure to reduce the cost. In this case, just beware of reserving too much capacity up front, and then discovering you have more reserved instances than are required to run SAP once the archiving is complete.

Data transfer

With the order of migration now planned, you need to consider how you will transfer data from your on-premises data center into Azure. This is key, as it directly influences the total downtime required. The right solution will depend on the amount of data to be transferred and the downtime available. There are two basic ways you can transfer data to Azure: either using an external device, or over a network. We'll discuss these individually in the following sections.

Transfer data using Azure Data Box

In theory, using Azure Data Box may seem like a simple solution to moving large amounts of data from your current data center to Azure. Data Box uses what is essentially a physical disk to move the data. After registering for the Data Box service, within a few days Microsoft will send a physical disk device that you connect to your network, upload the required files, and then send back to Microsoft. This is an approach that has worked successfully for many years.

However, Microsoft does not provide any precise information as to how long the uploading of data to the storage account will take as it heavily depends on the number of files and their sizes. The estimated time when your data will become available on cloud storage in Azure is around 10 to 14 days, which means you cannot possibly use it for migrating production workloads, although it can still be useful for proofs of concept, pilot migrations or migration of non-production systems.

Network-based data transfer

When transferring data via a network, the key factor that dictates the required time is the available network bandwidth. A stable and reliable connection to the internet is required, otherwise the connection can be interrupted, and depending on the tool used, the transfer may have to be repeated.

You should aim only to use tools that allow you to restart the copy process from where it stopped, such as Microsoft AzCopy, which is a dedicated tool to upload files to Azure Storage.

With many copy tools the process usually involves two steps:

- Firstly, you need to upload your data to Azure blob or file storage
- Secondly, you need to download the data to the target VM

The data can be transferred using various protocols. A recommended way is to use Azure AzCopy, which is rich in functionalities and tested by many other customers, but some people prefer an FTP server, which is supported by SAP copy tools in the heterogenous migration. You should avoid mounting remote file systems directly on the VM (for example, Azure File Share) – it usually offers a lower transfer rate and is a less reliable solution.

Many transfer tools, including AzCopy and FTP, work best when you simultaneously copy multiple files. A single copy thread will not use the entire network bandwidth. This is important if you plan to use database backup files, as you will need to split the backup into several smaller chunks.

The average time required to copy files to Azure Blob Storage is as follows:

	10 Mbps	100 Mbps	500 Mbps	1 Gbps
100 GB	22 hours	2.5 hours	30 minutes	< 30 minutes
500 GB	5 days	11 hours	2.5 hours	1 hour
1 TB	10 days	22 hours	5 hours	2 hours
2 TB	19 days	2 days	9 hours	5 hours
10 TB	88 days	9 days	2 days	22 hours

Table 3-2: Time taken to copy data using different network speeds

Based on the volume of data you need to transfer, and the downtime window available, you may have to consider how you can increase network bandwidth during the migration period. The most common solution is to set up additional temporary site-to-site VPN connections between your on-premises data center and Azure, but this does require you to have sufficient bandwidth available on your internet connection to support the additional VPN sessions.

If you have an ExpressRoute connection between your data center and Azure, then you can either supplement this with additional site-to-site VPN connections, or potentially increase the capacity of your ExpressRoute connection for the duration of the migration.

The latter option will depend on your telecommunications provider who provides the link to the Azure network peering, whether they are able to provide a temporary increase in network bandwidth, and what they will charge to do this. Increasing ExpressRoute bandwidth is generally more difficult for shorter periods of time, due to minimum contract terms, whereas for large complex migrations, it is likely that the bandwidth will be required for many months, both for testing and actual live migrations.

You also need to consider the security of your data while in transit. Some database management systems offer the option to encrypt the data during backup. It is always worth enabling this encryption, even if the file will be transferred over a secure connection.

Unless you have an ExpressRoute connection you will need to transfer the files over a public internet connection. In this case you should use transfer protocols that offer additional in-flight encryption, such as HTTPS or SFTP, otherwise it is possible that your data could be stolen. Microsoft AzCopy allows you to use the secure HTTPS protocol to upload the files.

In this section, we have looked at some of the key areas that you need to consider when planning a migration of SAP to Azure. However, there are a number of other areas that you will also need to consider, which we will look into in the coming sections.

Landscape review

As part of the migration, you should consider reviewing your landscape. As well as the **minimum Development (DEV)**, **Quality Assurance System (QAS)**, and **Production (PRD)**, it is quite likely that you have multiple additional non-production environments. These may include Sandbox, Training, Integration Testing, User Acceptance Testing, Project DEV, Project QAS and Pre-Production. Should all of these be migrated to Azure, or should only the key environments be migrated, and the rest created as required once the move to Azure is complete?

Once you have decided which environments need to be migrated, you will also need to decide whether to migrate each individual environment, or simply migrate production and copy back the production data into the other environments. This will depend to some extent on your current practices. You may already copy back production into QAS on a regular basis for testing purposes, but equally your development environment may contain custom data that has been specifically created for development testing. As development often has a much smaller database, it can be useful to test migration processes using the development database, as it will be much quicker to run tests, fail, and repeat.

Choosing the right migration method

To a large extent the migration method will depend on whether the migration is homogeneous or heterogeneous. In general, the migration is much easier if it is homogeneous and there are multiple different ways of performing the migration depending on the downtime window available. Heterogeneous migrations are always more complex, and if you need to minimize downtime then specialized tools may be required.

Homogenous migration

A homogenous migration is the easiest to execute, as the operating system, DBMS, and hardware platform remain the same and no data conversion is required. The database files use the same format and therefore they can be copied and attached to the new database. The simplest form of homogenous migration is a backup/restore, but, depending on the database size, this can be quite slow. An alternative can be to use DBMS replication to live replicate the database into Azure.

Migration using backup/restore

One of the simplest methods of homogenous migration is the backup/restore method. If the operating system and DBMS are already running on an x86-based hardware platform, using either Intel or AMD x86 processors, then it is possible to take a full database backup and restore it on the target virtual machine. If you run your SAP system on, for example, Microsoft SQL Server or Oracle and you do not want to change the DBMS, then the backup/restore offers the easiest way to migrate the system.

The backup/restore method does not provide any opportunity for any data conversion. If the source system is non-unicode then the target system will also be non-unicode. If a conversion is required, because, for example, the operating system has to change, then this either has to be done as another step or a different migration method, such as Export/Import or DMO, must be considered.

Each database has dedicated tools to perform the system backup and they should always be used. In general, data consistency is ensured by the backup process; if the backup is successful, then all data should be able to be restored on the target virtual machine. However, it does not guarantee that the backup itself is not corrupted. Therefore, during the migration it is recommended that you execute additional database consistency checks, an option offered by most of the database tools:

Chapter 3

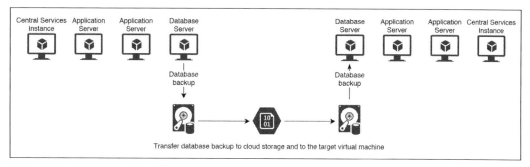

Figure 3-1: SAP homogeneous migration using the backup and restore method

As the database backup can be large, depending on the source database size, then compression should be used where available. A compressed backup is executed faster, as the main bottleneck is usually writing the backup to the target storage system, so the cost of a few additional CPU cycles to perform the compression is worth it in terms of the time saved writing the backup to disk.

While for day-to-day operational purposes it is quite usual to perform online "hot" backups, for a homogeneous migration you need a full copy of the database, and for this the backup needs to be taken when the database has been shut down. Otherwise, the data changed after the backup was started would not be copied to the target environment. The total downtime is the sum of the time required to perform the backup, the time required to transfer the files to Azure, and the time taken to restore from the backup.

The high-level process of executing the migration is as follows:

- Prepare target Azure environment
- Install database software on the target server
- Stop source SAP system
- Perform database backup
- Transfer backup files
- Perform database restore
- Run Software Provisioning Manager and install SAP binaries
- Start SAP system

Interestingly, Microsoft SQL Server does not require you to perform a system backup. When the database is shut down, it is possible to detach the database files, copy them to the target system, and then attach them to the new SQL Server instance. As you do not have to perform a backup or restore, this can significantly decrease the total downtime.

Downtime-optimized backup/restore

A simple way to reduce the downtime window when using the backup/restore method is to transfer most of the backup files in advance. A full system backup is taken in advance of the migration period, transferred to Azure, and the backup restored. It does not matter if this takes a few hours or a few days, as long as it is completed in advance of the cut-over.

After the full backup, each day an incremental backup is taken, also transferred to Azure, and restored. When it comes to the cut-over period, the SAP application is shut down to stop any further database changes, a final incremental backup is taken, and that is then transferred to Azure and restored. In normal circumstances, that final incremental backup will be very small compared to the full backup, and will be much quicker to complete, transfer, and restore.

Migration using DBMS replication

If the downtime-optimized backup/restore still does not meet your requirements, then there is a further option using DBMS replication tools. Instead of copying all data during the migration period, you can ship the database files ahead of time and enable DBMS replication between source and target environments. All records created or updated since the backup was taken will be transmitted and applied to the cloud using database-specific replication technologies, such as SQL Server AlwaysOn Availability Groups or SAP HANA System Replication. The configuration requires that both databases can communicate with each other, so it is essential to have network connectivity between the two databases, which may require ports on the firewalls to be opened both on-premises and in Azure.

When the application servers are prepared, you can change the DNS configuration and route users to the newly created database. Migrating the database using DBMS replication drastically reduces the downtime as you only need allow the final few transactions to complete, before you are ready to bring up the database in Azure and connect the new application servers:

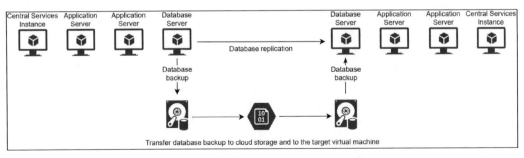

Figure 3-2: SAP homogeneous migration using the DBMS replication method

To copy the database backup, you can use the AzCopy tool, which uploads the files to the storage account and you download it to the target VMs. You could also provision a temporary FTP server in the cloud and transfer the files directly to a disk that you can subsequently mount to the database server. When the database backup is restored, you can establish replication between the source and target system. Be careful, as the replication usually requires that the source and target release of the database is exactly the same.

Migration using Azure Site Recovery

One final option for heterogeneous migrations is to use **Azure Site Recovery** (**ASR**). ASR was designed to provide a reliable disaster recovery solution, and it is mentioned earlier in this book for that purpose, but it can also be used to migrate SAP environments to Azure. ASR can support the replication of virtual machines currently running on VMware or Hyper-V, as well as physical servers.

When ASR replication is enabled on a system, all data stored on its disk is copied to Azure. For Application Servers that consist of mostly static files, this is a reliable solution. However, for database servers, an additional step is required to complete the replication and ensure that you have a consistent database. As you may remember from *Chapter 2* of this book, ASR does not support the replication of database workloads to Azure for DR, due to the lack of synchronization across multiple disks. The workaround for migration purposes is to shut down the database and wait for the next Application Consistent Snapshot. As there is no data being written to the data or log files, the latest changes are replicated to the cloud and the database is in a consistent state.

The migration is executed when you choose to failover the systems in ASR. Protected servers are re-created in Azure, based on the pre-defined virtual machine sizes, and the replicated disks are then attached to the newly created VM. Please note that the new virtual machines are an exact copy of the on-premises systems, including hostnames and data stored on the disks:

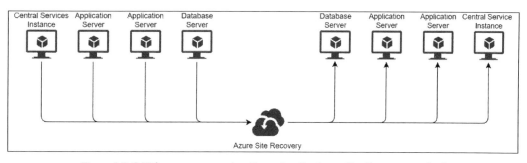

Figure 3-3: SAP homogeneous migration using the Azure Site Recovery method

The Azure Site Recovery method supports various operating systems including Windows Server, SUSE Linux Enterprise Server, and RedHat Enterprise Linux. The migration requires that operating system updates are installed. Always check whether your system is supported before starting replication.

Using Azure System Replication to migrate your system means you take everything as-is. All the files and entire configuration of the operating system will be transferred to the cloud, which is not a recommended approach and may result in higher operational costs. However, it may be a good solution to quickly migrate smaller systems.

Heterogenous migration

Whenever there is a change to the operating system, DBMS software, or the hardware platform, the migration becomes heterogeneous. Rather than some form of relatively simple copy process, all data residing in the source database must be exported to flat files in the source environment, copied to the target environment, and then imported into the target database. This Export/Import method is more complex than backup/restore, but it offers additional capabilities, and as the basic migration tools are supplied and fully supported by SAP, this is the recommended option if you plan a platform change.

More recently, SAP has enhanced the basic Export/Import solution with a relatively new option to migrate systems to the cloud with the Database Migration Option with System Copy. It offers the same capabilities as the Classical Migration, but in addition you can perform a system upgrade or Unicode conversion in a single step.

Because the export files are much smaller than the source database, the amount of data that needs to be transmitted across the network to Azure is reduced, thereby reducing the time to transfer the data or allowing the use of a network link with lower bandwidth.

Classical migration

In classical migration cases, all data stored in the database is exported to flat files. You can then copy the files to the target virtual machine in Azure and re-create the database instance.

As the extract uses a SAP-specific format that is not bound to any particular database, it is possible to import the data even if the target platform runs on a different platform, such as:

- **Different database** – for example, migration from Oracle to SAP HANA
- **Different operating system** – for example, migration from AIX to Linux
- **Different hardware architecture** – for example, migration from IBM Power or HP Itanium to Linux on x86

As the classical migration is complex, SAP requires that the system administrator that executes it has the SAP OS/DB Migration certification.

There are three main phases of the system Export:

1. **Generate the Data Definition Language (DDL) statements for non-standard database objects**: Some systems may contain additional objects that are not referenced in the ABAP structures. Usually this applies to the SAP Business Warehouse solution, but to avoid problems this step should be executed for all systems. Shortly before migration, non-standard database objects should be scripted to SQL using the SMIGR_CREATE_DDL report.
2. **Generate the structure files and compute the size of the database**: The R3SZCHK is called by the Software Provisioning Manager to perform size calculation for tables and indexes. The output is written to the DBSIZE.XML file. This can be run in advance of migration.
3. **Extract data to dump files**: Based on provided configuration, the data from the database is extracted to the filesystem. This is the longest export step. The process can be optimized to decrease time required for the extract.

There are three phases to the system Import:

1. **Install database software and create database**: The first import step requires you to install the DBMS software and provide connection details.
2. **Import data from the dump files**: Data from the files is read and imported to the target database. This is the longest import step and can be optimized to minimize the downtime.
3. **Post-import checks**: After the import, Software Provisioning Manager runs additional checks and then starts the instance.

Classical migration is highly flexible and enables a change in the operating system and database platform. It also reduces the data footprint that has to be transferred to the cloud system. Each step of the migration can be customized to reduce the overall execution time. In the following, we provide a few optimization techniques that you can evaluate.

Performance optimization

Classical migration takes a lot of time to execute. All data from the source database is exported as multiple files to a filesystem, transferred to Azure, and then imported to the target environment. It may be a challenge to execute all these steps sequentially during a short downtime window, therefore you should look for optimization techniques that decrease the time required to perform the migration.

Execute System Export Preparation ahead of time

Some of the steps take a lot of time but do not have to be executed during the downtime window. The database size calculation and creating DDL statements for non-standard database objects can be executed ahead of the migration.

Export/import process optimization

There are several optimizations that can be applied to the actual export and import processes, which are performed by the SAP R3Load process.

R3Load process configuration

The ABAP objects that are exported and then imported to the target database are grouped into packages that are then executed by R3Load processes. SAP allows you to parallelize them and execute the import and export of several packages at the same time. This doesn't mean that the more processes running the faster the execution is, as each process utilizes the processing power, memory, and storage on both the export server and the import server, so it is important to correctly understand the impact and the resource consumption.

Three to five processes per vCPU is a value recommended by SAP, but to achieve best results the migration should be tested multiple times to find the optimum number of processes for your system:

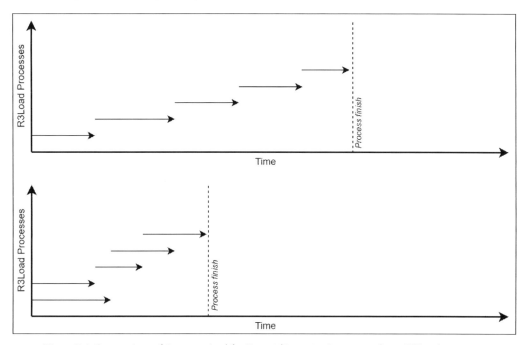

Figure 3-4: Comparison of time required for Export/Import using one and two R3Load processes

In the preceding example, we present how increasing the number of concurrent R3Load processes reduce the time of migration. If only one process is defined, all migration packages are executed one by one. If you create additional processes, export and import jobs can run in parallel, which reduces the overall time of execution.

Special care for large tables

Most of the data in the system is stored in a relatively small number of very large tables. Therefore, the export and import of these large tables can take the majority of the time, especially if the process is not optimized.

The migration is only complete when all data has been processed, so the correct order of table export and import, starting with the largest table first, impacts the overall time required:

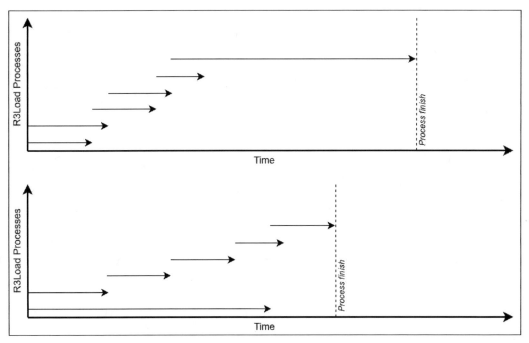

Figure 3-5: Comparison of time required for Export/Import depending on the order of processing packages

Very large tables should also be split into several smaller packages (table splitting) to avoid scenarios where the largest tables determine the total execution times. The packages for a single table should not be processed at the same time but mixed with others.

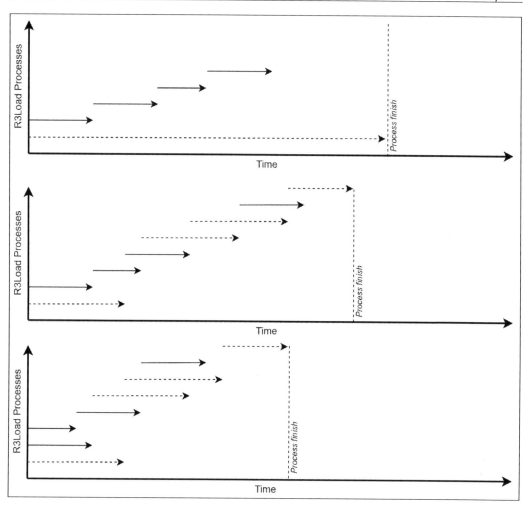

Figure 3-6: Comparison of time required for Export/Import with table splitting using two and three R3Load processes

As the table splitting results in a higher number of packages, you could also consider adding additional R3Load processes to increase the parallelism of execution. This will further reduce the time required for migration.

Parallel export/import

The data export and import can be parallelized. As soon as the export of a package is complete, the files for that package can be transferred to Azure and the import started, without waiting for the rest of the packages to be extracted. As the processes are executed in parallel, the total time to complete the migration is reduced:

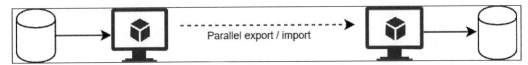

Figure 3-7: Parallel export/import

The data that is exported from the source system is immediately transferred to the target virtual machine, using, for example, the FTP server. Signal files inform the target system that the export of the package is finished, and the import process can start.

Use multiple R3Load servers

You can use multiple physical or virtual servers to allow you to run more parallel R3Load processes. Each server can be configured to process selected packages:

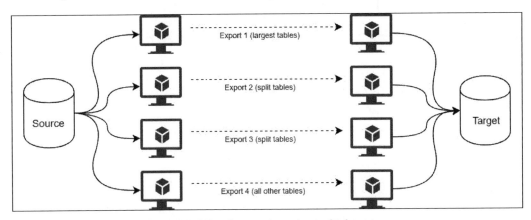

Figure 3-8: R3Load processing using multiple servers

Ultimately, the database server itself will become a bottleneck and it needs to be monitored. If this becomes a problem, performance can be improved during the export by creating temporary export database instances with copies of the production database. Note that this does require you to have access to additional hardware to create the copies:

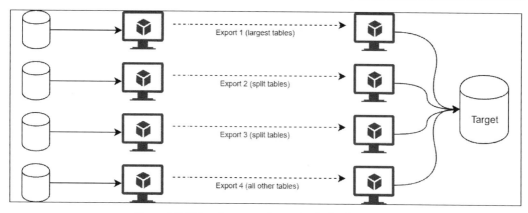

Figure 3-9: R3Load export using multiple database copies

Simultaneous exports from four copies of the source database can significantly reduce the time of the overall export. Such a scenario is, however, highly complex and requires specialized knowledge. Unless your source database is big and the migration window very small, you shouldn't consider this approach. We suggest engaging with SAP and Microsoft if you think this is the only way you can migrate your system.

Temporarily scale-up the Azure environment

One of the great features of the Azure cloud platform is that you can change the size of VMs. Adding more resources to the database server during the migration will allow you to run more R3load processes, and therefore reduce the time required to import all the data. When the process is finished, the VM can be scaled down to the size required for normal running.

Database Migration Option (DMO) with System Move option

SAP introduced the DMO to the **Software Update Manager (SUM)** originally to simplify the migration to the SAP HANA database. For many customers this requires a system upgrade and sometimes even a Unicode conversion. SAP introduced a new process that combines all steps and can even migrate the system to Azure. In the classical migration it would require two or three steps:

- System upgrade
- Unicode conversion if required
- Database Migration + Cloud Migration

Executing all these steps together reduces the time required for testing and automates the process.

However, the DMO process is highly complex and requires experienced system administrators to execute it. There are several limitations described in the SAP Notes, and additional time may be required during the exploration phase. DMO is designed for the ABAP stack, and it does not work for Java components. If the system is running as a dual stack, a split is required before the migration.

Since the release of SUM 2.0, SAP enhanced the range of supported databases during the DMO process. Now you can use it with most databases, including AnyDB and HANA.

For SAP NetWeaver 7.50 and higher, SAP does not deliver the non-unicode kernel binaries. If your system is non-unicode and you want to use DMO to upgrade the system to release 7.50 or higher, then Unicode Conversion is a pre-requisite and has to be performed in advance.

At the time of writing, the DMO process is available for:

- SAP ERP 6.0 or higher (for example EHP1, EHP2, EHP3)
    - Systems based on SAP NetWeaver 7.0 (for example SAP ERP 6.0) need at least SP17 for software component SAP_BASIS and SP19 for software component SAP_BW
- Systems as part of SAP Business Suite 7 or higher (SAP ERP 6.0 EHP4, SAP CRM 7.0, SAP SRM 7.0, SAP SCM 7.0)
- SAP SCM 7.0 (or higher)
    - An additional limitation for SCM systems with integrated liveCache: For the migration of an SCM liveCache to an integrated SAP HANA liveCache on an SAP HANA database within the SUM DMO procedure, the following minimum **support package** (**SP**) levels of the SAP SCM start releases are required: SAP SCM 7.0 as of SP11, SAP SCM 7.0 EHP1 as of SP09, SAP SCM EHP2 as of SP10, or a higher SAP SCM version. For further information, see SAP Note 1825703.
    - The SUM DMO procedure can execute all manual steps of this SAP Note automatically, except the installation of the SAP liveCache applications and the final liveCache test with transaction LCA03. Hence, make sure that SAP liveCache applications (SAP LCA or LCAPPS-Plugin) are installed on the SAP HANA database before you migrate an SCM liveCache.

Note:

This additional limitation of the SAP SCM start release SP level is not necessary for a migration of an SCM system without integrated SAP HANA liveCache.

- If you want to use planning object structures in an SAP SCM system installed on an SAP HANA database, you have to migrate planning object structures after the SUM DMO procedure, but BEFORE productive usage. For further information, see *SAP Note 1818080*.
- SAP BW 7.00 (or higher)
  - Systems based on SAP NetWeaver 7.0 require at least SP17 for software component SAP_BASIS and SP19 for software component SAP_BW

For the latest information check SAP Note 2798588 – DMO of SUM 2.0 SP06. This SAP note also lists which source databases support which target databases, as shown in the following table:

Target DB:	SAP HANA	SAP ASE	MS SQL	DB6	SAP MaxDB	Oracle
Supported Source DB:						
Oracle	X	X	X	X	X	
SAP MaxDB	X	X	X	X		X
Microsoft SQL	X	X		X	X	X
IBM Db2 for z/OS (DB2)	X	X				
IBM Db2 for i (DB4)	X					
IBM Db2 for Linux, Unix, and Windows (DB6)	X	X	X		X	X
SAP HANA						
SAP ASE	X		X	X	X	X

Table 3-3: Which source databases support which target databases?

By default, DMO performs an in-place migration to SAP HANA, which means that no switch of application server is possible, and cross data center migration is not supported due to network latency and throughput. However, SAP does allow you to use DMO for data center migration when it's executed with the System Move option.

DMO can be performed with any source database and almost any target database. However, when using DMO with the System Move option, only SAP HANA or SAP ASE is supported as the target database. DMO with System Move cannot be used for migration when the source system is already running on SAP HANA.

Using the DMO with System Move does not allow you to change the system ID. The process of migrating the system using DMO starts on the source system, where the **Software Update Manager (SUM)** is started. During the first phase, SUM executes system checks and prepares the system for the update. When running the DMO as part of a cloud migration (with the System Move option), there are two ways to transfer the extracted data to the target environment:

Sequential data transfer

Sequential data transfer works in a similar way to classical migration. All data is exported to a filesystem on the on-premises system. When the export is over, the entire SUM directory has to be transferred and then the import continues.

Parallel data transfer

In the parallel data transfer mode, the SUM directory is manually transferred to the target environment before the source system is fully exported. A file replication mechanism using SAP-delivered scripts transfer the data to the cloud and the SUM imports the packages to the target environment in parallel to the source export process. When all data has been imported, the SUM continues with the Update downtime phase. The parallel data transfer mode significantly decreases the total system downtime and is an effective optimization technique where the target database is SAP HANA or SAP ASE. The following *Figure 3-10* illustrates the process of parallel execution:

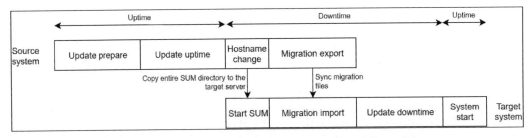

Figure 3-10: High-level migration phases using DMO with System Move

The DMO with System Move can also be executed if there is no intention to update the system when the source system is already running on the supported release.

The System administrator has limited capabilities to manually optimize the DMO run and their role is limited to identifying the optimal number of R3load processes. But unlike in classical migration the DMO has a built-in feature that learns from previous migration executions and optimizes the subsequent runs.

In the same way as for classical migration, the total runtime is very often determined by the export of largest tables. DMO will use table splitting to reduce long-tail processes, when only a few of the largest tables are still being processed. If the total number of active R3load processes drops below 90% of the configured number, which indicates that there are no more tables to extract, then DMO considers it as a tail. A downtime-optimized DMO is characterized by a short tail, as shown in *Figure 3-11*:

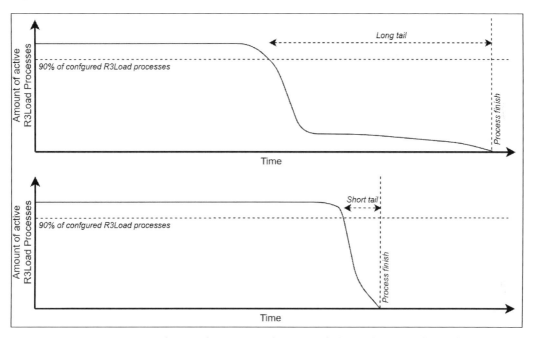

Figure 3-11: DMO showing the impact on downtime of a long tail versus a short tail

To enable the DMO to optimize each subsequent run, it needs information about the duration of each table migration from previous exports. Software Update Manager will use this data to optimize the performance of the next run by enabling automatic table splitting.

The optimization logic comprises four steps:

1. **Sorting by table size**: Based on the provided information, the SAPup process uses the table size or migration duration to sort the tables.

2. **Shuffle table sequence**: Export table sequence is reordered to achieve a good mixture of large and small tables.
3. **Table split determination**: SUM runs the simulation of the table splitting based on the number of configured R3load processes.
4. **Assignment to buckets**: The work packages from the previous step are assigned to the R3load processes to identify the best order of export/import.

Near-Zero Downtime Migration with DMO

If you are looking to migrate to SAP HANA and require the shortest possible business downtime, then you can take advantage of the SAP service, **Near-Zero Downtime Migration (nZDT)**. During the execution of the process, selected large tables are transferred during the uptime phase. The SAP LT Replication Server is used to create database triggers and replicate the data to the target HANA database.

Similar to the standard DMO process, nZDT can combine multiple activities such as database migration, system upgrade, and Unicode conversion. Migrating to the cloud was not initially supported, but the authors understand that this may change shortly.

Third-party options

If none of the preceding options allow you to migrate SAP to Azure within the maximum permitted downtime from your business, then there are some additional third-party options that you may wish to consider. Detailed discussion of these tools is beyond the scope of this book, so you will need to contact the relevant vendors directly for more information:

- **IBM DB2** – According to IBM documentation, IBM InfoSphere Change Data Capture can be used to perform SAP heterogeneous migrations, migrating DB2 databases between different operating systems. Contact IBM for further details.
- **Oracle Database** – Oracle have developed two solutions for migrating Oracle databases between different operating systems. The first is called Oracle to Oracle ("O2O" or "O2O Classic"), and the second is Oracle to Oracle Online ("Triple O"). The main difference is that O2O require the database to be shut down for the duration of the migration, while Triple O requires only very minimal downtime. Triple O uses Oracle Goldengate software for the online database synchronization. Contact Oracle for further details.
- **SNP Group** – SNP offer a range of different migration solutions covering all forms of heterogeneous migration. Contact SNP Group for further details.

Summary of migration options

The following *Table 3-4* provides a summary of migration options, along with their associated advantages and disadvantages:

	Backup/restore	Azure Site Recovery	Classical migration	Database Migration options	3rd Party Tools
Scope	Homogeneous Migration	Homogeneous Migration	Heterogeneous Migration	Heterogeneous Migration, upgrade and Unicode conversion	Heterogeneous Migration
Complexity	Low	Medium	Medium	High	High
Downtime optimization	Very High, except when using DBMS replication	High	Medium	Medium	Low
Flexibility	Low, the source and target platforms must match	Low, the source and target platforms must match	High, source and target platforms can be different	Very high, source and target platforms can be different. It's possible to combine upgrade and migration in a single process	High, source and target platforms can be different
Data footprint	High, entire database is copied	Very high, data from each server is copied	Low, only compressed data extract is copied	Low, only compressed data extract is copied	Discuss with vendor
Suggested data transfer	AzCopy or FTP server	Data copied as part of the ASR	AzCopy, FTP or file sync	File sync	Discuss with vendor

Table 3-4: Summary of migration options, pros, and cons

In this chapter, we have briefly discussed the available options to execute a technical system migration to the cloud. There is no universal answer as to which one is best. All of them should be carefully assessed.

The product type, the underlying source and target database, and, of course, business requirements such as the allowed downtime window, influence the possibilities you have to migrate your SAP systems to Azure. Sometimes, you may even do a trial migration to ensure your choice is correct and meets your situation and requirements.

Summary

While SAP migrations are potentially complex, any risks can be mitigated through detailed analysis and planning. You need to work closely with the business to agree the available downtime window and choose a date to perform the migration – you will normally want to avoid peak periods in your business due to the required downtime. In most cases the business will also need to be heavily involved in planning and executing the test plans used to validate the migration.

We cannot provide a definitive answer as to which migration option will be right for you, but we hope that this chapter gives you an idea of the options you have and the advantages of each of them. In many cases you will use more than one migration option, possibly using lift-and-shift for some SAP applications, and lift-and-migrate for others; for example, migrating from BW on AnyDB to BW on HANA. For many of the smaller systems, the downtime required will be fairly short and you may take a very simple approach to migration—backup/restore for lift-and-shift and classic R3load export/import for lift-and-migrate. While, if you have a large production ECC system with many TB of database that is required 24x7, then you will probably want to investigate some of the downtime-minimized options.

In the next chapter, we'll focus on the innovations that become available when running your system on Azure. We'll do a deep dive into identity, data, and integration topics to show you how modern companies use the SAP system to become a data-driven business. The architecture and migration chapters heavily focused on the infrastructure topics – we discussed a lot about networking, VMs, and storage. The innovations available in Azure move the discussion toward platform as a service offerings that are easy to consume and do not require manual installation and maintenance. You can use them to make your environment more open to fully utilize the power of your SAP data.

4
Transforming SAP in Azure

In the previous chapters, we mostly focused on the topic of infrastructure and presented the reference architectures for deploying SAP in the cloud. But Microsoft Azure is much more than just a next-generation data center, and **virtual machines** (**VMs**) are just a subset of the services that are available. Today's competitive market requires an organization to constantly innovate and build intelligent applications.

Satya Nadella, CEO at Microsoft, constantly repeats the message that "*every company is a software company*" and that the time of creating and maintaining single solutions is over. Organizations need to optimize and accelerate new services by building innovative digital capabilities that allow them to be closer to customers and receive immediate feedback. The ability to quickly adopt new technologies will be a major differentiator among competitors and access to the latest commercial platforms and tools will be essential for companies to survive. Organizations should prioritize tech intensity, as it helps to achieve optimal efficiency and productivity.

In this chapter, we would like to look at why enterprises that are on the digital transformation journey value the Azure cloud for its seamless experience of integrating SAP landscapes with platform services to increase the security and power of data. We will start by looking at the new concept of identity management and reducing the risk of data breaches, which is an especially important topic after the introduction of GDPR in the European Union. Then we'll deep dive into data and explore the tools and best practices for eliminating data silos and helping organizations to become data-driven.

Identity and access management

User directory software has been used in various forms since the birth of computing. The idea was developed in the early 1980s, and now one of the most commonly used directory services is Windows Active Directory, which was released in 1999.

20 years is a long time in the IT industry, and while Microsoft has always innovated with its products over time, the rise of cloud computing and cloud services has significantly changed organizational requirements in the area of access management. Currently, companies often rely on **software-as-a-service (SaaS)** solutions, like Office 365 or Salesforce, where they don't have to maintain infrastructure and users access the application over the internet instead of the local network.

It may sound like a little change, but in fact it has a big impact on authentication and user management. The traditional IT landscape partially relied on the physical access. Only if you entered the company building could you access the network and IT services. The cloud is different; as most services are available over the internet, the physical barrier is no longer relevant. You need to ensure that once the employee leaves the organization, their access is revoked from all systems.

Let's consider an example. In the past, the SAP system would be reachable only through a local network. Even if a hacker knew a username and password to get in, they wouldn't be able to gain access as this would require plugging their computer into a network socket within the building. Today, users can access SaaS solutions from home – over the internet, even without a VPN connection. That means obtaining a user's credentials is enough to access the system and to steal company confidential data. Moreover, as the hacker can access the system in the same way as the normal user would, it's almost impossible to differentiate an attack from a legitimate request. Strict firewall rules and regular system patching won't help in this situation.

Twenty years ago, almost every application was released with a specialized client. Even today, most SAP users access the system using SAPGUI. But over the years, web browsers became the primary application to access the system. SAP Fiori, which is the new and recommended user interface for SAP S/4HANA, doesn't require any dedicated client. Users access the system using a web browser, exactly the same as they would access something like Gmail. This triggered another change in the underlying authentication protocols. Kerberos, which is the foundation of the Windows Active Directory, is being replaced by modern alternatives like SAML and OAuth, which are designed to work with web applications.

Therefore, Microsoft released a completely new product, **Azure Active Directory (AD)**, which shifted the focus from user and device management to identity management. While at first glance the services are very similar to each other, they are in fact independent, and the architecture and use cases of the cloud directory are completely different.

Azure AD is organized into tenants, each tenant being a separate and dedicated directory instance created when an organization signs up for a Microsoft cloud service like Office 365 or Azure. Each tenant can host many user identities and enable access to many applications. Azure AD is the default access management solution for all resources created within Azure. The Kerberos protocol is deprecated and instead, customers can use SAML, OAuth, and OpenID, which are the de facto standards in web applications. Similarly, the LDAP protocol is no longer supported and Azure AD can be queried through a rich RESTful API.

Windows Active Directory and Azure Active Directory can be used in parallel, which is important for organizations that use legacy applications such as SAP NetWeaver-based products. Microsoft caters a great deal for customers with hybrid deployment models. Almost all companies already use Windows Active Directory and they don't want to provision an entirely new directory and maintain user data in two places. They use the Windows domain to manage SAP service accounts or use Kerberos-based single sign-on, and at the same time, they would like to leverage Azure AD capabilities and enable seamless access to SAP cloud products like SuccessFactors or Ariba. It is possible to both integrate directories and replicate users, groups, and attributes to Azure AD:

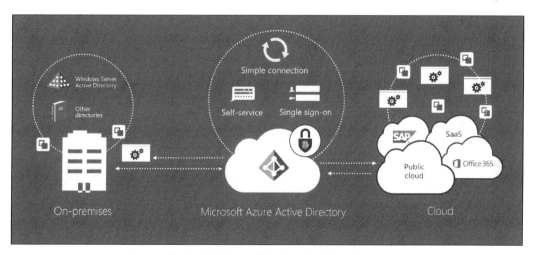

Figure 4-1: Azure AD integration scenarios

When migrating SAP systems to the cloud, it is very important to correctly handle user and application requirements for a directory service. Unfortunately, most SAP NetWeaver-based solutions still rely heavily upon the Windows Active Directory, and possible integration with Azure AD is currently limited to single sign-on, which we discuss in the next section.

If you use the domain to centrally manage SAP service accounts, or if you use Kerberos-based single sign-on, you need to ensure that the domain is constantly accessible in the cloud as well as on-premises to support user authentication and access to local resources.

Having a single domain controller is not a good solution. If the network connection between cloud and on-premises infrastructure breaks, part of the workload won't be able to access the Windows Active Directory and may stop working. The common solution is to extend the domain to the cloud by deploying an additional domain controller and synchronizing the data. This way, you ensure that no matter where the workload is located, the Windows Active Directory is always available.

A SAP migration is a good time for organizations to think about the new capabilities that are available with Azure AD. One of these new capabilities is improved single sign-on. If you require employees to type their username and password every time to need to access the system, you can consider implementing SAML authentication to improve the security of your SAP landscape.

SAP Single Sign-On with Azure AD

A common problem in accessing IT systems is authentication. The average person logs in to around a hundred services on a regular basis, and the most common authentication mechanism is a password. Following industry standards[1], a secure password should be at least eight characters long and include uppercase and lowercase letters and special characters. A sample secure password could be "10fudf=@a2a~" or "3bagictcla8+". To make it even more difficult, some services require the changing of the password on a regular basis, for example every three months.

Unfortunately, memorizing passwords is not easy, and the average person will encounter problems if they have to remember more than a few. This inevitably leads to many users writing their secret codes on post-it notes that are then attached to the monitor, for instance, or re-using the same password for multiple services. Ironically, the supposedly security-strengthening regulations usually lead users to adopt security-compromising habits. According to Verizon's Data Breach Investigations Report[2], the use of stolen credentials is the most common source of data breaches. Interestingly, software vulnerabilities are responsible for less than 20% of successful attacks.

The problem of authentication should be tackled in two ways. Firstly, the organization should empower users to use complex passwords.

---

1 OWASP, Password Cheat Sheet
2 `https://vz.to/2r6VNlV`

The easiest solution is to implement single sign-on, which reduces the amount of passwords that need to be remembered. Once the user is authenticated during the initial log in they should be able to connect to the desired service without providing additional credentials. As they only use a single password, it can be long and complex. We should also introduce an additional layer of security that won't allow access to the system even if the password was stolen—it's called multi-factor authentication, and basically requires the user to provide additional information during login, like a code sent to a mobile device.

SAP NetWeaver-based systems have supported single sign-on for a long time. The most usual form of support is Kerberos, which re-uses Windows domain authentication. It's a reliable solution for customers who manage a domain and require access using an SAP GUI client. But with the introduction of the SAP S/4HANA system and SAP Fiori, the default user interface is changed to a web browser. If your organization plans to modernize its SAP landscape together with the migration to Azure, that's a good opportunity to implement the new single sign-on mechanism as it brings additional advantages on top of eliminating the need for typing passwords.

In SAML authentication there is the identity provider that acts as an authentication service, and one or more service providers, which trust the identity provider. When a user logs in, the SAP system generates the authentication request and redirects the browser to the identity provider. If the user has already authenticated, the SAML response is passed to the SAP system, which verifies it and decides to authorize the user to access the system.

SAML authentication can easily be extended by additional security features that were difficult, or even impossible, to have when using Kerberos or certificates. When a user logs in, they may be asked to confirm their identity by typing a verification code sent to their mobile or email address. With the use of conditional access policies system administrators can create safe zones—like a corporate network or an entire country. If the connection is initiated from a safe zone, it's treated as trusted and doesn't require further confirmation. Similarly, if an access request comes from a country that is not included on the white list, or comes from an untrusted network like Tor, Azure AD automatically challenges the request and asks for additional authentication.

The advanced login protection constantly monitors the traffic and if there is a valid suspicion that the access request isn't initiated by a legitimate user it will be immediately blocked. All data stored in the SAP system is protected without enforcing complex policies for users.

Conditional access can be explained as a simple if-then action. **If** a user wants to access the resource, **then** they must complete an action. The following table shows the triggers available for multi-factor authentication:

Condition	Description
Users and groups	Users and groups affected by the conditional access policy
Cloud apps	Applications that are included in the conditional access policy, for example, SAP systems
Sign-in risk	An indicator of the likelihood that a sign-in was made by a legitimate user
Device platform	Operating systems that run on the device from which the request was made
Device state	Device identity state (domain-joined or compliant)
Location	User location (network, country, or region)
Client apps	Software used to access the resource

Table 4-1: Single sign-on access conditions in Azure AD

An access control is a set of actions that are executed if the conditions are met. The action can be as simple as the blocking of access, but it is possible to build a list of additional controls to be enforced. The administrator can select whether all or just one of the additional controls should be satisfied to authenticate a user.

Control	Action
Require multi-factor authentication	User is asked to provide an additional authentication code
Require device to be marked as compliant	The device has to be marked as compliant by mobile device management (MDM) software (Microsoft Intune)
Require a hybrid Azure AD-joined device	Computer has to be domain-joined
Require approved client app	Access only allowed when using the selected app

Table 4-2: Single sign-on access controls in Azure AD

The configuration of advanced access controls is managed from the Azure portal using a GUI. It allows you to build rules that have to be fulfilled before letting a user access a system:

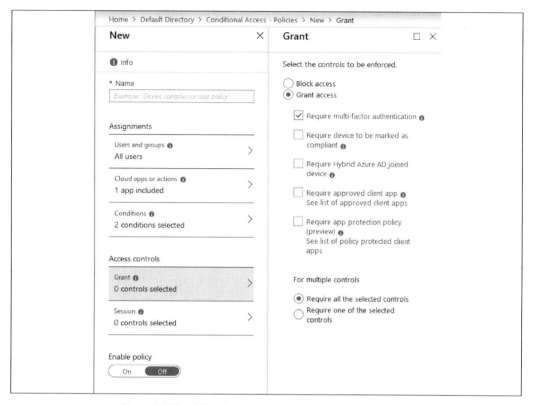

Figure 4-2: Conditional access configuration in the Azure portal

The conditional access feature allows you to integrate a sophisticated authentication platform with your SAP system, where the correct username and password is just one element that is analyzed when access is being granted to the user.

The SAP also offers its own set of products for managing users in both on-premises and cloud environments. SAP's Identity Authentication service is the access management platform for SAP Cloud Platform applications. However, using two identity solutions within a single landscape causes big administration overheads and inconsistent login experience.

Users that are forced to use multiple login screens pay less attention to detail, and may not notice when they are about to become victims of phishing attacks. Therefore, Microsoft and SAP decided to work together and integrate both identity platforms. Customers using SAP's identity solution can leverage the single sign-on mechanism with all the advanced threat protection capabilities and create a unique and consistent cross-cloud experience.

In addition, the Azure AD's provisioning service allows the automatic creation of user accounts in the SAP Identity Authentication service, which reduces the administration effort required and reduces the risk of having inconsistent user data across the landscape. When an employee leaves the organization, their account can be centrally locked and the change is propagated to all systems.

As organizations continue to adopt cloud services, they should focus on protecting employee identities, as compromised credentials are the main reason for data breaches. New features available in Azure AD are the result of huge Microsoft investment in the security area. Microsoft continues to spend over 1 billion[3] dollars every year to make data safe and protected against unauthorized attacks. Close partnership with SAP allows companies to benefit from Azure security features in the SAP landscapes they use to store their most critical data. The close integration of identity solutions is just one example of how Microsoft and SAP work together to improve the customer's experience and enrich their platform functionalities. By reading the next section, which is focused on data management, you'll discover more ways in which the Azure platform can solve current business challenges and improve company operations.

Data platform

Information is a valuable organization resource and most enterprises recognize data as an asset that differentiates them among competitors. During the last 20 years, the amount of information collected has been constantly growing and the trend will continue to accelerate in the future. Common access to the internet has changed the world we live in. Mobile phones, social media, and devices with constant access to the global network have made us all digitally connected.

The cloud software company Domo, in its 7th annual report[4], tried to estimate the amount of data that has been generated. Every minute we send more than 18 million text messages and 500,000 tweets. YouTube users watch 4 million videos and Uber takes almost 10,000 rides. IDC estimates that in 2020, we will have more than 40 zetabytes of data, which equals 40 trillion gigabytes. To understand how data generation accelerated last year, you can compare it to the amount of data available in 2010, which was estimated to be only 1.2 zetabytes. Moreover, IDC predicts that the total size of data will double every five years. Similar conclusions come from other reports.

---

3   https://reut.rs/33QmIzt
4   https://www.domo.com/learn/data-never-sleeps-7

In 2017 IBM estimated that 90% of available information was created only during the last two years. The preceding statistics, while they may sound overwhelming, have a common cause, which is more common access to the internet. In 2005 only 16% of the world's population had access to the internet. In 2019 more than 50% of us access the web on a regular basis. The number of connected devices is also increasing. At the end of 2018 the amount of connected devices reached 22 billion[5] and it's predicted to grow further to 50 billion in 2030.

This digital transformation, which we can observe in every aspect of our lives, is encouraging companies to see the data surrounding them as one of the most important advantages they can have over their competitors. The world's economy is also changing, and organizations are shifting from producing goods to offering services. Data collection and analytics plays a major role in this transformation. In 2016, Phillips Lighting announced a new pilot project to improve the lighting system in Los Angeles, which consists of 215,000 streetlights distributed across 7,500 miles. Traditionally, management was relying on the employees, who were responsible for identifying light outages and fielding more than 40,000 calls from citizens. CityTouch technology was introduced, which allows the monitoring and control of city lighting through a secure portal and reduces maintenance costs by 20% by automatically reporting faults.

This is just one example of how data is changing businesses. The financial sector often uses artificial intelligence to avoid fraud. Companies dealing with energy and utilities benefit from predictive analytics to detect outages or plan network capacity. The **Internet of Things (IoT)** is changing the manufacturing industry with real-time signals and robotics. Autonomous cars will completely change the logistics sector. Businesses must innovate and the biggest differentiator will be the usage of collected data.

With the increased importance of data, companies face new challenges that did not exist before. Never before did we need to store and analyze such massive amounts of information. Data as such is not valuable—but the ability to process it and draw conclusions from it is one of the most significant success factors in our data-driven economy. Modern technology provides tools and solutions to solve the biggest challenges in becoming a data-driven organization:

- **Data sourcing**: We are surrounded by data, but according to Forrester Research, companies on average analyze only 12% of the data they have. Information is distributed to many systems with strict functionality. We use different software for accounting for and monitoring customer experience.

---

[5] https://bit.ly/2s1JkQf

The lack of correct classification, categorization, and the ability to search creates isolated data silos that are difficult to manage and don't represent value.

- **Data storage**: As the amount of collected information grows, companies need new technologies to store it. In the past, the core of enterprise data was stored in relational databases composed into rows and columns. However, the significance of unstructured data like social media data, images, or videos is growing. Companies require data stores that can be easily scaled on demand without long procurement processes, but their current infrastructure isn't limitless.

  Keeping data in relational databases is also expensive and customers are looking for optimization techniques to make in-memory calculations more cost-effective.

- **Data quality and processing**: Distributed data stores and a lack of clear ownership of data lead to conflicts, logical errors, and data duplication. Analytics based on invalid or outdated information will produce misleading conclusions and eventually incorrect decisions.

- **Data analytics**: Businesses change dynamically, and answers should be available immediately. The era of overnight reports is over, and companies are more and more interested in real-time analytics. Processing power should be available on demand.

- **Data visualization**: A simple chart very often says more than a raw table. A data visualization engine should contain a set of analytics capabilities to empower users to find patterns and correlations, which is a new requirement in the world of big data.

- **Security and privacy of data**: At least some company data will always be confidential, and access to it should be limited to a set of authorized users. Data leaks and usage abuse lead to legal consequences.

The journey to becoming a data-driven organization is not easy. It requires tools that empower employees to explore new ways of solving problems. Solution engineering should allow rapid prototyping and constant innovation. When choosing the right IT platform, companies should focus on unlocking and taking advantage of their data.

Microsoft Azure is designed to support enterprises of any size. It's an open and highly scalable platform that enables companies to benefit from the newest technologies. With Azure, companies can build modern intelligent applications and take advantage of their data. SAP systems are one of the most important sources of information and Microsoft dedicates special attention to unlocking their power.

In the remainder of this chapter, we would like to guide you through the various services available on the platform, explain their purposes, and teach you how to use them in the SAP landscape. We will start with a short introduction to the storage types that you can use to create a common data store. Then we'll move onto data extraction topics and we'll explain how Hadoop services could be used in combination with SAP software. SAP data should be included in the common data store and blended and analyzed with information coming from other sources. Finally, we'll show you the possibilities around data visualization and how the correct data classification empowers employees to make data-driven decisions.

Storage types in Microsoft Azure

Eliminating data silos requires data to be available for processing and analytics. We've talked about the massive amounts of information that come from various sources: we need a highly scalable solution that is able to host structured and non-structured data. The commonly implemented solution uses intermediate storage. It combines information from many source systems and creates a foundation layer for data engineers and data scientists. Keeping all the information together simplifies management and helps in data governance.

Microsoft Azure offers the following storage services:

- Blob storage: An object storage solution available in the cloud for unstructured data like text, images, videos, or binaries
- File storage: Highly available file share that can be accessed using the SMB protocol
- Table storage: Schemaless tables providing a key/attribute store
- Queue storage: Messaging queues to store and retrieve information
- Data Lake storage: Enterprise-ready scalable storage optimized for big data analytics

Seeing so many storage types at the beginning may cause you to feel uncomfortable, but each of them has a number of use cases. Blob and Data Lake storage are the best choices for creating a common data store. They are designed to host petabytes of data and trillions of objects. They offer seamless integration with other Azure services, including identity, management, and security solutions. Table storage keeps key/attribute pairs organized into entities.

You could compare it to a simple database table. Finally, queue storage is used to deliver messages between applications and services.

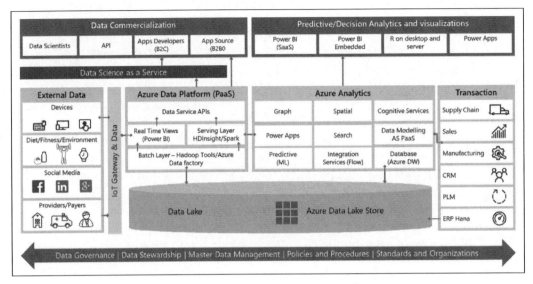

Figure 4-3: SAP and Azure data integration architecture

The data in a common store is a source of raw information that will then be transformed and consumed. *Figure 4.3* shows how Azure Data Lake can be integrated with other Azure services. SAP is a valuable source and you should consider opening the data it stores. In the next section, we focus on the data extraction process and include guidance on the common challenges you may encounter.

Data extraction

An enterprise may use many IT solutions to run their business, from e-commerce platforms, through social media monitoring tools, to large systems like SAP ERP. Each application works in isolation, sometimes supported by a few interfaces. A customer-facing internet shop collects orders and manages deliveries. Twitter or Facebook act as other communication channels. They all do what they are specialized to do; however, a lack of information exchange creates data silos.

Imagine a slightly different world, where all data is shared. Where social media and e-commerce telemetry data could be an input to forecast planning and collecting instant feedback. Where data coming from the ERP system could be used to update customer order statuses and predict delivery dates. Where, based on tweets, you could identify the part of the country where there is the greatest demand for your product, allowing you to plan distribution accordingly.

It's not science fiction—you can do it today using existing tools on the condition that all data is shared between applications.

A SAP system stores the most important organization data. Extracting it and blending it with information coming from other sources opens the door to new possibilities. But working with ERP data is not easy. During initial analysis, it may sound tempting to extract everything and let your data scientists discover new correlations, but usually that's not a good option. In this section, we would like to highlight the most important aspects of SAP data extraction to get the most out of the process without compromising security.

Finding a use case

Finding a good use case for data extraction is one of the most important tasks during initial analysis. There are many valid reasons to make data accessible. You can blend data with information coming from other systems to get new business insights or build advanced AI/machine learning models. Current reporting tools could be enhanced by the data stored in an SAP system. A use case dictates the data extraction scope and security conditions. One set of tables may be considered for sales order reporting in Power BI, while a different set may be considered for automating credit score calculations. A use case is also a key input when choosing the correct extraction tool and planning an execution schedule.

It's never a good idea to start with data extraction before considering and understanding the use case. Such an approach causes security issues and additional storage charges, all of which could be easily avoided if only relevant data was extracted.

Data exploration

When a use case is specified it is possible to identify the data that's relevant to the task. A SAP data model is highly complex—it consists of at least 50,000 related tables. A single business object, like a sales order, can be partially stored in many tables at the same time—the VBAK table stores sales document header information, while the line items can be found in VBAP. Knowing the underlying architecture and data model is essential to designing a reliable and scalable solution.

Some companies decide to design a common data model for all their data and to enforce the data transformation during the extraction process. That requires additional work during the initial project phase, but it results in easier data management and consumption. Data scientists or data engineers won't necessarily know the SAP architecture, and they wouldn't know how all the information is connected. By creating a common data model for your company, you also ensure that data can be easily blended with information stored in other systems.

Data security

Authorization in SAP is highly complex and reflects the organization's hierarchy. Users have the right to access or change only selected records based on their authorization profile. External tools may not have as sophisticated access controls and usually work on the table level.

The SAP authorization model is not easy to replicate, and access to extracted information should be considered during the planning phase. As SAP stores highly sensitive or even confidential information, it is extremely important to ensure that only selected people access it. Developers should work on randomized sets of data and access to intermediate storage with extracted information should be forbidden for all users. The extraction process can be chunked into smaller pieces and it is possible to implement segregation of duties. Administrators can set up jobs and perform troubleshooting without needing to see data. Developers and data engineers can work on selected, ideally anonymized parts of a dataset, and their algorithms are then applied to the entire set.

Delta extracts

Many SAP tables store millions of rows. Working with such large datasets requires special handling, as usually the daily extraction of an entire table is not an option. It highly impacts application server performance and consumes a lot of network bandwidth. Storing multiple copies of the same data also increases the cost of a solution, not to mention the associated cost of storing multiple daily replicas.

SAP NetWeaver and SAP HANA databases don't have native change-data-capture capabilities that track all changes on the table level. But even without such capabilities, you can overcome the issue and identify new and updated records. The most reliable solution uses the last change date and time, which is available for most transactional tables. You can use that information to identify the changes made since the last extract and then copy only new or updated records.

You could also consider SAP data extractors; however, their usage is very limited as only SAP applications like SAP Data Services and SAP Data Hub can access them.

Schedule

Another key question to consider is how often data should be replicated. Some scenarios may not require frequent data updates, while for the others, real-time replication is essential. Imagine an internet advertising campaign that aims to sell particular products. It is important that there is available stock. In most cases, the advertising of products that are out of stock simply results in a waste of money.

The customer experience would be poor as the goods are not available, while you would still have to pay for the ad. Integration with real-time stock information changes everything. Using replicated data, the software could suspend the campaign and start a new one for other, actually available, products.

The right tool

There are different ways to access SAP data. It is possible to connect directly at the database level and fetch data using the ODBC protocol. But it doesn't allow the fetching of information stored in a pool or cluster table. In addition, it also requires a full-use database license, which is significantly more expensive than the runtime license bought together with the SAP system. You can also use the RFC protocol to read data from the application server. It doesn't require an additional license, but it is usually slower and may impact the overall performance of the SAP system.

For real-time data integration, you should consider a third-party product that uses database triggers to capture new and updated information or a solution that consumes database transaction logs to identify delta changes. Their additional advantage is minimizing the performance impact of data extraction.

When you understand what data residing in the SAP system is required and how often you need to refresh it, you can design the extraction process and implement it. In the next section, we will take a closer look at Azure Data Factory—a cloud solution that is designed to integrate data across the landscape using ETL and ELT processes.

Azure Data Factory

Azure Data Factory is a Microsoft solution for integrating data from many sources. The cloud service allows the building of advanced pipelines to automate data movement and transformation. The target for the data can be any other Azure storage service—from Azure Data Lake to Cosmos DB. The source data coming from databases, file shares, web applications, or SAP systems is extracted into a centralized store for further processing using an Azure data platform solution.

Most applications offer a way to communicate with the external world using an **application programming interface (API)**, which is a set of functions that can be executed on a target system and return results. Very often they are unique to the particular application. Let's look at databases. They expose the ODBC API, which is aimed at being independent of the database and operating system, but they require a specialized driver that implements communication. Similarly, a SAP system can be accessed using an API but requires specialized libraries to facilitate communication.

To achieve great flexibility and allow communication with hundreds of various applications, Azure Data Factory implements connectors. You can think of them as specialized software units that are designed to work with an application and implement the main Data Factory capabilities, like data copying. Some of the connectors available in Azure Data Factory require an integration runtime, which acts as a proxy between the cloud service and the data source. Using the integration runtime allows you to establish cross-premises connections and extract data from SAP running in your own datacenter without needing to expose the system to the internet. There are three types of integration runtime:

- **Azure Integration Runtime**: This works with publicly available endpoints, like web-based applications or SaaS offerings including SAP Cloud for Customer. Azure supplies the runtime as a managed compute instance that is deployed without the need for manual software installation.
- **Self-hosted integration runtime**: Designed to work in on-premises networks or virtual networks in Azure, this integration runtime has to be installed manually on a server in the cloud or on-premises. It's required when extracting information from SAP NetWeaver-based systems using the RFC protocol.
- **SSIS integration runtime**: This is designed to lift and shift existing SSIS workloads over to Azure.

Most of the SAP connectors available in Azure Data Factory use the integration runtime to communicate with the SAP system and therefore the installation of this component is mandatory to enable data replication.

SAP connectors in Azure Data Factory

Azure Data Factory currently offers six connectors to the SAP systems, which will be detailed in this section.

SAP ECC

OData is a data access protocol based on HTTP. SAP commonly uses OData for communication between systems—Fiori apps rely on OData services exposed by the backend system. The ECC connector can re-use those services to fetch tables, views, or other entities that are exposed through the SAP Gateway system. The connector name suggests it works only with the SAP ERP but in fact, it can be used with any OData service exposed by an SAP NetWeaver-based system.

The OData protocol is not the best choice when working with large sets of data and should be avoided if a single extract contains more than 1 million rows. OData queries can be customized and include filtering expressions.

SAP Table

The SAP Table connector uses RFC to connect to the source system. At the application layer, the tool executes the /SAPDS/RFC_READ_TABLE2 function module to extract data. It supports tables (including cluster and pool tables) and views as the data source. Filtering can be applied using table options—a small chunk of ABAP code that is passed as a parameter to the function module. This way it's possible to write even extensive WHERE clauses and, together with expressions available in Azure Data Factory, it can be used to implement delta loading.

The connector supports load balancing using the SAP message server, but the application server can also be pointed to explicitly.

The self-hosted integration runtime and the SAP connector for .NET are required to connect to the SAP system.

SAP Business Warehouse (BW)

The data stored in the SAP BW system can be fetched using the respective connector available with Azure Data Factory. It connects to the system using RFC and selects data from InfoCubes and QueryCubes using MDX queries.

The self-hosted integration runtime and the NW RFC SDK are required to connect to the SAP system.

SAP BW Open Hub

The Open Hub service is a service available in the SAP BW system to distribute BW data to an external application. Any objects supported by SAP **Data Transfer Process (DTP)**, like a datastore, InfoCube, or datasource, can be used as a source for Open Hub.

The data extraction is executed in two steps:

1. The data is collected and prepared by BW DTP, which copies the data from a supported object to the Open Hub table. Each extraction has a unique request ID that is used by Data Factory to identify delta changes.
2. Azure Data Factory extracts data from the Open Hub table.

The steps are executed asynchronously during the execution of the pipeline. By default, to ensure that no data is lost during extraction, Azure Data Factory doesn't fetch the last delta from the system. This behavior can be customized using parameters in the copy activity.

To ensure that the delta is handled correctly, only one DTP is allowed for each Open Hub table. For two independent extraction processes, there should be two Open Hub destinations defined at the SAP level.

The self-hosted integration runtime and the SAP connector for .NET are required to connect to the SAP system.

SAP HANA

A SAP HANA database is a valid source for Azure Data Factory. Using the dedicated connector, it is possible to extract data stored not only in the tables and views but also from information models like analytical or calculation views.

The SAP HANA connector can be used only to fetch data from the database. To insert new records you should consider a generic ODBC connector.

The self-hosted integration runtime and the SAP HANA client are required to connect to the SAP system.

SAP Cloud for Customer

Azure Data Factory supports extraction from SAP Cloud for Customer using an OData endpoint exposed by the system. It is also possible to upload data from external systems—such a scenario requires the Azure Integration Runtime:

Connector	Source systems	Protocol	Integration runtime required?	Processing mode
SAP ECC	SAP NetWeaver version 7.0 and later with SAP Gateway	OData	No	Batch
SAP Table	SAP NetWeaver version 7.01 and later	RFC	Yes—self-hosted	Batch
SAP BW MDX	SAP Business Warehouse version 7.X	RFC	Yes—self-hosted	Batch
SAP BW Open Hub	SAP Business Warehouse version 7.01 and later	RFC	Yes—self-hosted	Batch
SAP HANA	Any SAP HANA release supported by the database client	ODBC	Yes—self-hosted	Batch

Connector	Source systems	Protocol	Integration runtime required?	Processing mode
SAP Cloud for Customer	SAP Cloud for Customer including the SAP Cloud for Sales, SAP Cloud for Service, and SAP Cloud for Social Engagement solutions	OData	Yes, when SAP C4C acts as a sink store	Batch

Table 4-3: SAP connectors available in Azure Data Factory

Once the extracted information is available in the common storage, it is easily available for analytics and machine learning services in the Azure cloud.

Using Azure Data Factory you can integrate data from many sources and then make it available for consumption by other cloud services. It is the initial step toward eliminating data silos and using data in a wider way. The next section focuses on big data analytics in Azure and describes two main services—Azure HDInsight and Azure Databricks. Both services can be used together with SAP applications.

Big data analytics

Modern organizations are powered by data. They use data to get new business insights, to gain competitive advantage, and make data-driven decisions. But as we already described in the introduction to the Azure data platform, the amount of information that has been collected has grown tremendously in recent years. Solutions have become insufficient; relational databases are not designed for such workloads. They are fast, but at the same time they are difficult to scale, and enforce a data structure that is very often impossible to apply. They require high-end infrastructure with large amounts of memory and fast storage, which makes them inefficient when working with massive datasets.

Hadoop solves these problems. It's a combination of a distributed file system (**Hadoop Distributed File System**, or **HDFS**) and a collection of open source data software designed to work with massive amounts of data. For example, one Hadoop component, the data engine Spark, splits processing into smaller jobs that are concurrently executed on many nodes at the same time. Hadoop clusters can scale up to hundreds or even thousands of servers, which is just not possible using relational databases. But it doesn't mean that relational databases are now obsolete. The solutions complement each other and the tight integration of both solutions is a very important topic to study.

Microsoft Azure supports running a Hadoop as a service or as a managed instance. It's possible to deploy and run a cluster without manual installation or maintenance. Using the cloud for Hadoop deployments means you'll benefit from higher availability and flexibility, as you can dynamically change the number of compute nodes. It also decouples storage from processing power and allows each to scale independently. The traditional on-premises deployments require them to scale together, which cost a high price, and in any case the requirements for storage and compute don't grow at the same rate. That means if you need more space on the disk but you don't require more processors, you need to buy a whole server anyway. Cloud deployment is different. Hadoop uses VMs as the processing layer, but data is stored in an Azure storage service.

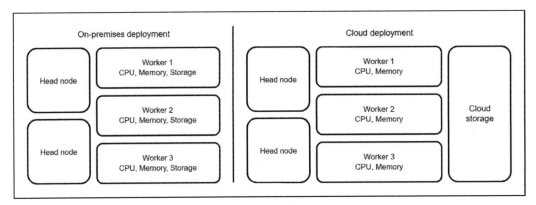

Figure 4-4: Comparison of on-premise and cloud Hadoop deployment

There are two Azure services that are designed to work with big data. HDInsight is a cloud implementation of a Hadoop cluster and is available in many flavors specialized for specific workloads. If you focus on data analytics and you don't require additional components like Kafka or Storm, you should consider Azure Databricks, which is a managed Apache Spark cluster that offers additional collaboration and scaling capabilities.

Azure HDInsight

Azure HDInsight is the Microsoft cloud implementation of a Hadoop cluster. It allows you to effortlessly deploy a scalable platform that is capable of quickly processing massive amounts of data. There are seven cluster types dedicated to running various workloads, from batch processing to machine learning:

Cluster Type	Description
Apache Hadoop	A framework that uses HDFS, YARN resource management, and a simple MapReduce programming model to process and analyze batch data in parallel.
Apache Spark	An open-source, parallel-processing framework that supports in-memory processing to boost the performance of big data analysis applications.
Apache HBase	A NoSQL database built on Hadoop that provides random access and strong consistency for large amounts of unstructured and semi-structured data — potentially billions of rows times millions of columns.
ML Services	A server for hosting and managing parallel distributed R processes. It provides data scientists, statisticians, and R programmers with on-demand access to scalable, distributed methods of analytics on HDInsight.
Apache Storm	A distributed, real-time computation system for processing large streams of data quickly. Storm is offered as a managed cluster in HDInsight.
Apache Interactive Query	In-memory caching for interactive and faster Hive queries.
Apache Kafka	An open-source platform that's used for building streaming data pipelines and applications. Kafka also provides message queue functionality, which allows you to publish and subscribe to data streams.

Table 4-4: Available HDInsight clusters (Source: microsoft.com)

HDInsight consists of VMs and storage. The number of allocated servers can be changed, but it's not possible to temporarily shut down the server. Instead, the server must be deleted and re-created using the existing configuration.

Azure Databricks

Azure Databricks enhances the capabilities of Spark analytics and is focused on collaboration, where using a common user interface allows data engineers, data scientists, and business users to work together, making the development process more productive. Spark clusters are provisioned through the management console — it's not necessary to manually install Hadoop services. Each server can easily be scaled out and terminated if no longer in use, which leads to savings in running the Hadoop environment.

The Azure Blob or Data Lake services can be used as the storage layer for Azure Databricks. But you can also easily connect to other Azure services like a globally distributed database, such as Cosmos DB, or expose the data for further analytics in Azure SQL Data Warehouse. The big advantage of using Azure Databricks is the native integration with surrounding components. You can use Azure AD as the user management layer and assign permissions.

Microsoft Azure is the only cloud that runs Databricks as a platform service:

Figure 4-5: Displaying Databricks cluster information

Azure HDInsight and Azure Databricks can be integrated with the SAP landscape. Connecting the world of massive amounts of unstructured data with the world of highly structured SAP solutions reduces the cost of ownership and helps to make better decisions.

Integration between SAP HANA and Hadoop

SAP HANA offers very fast data processing; however, it comes at a price. The database keeps all data in memory, which greatly improves the speed of query execution, but at the same time the memory is significantly more expensive when compared to persistent storage like hard drives. We briefly discussed this topic earlier in the book. Correct data management is essential to keep SAP HANA infrastructure costs under control.

Depending on the data access rate we can define a data temperature. The financial information from the last year, for instance, may be accessed frequently, therefore keeping it in server memory is justified. But is there a reason to store in memory old sales orders that were completed years ago and that nobody uses on a regular basis? They could be safely offloaded to a Hadoop cluster with low-cost disk storage and retrieved only when required. Depending on the access and change frequency we can distinguish three levels of data temperature:

- **Hot**: Data accessed or changed very frequently, essential to running the business
- **Warm**: Data accessed or changed rarely
- **Cold**: Archived data, usually not accessed or changed

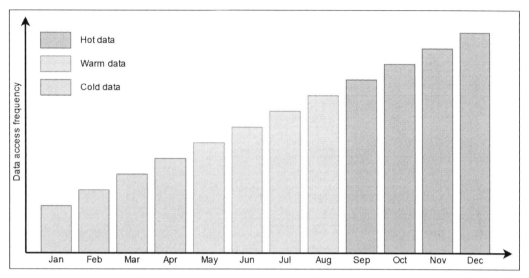

Figure 4-6: Data access frequency and data temperature

SAP HANA accounts for the data temperature paradigm and has built-in tiering capabilities to partition tables and keep part of them on disk or extension nodes. When a user executes a query that requires information from the warm area, the respective partitions are loaded to memory and used for calculations.

Obsolete data that is not required in the database can be moved to cold storage. The Smart Data Access technology available in SAP HANA allows access to external data stores online. A linked system is represented as a set of virtual tables that can be queried and joined as though they were part of the same database. The SAP HANA query processor analyzes queries and executes relevant parts on the target database, then uses the returned values to complete the operation.

Cold data tiering uses Smart Data Access to retrieve archived information. You can use SAP Data Hub or HANA Spark Controller connections.

Cold data tiering using SAP Data Hub

The Kubernetes-based SAP Data Hub distributed runtime, which was previously known as SAP Vora, can store cold data in disk-based streaming tables, which are then accessed in SAP HANA using virtual tables.

It allows you to reduce the amount of processed information to the rowlevel, which optimizes query execution performance. This type of connection allows us to select, insert, update, and delete records. Data lifecycle management tools can facilitate data movement between hot and cold storage.

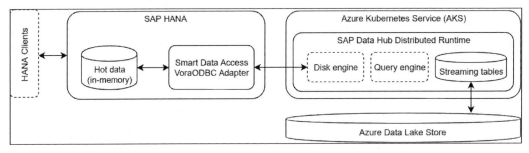

Figure 4-7: Architecture of cold data tiering using SAP Data Hub

Cold data tiering using SAP HANA Spark controller

Customers that don't want to use the SAP Data Hub software can directly connect Azure HDInsight with their SAP HANA database using HANA Spark controller, which provides access to data stored in Azure Data Lake storage. Similarly to the data tiering using SAP Data Hub, the cold store is accessed using virtual tables that represent data in the Spark cluster. Data is accessed at the file level:

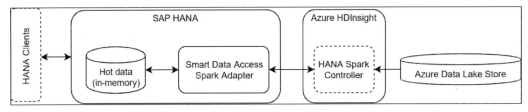

Figure 4-8: Architecture of cold data tiering using HANA Spark controller

Hadoop clusters work on a petabyte scale and distributed file systems like Azure Data Lake are good storage solutions for data that was never meant to be kept in relational databases. Cold data tiering is not the only use case for integration between Hadoop and SAP HANA. Unstructured data like images, videos, social media data, or data extracted from other applications to the common store can be used together for analytics. Connecting all that data with data stored in SAP HANA delivers business value that is not available in traditional data warehouse scenarios.

But ETL processes, which we covered in the previous section, are not always desirable. Such processes require the movement of data between stores, which is lengthy and unless it involves real-time replication, it only represents the state of data at a point in time.

Reports available in SAP Business Warehouse could be enhanced with large sets of data stored in a data lake, but as we explained before, keeping everything in memory is expensive. Therefore, customers look for more cost-efficient solutions.

Smart Data Access solves this problem. Firstly, it eliminates the need for ETL processes so there is no need to duplicate data and store it in memory. It also accesses data in real time and so the returned data is always current. The challenge is performance degradation. Each time the SAP HANA database communicates with an external system, the query and results are transferred over the network and the execution time may increase manifold. Accessing server memory is fast, but network latency and limited bandwidth also play a role in influencing query execution times, and therefore you must ensure that there is sufficient bandwidth available so as not to bottleneck data access and transfer. Additional attention should be given to the efficiency of the code; calls to external stores should be limited and the scope of the query narrowed. You should also consider implementing a caching strategy in calculation views if the data lake store is accessed frequently.

What about the analytics jobs executed in the Spark cluster that require access to information kept in the SAP HANA database? Although creating a common data store brings advantages, in real life extracting SAP data is not always possible. Due to the confidentiality of information kept in SAP, many customers don't allow the copying of data. Analytics may also require the use of real-time data, which is not possible with ETL processes. In such cases you should consider using ODBC connections to access the database. It provides an additional level of security as you can assign limited permissions to the user that executes the query and use the built-in database functionality to reduce the amount of information being accessed. Direct database calls always return real-time values.

Unfortunately, such an access strategy can negatively influence the overall performance of the database and before implementing it you should ensure that the current infrastructure can withstand the additional workload. Customers who want to implement ODBC connections should also carefully check the database licensing. Very often, databases bought together with SAP software don't allow access using anything other than SAP software.

Data lakes and distributed processing complement the fast engine of the SAP HANA database. Both technologies should be used in parallel as each solution addresses a specific and unique workload. Keeping data in memory is expensive and doesn't necessarily provide business value. Data lakes store petabytes of data that can easily be accessed using Smart Data Access. Implementing a data-tiering strategy can drastically reduce the cost of running a SAP HANA database as archived information is offloaded to external stores and accessed only when needed.

At the same time, rich integration options between the SAP HANA database and Hadoop clusters allows customers to build modern data science platforms that derive from the company's core systems. But blending data is not the end of the story. To get the full value of implemented analytics, employees should be empowered with a reliable visualization solution that helps them to identify patterns and correlations. Microsoft Power BI is the natural choice as it offers tight integration with all Azure services and through a set of connectors can also be used in a SAP landscape.

Data visualization and business intelligence

Connecting information from many sources is essential to make smart decisions and be ahead of the competition. Data visualization and business intelligence play a key role in the process of eliminating data silos and becoming a data-driven company. A single dashboard that displays aggregated results collected from multiple IT systems, including SAP software, empowers employees to identify trends and patterns that wouldn't be discoverable when data is locked within a single application. Transactional data enhanced with telemetry and social media data exposes sales insights that allow users to understand customer behavior and improve sales processes.

In a data-driven organization, every employee is partially a data scientist, and companies are interested in software that supports them in making decisions based on collected information. The output of the complex algorithms used in analytic processing to describe what happened and why it happened, or even predict the future, can be represented in a graphical format to make it easy for people to consume.

Microsoft's Power BI is an ecosystem of products and technologies that work together to unleash the power of data. Individual users access data sources through a desktop application and transform it into meaningful reports and dashboards that can be shared across the organization using the cloud-based Power BI service. Access to business insights is not limited to desktops—data can be taken with you on a business trip and accessed from mobile devices:

Figure 4-9: Power BI on various platforms (Source: microsoft.com)

Power BI Desktop is a free application that individual users, including data engineers or data scientists, can use to transform and visualize data. The journey starts by accessing the data sources. Power BI currently supports connections to 29 databases (including SAP HANA) and many online services like Google Analytics, Salesforce, and Facebook. It's even possible to fetch data directly from a website. Next, the collected data is transformed and cleansed using Query Editor—the field format can be easily adjusted, and the collected information can be trimmed as per the user's requirements. Finally, the user can choose from more than 30 ways to present the data—each containing a wide range of possible adjustments.

The Power BI service enhances data visualization capabilities with collaboration. There are four building blocks that make resources available to everyone. **Reports** contain data visualizations that are created using Power BI Desktop and shared across the organization. A report can also be included as part of a dashboard. **Dashboards** are collections of many visuals and underlying **datasets**. All those resources are contained in a private or shared **workspace**.

Accessing a data source may require different data handling. Some systems or databases can be queried directly (DirectQuery mode), while others benefit from an automatic data refresh that runs on schedule (Import mode). In the first approach the user always sees live data and Power BI fetches data whenever a user interacts with the visualization. In DirectQuery mode it's not possible to implement data transformation and only a single source is supported. The second approach is useful especially when the end users can work on a copy of the data, thereby minimizing the performance impact on the source system. However, to see any data changes, another import job has to be executed to refresh the Power BI datastore. This approach is also useful for blending data coming from many sources.

As SAP systems contain the most critical company data they are valuable sources for Power BI. Financial, sales, or manufacturing data can be presented in a visual format that makes it easy to understand and interpret.

When it comes to building visualizations on SAP data or blending SAP data with external data sources, Power BI is a good solution. Organizations that have SAP BW can enhance their current analytics capabilities by implementing Power BI as the visualization layer for existing models and queries. For smaller customers, Power BI can eliminate the need for data warehouse solutions altogether. Developing a new model in SAP BW is usually a long and expensive process, but if you don't require data warehouse features Power BI can be a good replacement that is focused on analytics.

You can connect Power BI with SAP BW to visualize data that resides in cubes or BEx queries. SAP HANA calculation views are also supported. Using an OData connector you can fetch information from any SAP NetWeaver-based system through a SAP Gateway.

Supported SAP data sources:

- SAP Business Warehouse and BW/4HANA:
    - BW cubes
    - BEx queries
    - **Advanced DataStore Objects (ADSO)**
- SAP HANA:
    - Calculation views
- SAP NetWeaver-based systems:
    - OData services

Accessing SAP data sources requires additional libraries that need to exist on either the local user's computer or on the data gateway. In order to connect to SAP BW you need to download and install SAP .NET Connector 3.0. Database client libraries (ODBC drivers) are required for fetching data from SAP HANA. No additional software is required for accessing OData services.

A DirectQuery connection to the data source allows us to customize user credentials so that visualizations will reflect the authorizations set in the SAP system. Import jobs connect to the SAP system using a predefined user that usually has greater permissions and additional work is required to restrict the data that is visible in Power BI. At the same time the import approach is more flexible as it allows us to perform data transformations and blend data with data coming from external sources.

Both access methods support single sign-on. The import connection takes the user that runs the data gateway software, and for DirectQuery it's always the user who interacts with the report.

SAP is just one data source, and there are many ways to retrieve stored information. With limited documentation, users may feel lost and even not interested in designing solutions that help with their daily jobs. It's important to support them and share knowledge between teams. Microsoft Azure, as part of its data platform, offers solutions that through collaboration empower employees to easily identify valuable data sources and use them in their daily activities.

Azure Data Catalog

With so many systems currently deployed in an organization, users suffer from not knowing where to look for information that they require in their daily jobs. Information about sales orders can be stored in many systems at the same time. But which is the correct source?

Some data sources may even be hidden so deeply that employees may not even know that they exist. The knowledge is chunked and distributed across the team, with no single person that takes ownership. Data is locked in silos that are difficult to access and consume. Interfaces running in the background that should automate business processes due to logical data errors cause employees to spend time fixing the issue instead of focusing on innovation.

Systems that store sensitive information like personal customer data and credit card numbers should have an additional security layer. The law requires companies to implement solutions that register every access attempt. But without understanding where the data is stored there is no chance to ensure satisfactory protection.

A single data directory that keeps records of all company data is the first step toward becoming a data-driven company. Microsoft understands the challenge. Data Catalog fills this gap and allows discovery and classification enriched by team collaboration to ensure that you're compliant with the rules. At the same time, Data Catalog makes data sources available for employees who can use them in their daily jobs.

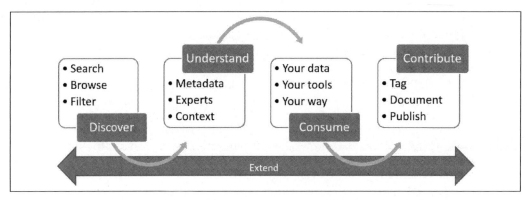

Figure 4-10: Data crowdsourcing with Azure Data Catalog (Source: microsoft.com)

The crowdsourcing approach to capturing documentation reflects the distributed knowledge about existing data sources and empowers employees to provide their insights. The system administrator provides connection instructions, but they most probably won't be able to answer questions about related business processes. Similarly, the functional expert contributes by providing the meaning of information but may not know all ways to consume the data. When all employees take part in the discovery process the collected information becomes complete. The documentation of data sources becomes a valuable and trusted asset for users.

Azure Data Catalog delivers connectors to automatically retrieve metadata and makes the discovery process fast and simple. SAP Business Warehouse and SAP HANA are on the list of supported systems that benefit from automatic discovery. Instead of a manual process of providing basic information, users focus on what they know best, while the application automates the initial registration job and minimizes the chances of mistakes.

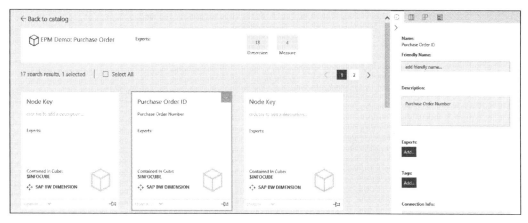

Figure 4-11: Data source view in Azure Data Catalog

The foundation of a modern organization is data. Challenges related to data discovery and classification can be easily solved using automated processes offered by Azure Data Catalog. It's an important step toward eliminating data silos and ensuring a proper level of protection for sensitive information.

Integration

We live in a world of connected applications. In the previous section we focused on integrating a data layer to uncover new business insights and develop new ideas. But that's not the only area where Microsoft Azure can improve IT operations. Integrating applications and business processes can dramatically change how your company operates. Manual repetitive activities can be automated and executed on schedule or triggered by events. We can distinguish four main areas of integration:

- **Application-to-application (A2A)**: A2A integration focuses on the integration of many applications inside a single organization. It has been used for many years and through exchanging messages you can optimize distributed business processes; for example, production data coming from manufacturing systems can be automatically posted in ERP.

- **Business-to-business (B2B)**: B2B integration automates business processes between trading partners, similarly to how A2A integration is commonly used today. Data formats and communication methods follow EDI standards like X12 or EDIFACT.

- **Software-as-a-Service (SaaS)**: SaaS integration involves exchanging data between cloud-based applications like Salesforce or Dynamics 365 and traditional systems running on-premises or in the cloud.
- **Internet of Things (IoT)**: IoT integration connects applications and devices.

Azure Integration Services is designed to work for all four integration domains. The services provided solve most common integration challenges and are in line with modern development processes. It's a platform consisting of four cloud services to integrate data and processes. Azure Logic Apps is used to build and schedule the execution of workflows that connect cloud and on-premises applications. API Management provides governance and an additional layer of security for applications that exposes REST or SOAP APIs. Service Bus is an enterprise messaging platform and Event Grid is a service that manages communication using events. All services complement each other and provide a powerful integration framework.

Integrating SAP applications used to be a long and expensive process. That was partially caused by complex business processes that required careful testing, but it was mostly due to the deficiencies of the existing integration platforms. There was no universal service that offered a technical layer for exchanging messages with many services out of the box, so even if the external application supported communication using SOAP or REST APIs the integration had to be preceded by analysis, manual implementation of the calls, and error handling. Connecting a SAP system with an external database required installing drivers on the application servers and writing a custom report. In addition, the system administrator had to manually define the connection. Calling external web services required a tedious process of defining proxy objects, which usually resulted in hundreds of new repository objects that had to be maintained during system upgrades. Technical limitations made implementing even the most basic integration inefficient and costly.

Logic Apps changed the way integration is built. The execution of workflows that natively offer communication with hundreds of systems and services allows us to streamline the process and reduce the cost of connecting SAP with other systems. Instead of coding, you can implement integration logic using building blocks that are executed in a specified order. Building a workflow doesn't require programming skills and it can be designed using a graphical editor. Through integration with Azure DevOps you can automate the deployment process, which allows you to deploy workflows in a consistent way across many SAP environments.

Each workflow consists of a trigger and a chain of actions that are executed. There are various triggers available. The generic one waits to receive an HTTP request or executes the workflow on a schedule. A trigger can also be an event from an external application.

This way, the workflow can start when a new record is inserted into Salesforce or when the SAP system sends a message using RFC. Logic Apps supports more than 200 applications, and almost all of them implement at least one trigger.

An action is an activity performed during the execution of a workflow that interacts with an external application. It can be a basic activity like sending an email notification. There are connectors available for accessing FTP servers, connecting to databases, or fetching data from social media. Enterprise applications are also supported. Logic Apps can seamlessly communicate with SAP systems using RFC and post IDOCs or call BAPIs. Conditional expressions and loops allow the implementation of advanced logic so that developers can avoid spending time manually implementing API calls.

Using Application Gateway, which is a small application installed in the DMZ part of the network, you can connect on-premises applications without having to expose them to the internet. It works in a similar way to SAP Cloud Connector and enables the building of hybrid integrations:

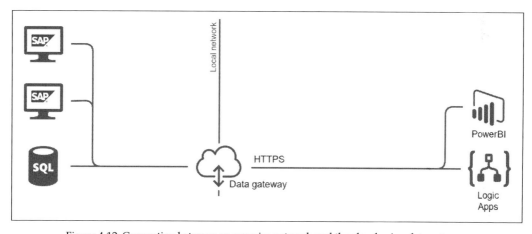

Figure 4-12: Connection between on-premise network and the cloud using data gateway

Customers who require an additional layer of security can create private and isolated instances of the Logic Apps service. The integration service environment is separated from the main service and runs on dedicated infrastructure. It's deployed to the virtual network and depending on requirements, the origin of the incoming requests can be limited to that network, which even further increases the security of the environment. The dedicated instance of Logic Apps provides the same user experience and similar capabilities as the public one.

Reliable communication with trading partners is essential in every SAP deployment. Customers automate business processes through exchanging documents like invoices and orders. Digital communication improves the transfer of goods and reduces the complexity of collaboration. B2B messaging is fully supported on Microsoft Azure and takes advantage of the modern integration development on Logic Apps.

Organizations can implement communication using standard protocols like EDIFACT, X12, AS2, and RosettaNet. Each protocol has a dedicated connector to process messages and handle the encoding and decoding of the provided body. For EDI message types the respective connectors calculate the interchange control numbers and validate schema. The prepared message is then serialized and sent to an HTTP endpoint. An IDOC containing a purchase order generated in the SAP system can trigger a workflow that encodes the information into an AS2 message and sends it to a trading partner through a secure channel. The received delivery notification is then saved to the selected storage solution. The message structure can be validated against schema. Maps allow us to perform format changes using XSLT transformations.

Azure Integration Account facilitates the communication. It's the central place for storing all B2B integration artifacts like the definition of trading partners and agreements. To even further increase the security of exchanged messages, private keys used for data encryption and digital signing are stored by the Azure Key Vault service, which uses a hardware security module to safeguard keys and passwords. Access to the private keys is tightly controlled and restricted to the selected Azure service. While developers are still able to reference keys in their workflows, they can't see or download them, which makes the development process highly secure. Access to the protected Key Vault store is logged and the usage can be monitored and audited.

Basic Integration Account artifacts are described in the following table:

Schemas	Message format
Maps	A transformation that can be applied to outgoing and incoming messages. Supports XSLT, Liquid, and HIDX types.
Assemblies	A custom set of functions written in .NET that can be invoked from the XSLT map.
Certificates	Stores private and public certificates to verify message authenticity and integrity.
Partners	Definition of a trading partner.
Agreements	Defines communication settings including message compression and encryption requirements or delivery notification.

Connections to external partners can be monitored. Logic Apps and Integration Account generate runtime logs that are saved in Azure Monitor. The B2B monitoring add-on available in Azure Monitor can access and analyze information coming from a workflow and present it in a graphical and easy-to-use format. The add-on supports the following metrics:

- Message count and status
- Acknowledgment status
- Detailed error descriptions for failures

Logic App B2B monitoring generates a dashboard that displays information about processed messages, received acknowledgments, and allows users to track communication problems:

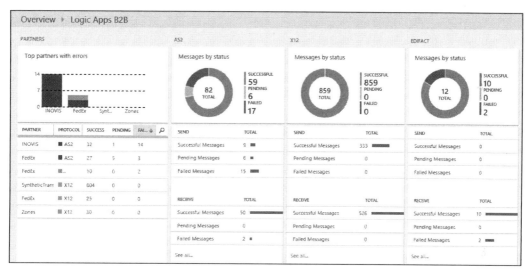

Figure 4-13: Logic App B2B monitoring dashboard

Creating the first integration workflow is easy; however, as always, a detailed analysis of the use case should precede the implementation. Logic Apps allows communicating with the SAP system using an RFC connection. This way, it is possible to post an IDOC or execute BAPI. SAP systems with a Gateway component expose hundreds of available OData services that can also be invoked from the workflow.

All SAP connectors support **Secure Network Communication (SNC)** and single sign-on using Kerberos. A user that runs the data gateway can be mapped to an SAP user, thereby allowing communication without transmitting user credentials. During the development process you can't forget about testing. Each workflow should be carefully validated before enabling communication with the production landscape.

The source control and continuous integration/delivery features available in Logic Apps can be used to support the process of transporting changes between SAP environments, minimizes the chances of errors in production.

Azure Logic Apps is a powerful framework for building enterprise-scale integration between applications, trading partners, and cloud services. It's a truly serverless technology that doesn't require a long process of hardware procurement or software maintenance. It eliminates the need for other integration engines. However, it can also work together with existing SAP integration systems. Microsoft Azure heavily relies on Logic Apps for communicating with the IoT, which is another advantage as it opens the door to SAP integration with connected devices.

Internet of Things

In the introduction to the *Integration* section we discussed how we live in a world of connected applications. That's of course a valid statement, but when we take a look at how technology has evolved in recent years we can easily see that common internet access has created another integration domain. We live in a world of connected devices. Smartphones, which we use on a daily basis, send usage data to software vendors. Printers are connected to the internet and automatically order new cartridges when the ink level is low. Coffee machines can be programmed using smartphones, and, similar to printers, they can also automatically order supplies. The automotive sector heavily invests in car telemetry, which involves cars constantly sending data using the mobile network.

The manufacturing industry is focused on the optimizing of production lines. Unplanned maintenance due to overused parts causes serious problems and leads to production delays and unsatisfied customers. By implementing IoT devices, manufacturers can constantly collect telemetry data to monitor the performance of equipment and use advanced analytics to predict when maintenance will be necessary. For retailers a common problem is tracking items on shelves to ensure that they never run out of stock. Installing weight sensors automates the monitoring and triggers notifications when stock levels are running low.

The IoT improves customer engagement and helps to shift the focus from selling products to selling services and experiences. With the ability to communicate with their devices over the internet, device manufacturers can monitor consumption and react in real time to ensure that the customer never runs out of coffee or ink.

This new technology raises a variety of integration challenges. A device that is distributed with a security vulnerability becomes an easy target for hackers, who can take control of the hardware and cause major problems. Infected devices may be part of a worldwide botnet but also cause physical damage.

Breaking an IoT infrastructure may result in data leaks that contain sensitive customer information like medical histories. We also can't forget that through the tight integration of external devices and the company network, hackers may get access to corporate data and infiltrate resources. It may sound like science fiction, but an unsecured washing machine may act as a backdoor to your central SAP system.

You can't look at the IoT as an isolated technology. It is part of all the other company assets that benefit from communication with existing systems. As SAP plays a central role in every organization, sooner or later data from SAP and IoT will need to be blended for that additional advantage over the competition. Data coming from IoT devices is an important input for automating processes running in a SAP system. For example, you can enhance the functionality of existing SCADA solutions, and the device telemetry information could be used in the SAP Predictive Maintenance. Electronic sensors kept in a cold room can detect temperature anomalies and change the best-before dates of the products stored in that room accordingly. Finally, live delivery information allows us to establish just-in-time manufacturing processes and reduce production cycles.

Microsoft Azure is the leader in the domain of connected devices and offers an entire portfolio of services that allow users to efficiently and securely implement large deployments. Azure IoT Hub is the main service that connects devices with other Azure services. It facilitates communication and takes care of registration processes and configuration updates. The messaging channel is secured using per-device authentication that supports tokens and certificates:

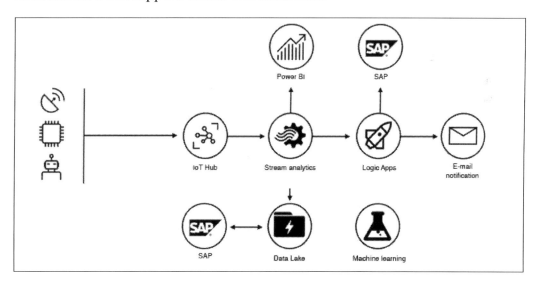

Figure 4-14: IoT integration with Azure

Microsoft Azure provides a technical foundation for IoT solutions. Through a set of integrated services, signals coming from devices can be used to streamline business processes. To accelerate development processes, Microsoft prepared a unique solution that out of the box, without tedious development processes, allows us to consume core IoT functionalities in a secure fashion. IoT Central is an application platform that offers pre-built and customizable templates for customers from many industries. You can use them as a starting point and adjust them to fulfill your requirements. While IoT Central offers a simplified implementation experience, in the background it is powered by the Azure platform and it offers the same integration possibilities including connecting with the SAP landscape.

SAP also understands the value of integrating the IoT with business applications. The recently launched SAP Leonardo IoT platform promises greater business value and stronger competitive advantages through the collection and ingestion of data into SAP S/4HANA. The solution is still in the development process, but we already know that SAP Leonardo IoT and Microsoft Azure will complement each other.

Customers who would like to take advantage of the SAP business solution can use Azure IoT services in the connectivity and device management layer. Collected data is automatically synchronized with SAP Cloud Platform and customers can benefit from the advanced security features offered by Azure together with the optimized business processes prepared by SAP without any additional investment being required to integrate the platforms.

Implementing IoT solutions allows companies to act faster and offer a unique customer experience. While at the moment most of them are custom-built, we observe that software vendors like Microsoft and SAP are working to reduce the customer development effort required by creating solution templates that are based on industry best practices. This way, the implementation process is faster and customers can benefit from a quicker return of investment.

Summary

Implementing SAP on the Azure platform shouldn't focus only on infrastructure and virtual machines. Through integrated services that are already capable of working with SAP systems Azure empowers customers to make their data meaningful and shared across the landscape. Employees that access them will make better decisions that allow a company to grow. Technical integration and the automation of business processes, followed by advanced analytics and artificial intelligence, can reduce operational costs, which lets you focus on what is most important—providing the best customer experience you can.

Microsoft Azure is designed to support IT and business operations and every company, no matter what size, can use its technical capabilities to transform and be successful in the digital data-driven world. In this chapter, we covered just some of the possibilities provided by the cloud platform. Identity, data, and integration are the three main areas that customers should focus on. As you start your journey, you'll discover more services that further optimize business processes and allow you to react quicker to a constantly changing market. Customers expect product innovation and are willing to pay for a great experience. Azure will allow you to deliver that experience.

Index

A

Accelerated Networking (AN) 36
action 215
Activity Logs 94
Additional Application Server (AAS) 66
Advanced Analytics (AA) 20
advanced analytics, on big data
  reference link 21
Advanced DataStore Objects (ADSO) 210
agile and trusted SAP environment, on Microsoft Azure
  reference link 22
alerts 94
ANF for SAP HANA VM
  benefits 60
Apache Hadoop 203
Apache HBase 203
Apache Interactive Query 203
Apache Kafka 203
Apache Spark 203
Apache Storm 203
application-consistent recovery point 79
application programming interface (API) 197
application server disaster recovery 79, 80
Artificial Intelligence (AI) 20
ASR limits, and data change rates
  reference link 80
asynchronous replication 73
Availability Zones, in Azure
  reference link 13
Azure
  best cloud platform, for SAP workloads 6
  customer stories 3-6
  for business-critical systems 1-3

Azure Active Directory (AAD)
  about 9, 184
  SAP Single sign-on 186-190
Azure Active Directory single sign-on (SSO) integration, with SAP Fiori
  reference link 9
Azure Advisor 95, 96
Azure backup
  about 88
  for databases 89
  for SAP HANA 140
  for virtual machines 88
Azure Blob Storage
  archive 91
  cool tier 91
  for backup 90
  hot tier 91
Azure Blueprints service
  reference link 20
Azure Compute (IaaS) 76
Azure Data Box
  used, for transferring data 161
Azure Databricks 203, 204
Azure Data Catalog 211-213
Azure data factory
  SAP connectors 198-201
Azure Data Factory (ADF) 4, 21, 197
Azure Data Lake Store (ADLS) 21, 144
Azure Data Lake Store Gen2 (ADLS Gen2) 4
Azure diagnostic extension 92
Azure Enterprise Scaffold
  reference link 17
Azure, for hosting and running SAP workload scenarios
  reference link 3

Azure governance documentation
  reference link 47
Azure HDInsight 202, 203
Azure Integration Runtime 198
Azure Integration Services 214
Azure Kubernetes Service (AKS) 34, 144
Azure landing zone 42-44
Azure Logic Apps 214, 218
Azure Managed Disks
  Premium SSD 55
  reference link 55, 56
  Standard HDD 55
  Standard SDD 55
  Ultra SSD 55
Azure management hierarchy 47
Azure Monitor 93
Azure monitor application Insights
  for Java 153
Azure monitoring extension for SAP 92
Azure NetApp Account 58
Azure NetApp Capacity Pool 58
Azure NetApp Files (ANF)
  about 58, 67
  premium tier 59
  standard tier 59
  ultra tier 59
Azure NetApp Volume 58
Azure Network Appliances
  reference link 136
Azure Reserved VM Instances (RIs)
  reference link 63
Azure Resource Manager (ARM) 36
Azure resources
  reference link 47
Azure Security Group (ASG) 107
Azure Site Recovery (ASR)
  about 17, 77, 167
  using 167

B

backup
  about 85
  Azure backup 88
  Azure Blob Storage for backup 90
  database backup 86, 87
  database snapshot 87
  database streaming backup 88
  disk snapshot 86
  filesystem backup 85
  third party backup solutions 89
  versus disaster recovery 85
backup/restore
  using 164, 165
big data analytics
  about 201, 202
  Azure Databricks 203, 204
  Azure HDInsight 202, 203
Brownfield migrations 29
business continuity and disaster
    recovery (BCDR)
  reference link 76
business intelligence 208-210
Business Warehouse (BW) 5, 20

C

caching, for VMs and data disks
  reference link 57
cancel, exchange and refund policies
  reference link 63
Carlsberg Analytics Platform (CAP) 4
central services disaster recovery 82-84
Chief Digital Officer (CDO) 1
Chief Information Officer (CIO) 1
Chief Technology Officer (CTO) 1
classical migration
  about 169, 170
  export/import process optimization 170
  performance optimization 170
  System Export Preparation, executing 170
Cloud Adoption Framework (CAF) 17, 42
Cloud Operating Model
  reference link 17
Cloud Service Provider (CSP) 18
Cloud Solution Architects (CSAs) 38
Coke One North America (CONA) 5
cold data tiering
  with SAP data hub 205, 206
  with SAP HANA spark controller 206-208
colocation (Colo) 7
Conditional Access (CA) 9
configuration management database
    (CMDB) 20

Content Delivery Network (CDN) 151
cost conscious Azure storage configuration
  reference link 58
crash-consistent recovery point 79
cross-region activities
  reference link 76
Customer Stories, Carlsberg Group
  reference link 4

D

dashboards 95, 209
data analytics 192
database backup 86, 87
database management system
    (DBMS) 8, 49, 155
Database Migration Option (DMO)
  about 30
  Near-Zero Downtime Migration (nZDT),
    using 180
  parallel data transfer 178, 179
  sequential data transfer 178
  third party options 180, 182
  with System Move option 175-178
database server disaster recovery 80, 82
database snapshot 87
database streaming backup 88
data center
  advantages 160
data exploration 195
data extraction
  about 194, 195
  schedule 196
data platform 190, 191
data privacy 192
data processing 192
data quality 192
data security 192, 196
datasets 209
data sourcing 191
data storage 192
data transfer
  about 161
  Azure Data Box, using 161
  network based data transfer 161, 162

Data Transfer Process (DTP) 199
data visualization 192, 208, 209, 210
DBMS replication
  using 166
DBMS replication technologies, to provide
    high availability
  IBM Db2 74
  Microsoft SQL Server 74
  Oracle Database 73
  SAP Adaptive Server Enterprise (ASE) 74
  SAP HANA 73
  SAP MaxDB 74
delta extracts 196
Demilitarized Zone (DMZ) 7
Department of Defense (DoD) 8
disaster recovery (DR)
  about 4, 15, 75, 77
  application server disaster recovery 79, 80
  Azure Site Recovery (ASR) 77-79
  central services disaster recovery 82
  database server disaster recovery 80-82
  landing zone 77
  versus backup 85
  /sapmnt directory, handling 85
disaster recovery, ExpressRoute
    private peering
  reference link 46
disk snapshot 86
disk types, Azure
  Premium SSD 120
  reference link 55
  Standard HDD 120
  Standard SSD 120
  Ultra SSD 120
Downtime Minimized Option (DMO) 158
downtime-optimized backup/restore 166
Dynamic Random Access Memory
    (DRAM) 119

E

Enhanced Managed Services (EMS) 25
Enqueue Replication Server (ERS) 17, 68
enqueue replicator 2 (ER2) 68
enqueue server 2 (ENQ2) 68

Enterprise Resource Planning (ERP) 22
essential business function (EBF) 23
export/import process optimization
   Azure environment, scaling-up 175
   large tables 171, 173
   multiple R3Load servers, using 174
   parallel export/import 174, 175
   R3Load process configuration 170
ExpressRoute 44
ExpressRoute connection establishment methods
   Any-to-any (IPVPN) Connection 45
   Cloud Exchange Co-location 45
   Point-to-point Ethernet Connection 45
ExpressRoute connectivity models
   reference link 44
ExpressRoute partners, and peering locations
   reference link 45

F

FastTrack for Azure
   reference link 38
fault domains (FD) 12
filesystem backup 85

G

geo-redundant storage (GRS) 16, 56, 90
geo-zone-redundant storage (GZRS) 56, 90
Giga Bytes (GB) 53
global strategic service partners (GSSPs) 24
Global Systems Integrators (GSI) 25
Greenfield migrations 29

H

Hadoop
   SAP HANA, integrating with 204, 205
Hadoop Distributed File System (HDFS) 201
HANA backup
   to filesystem 139, 140
   with filesystem snapshot 141
   with third-party tools 141, 142
HANA database backup
   about 139
   monitoring and performance optimization 143
HANA disaster recovery 136-138
HANA Enterprise Cloud (HEC) 23
HANA Large Instance (HLI) 10, 115
HANA System Replication (HSR) 129
HANA System Replication synchronous (HSR sync) 131
Hardware and Cloud Measurement Tools (HCMT) 115
Hardware Configuration Check Tool (HWCCT) 57
heterogeneous migration
   about 168
   classical migration 168, 170
   Database Migration Option (DMO), with System Move option 175-177
   examples 157
heterogeneous system copy 31
high availability (HA) 4
homogeneous migration
   about 32, 164
   examples 157
hub-spoke network topology, with shared services
   reference link 43

I

IBM DB2 180
Icertis Contract Management (ICM) 5
identity and access management 183-186
Identity and Access Management (IAM) 9
Information Technology (IT) 1
Infrastructure as a Service (IaaS) 1
Infrastructure as Code (IaC) 36
integration
   about 213-217
   application-to-application (A2A) 213
   business-to-business (B2B) 213
   Internet of Things (IoT) 214
   Software-as-a-Service (SaaS) 214
Internet of Things (IoT) 5, 191, 218, 219, 220

K

key performance indicators (KPI) 116

L

landscape planning 41, 42
live migration
  reference link 64
locally redundant storage (LRS) 56, 90

M

Machine Learning (ML) 20, 64
management groups 47
Megabytes per second (Mbps) 57
Microsoft Azure
  about 219
  storage types 193
Microsoft Azure Training
  reference link 37
Microsoft Cloud Adoption Framework, for Azure
  reference link 17
Microsoft Consulting Services (MCS) 38
Microsoft Enterprise Edge Routers (MSEE) 45
Microsoft Trust Center
  reference link 7
migration method
  Azure Site Recovery (ASR), using 167
  backup/restore, using 164, 165
  DBMS replication, using 166
  heterogenous migration 168
  homogenous migration 164
  selecting 164
migration options
  advantages 181
  disadvantages 181
minimum Development (DEV) 163
ML Services 203
monitoring
  about 91
  Activity Logs 94
  alerts 94
  Azure Advisor 95, 96
  Azure diagnostic extension 92
  Azure Monitor 93
  Azure monitoring extension for SAP 92
  dashboards 95
Multi-Factor Authentication (MFA) 9
multiple components on one database (MCOD) 109, 110
multiple R3Load servers
  using 174, 175
multiprotocol label switching (MPLS) 7, 45
Multitenant Database Containers (MDC) 113

N

National Systems Integrators (NSI) 25
Near-Zero Downtime Migration (nZDT)
  about 180
  with Database Migration Option (DMO) 180
net present value (NPV) 2
NetWeaver Application Server for ABAP (NW AS ABAP) 68
Network address translation (NAT) 146
network based data transfer 161, 162
network connectivity 44-46
Network Security Group (NSG) 107
network sizing
  about 103
  latency 103
  throughput 103
Network Virtual Appliance (NVA) 36, 43, 107, 136
network zones, SAP
  client 119
  internal 119
  storage 119
new procurement system (NPS) 4
NFS v4.1 volumes, on Azure NetApp Files
  reference link 60
non-NetWeaver applications 34
non-production environments
  reviewing 163

O

OData 198
on-premises network, connecting to Microsoft Azure virtual network
  reference link 44
Open Data Initiative (ODI) 23
operating system (OS) 31, 49, 155

Oracle Database 180
Oracle Real Application Cluster (RAC) 9, 73

P

Page Blobs
   reference link 55
parallel data transfer 178, 179
pay as you go (PAYG) 61
planned downtime 64, 65
Platform as a Service (PaaS) 1
Power BI Desktop 209
Primary Application Server (PAS) 66
process optimization
   importing 170
Production (PRD) 163
production storage solution, with Azure Write Accelerator
   reference link 58
Proximity Placement Groups (PPG) 104

Q

Quality Assurance System (QAS) 163

R

R3Load process configuration 170
read-access geo-redundant storage (RA-GRS) 25, 56, 90
read-access geo-zone-redundant storage (RA-GZRS) 56, 91
Real Application Clusters (RAC) 9, 73
recovery point
   application-consistent recovery point 79
   crash-consistent recovery point 79
recovery point objective (RPO) 16, 73
recovery time objective (RTO) 16
Red Hat Enterprise Linux (RHEL) 31
Redundant Array of Independent Disks (RAID) 55
rehosting 49
replatforming 50
reports 209
reserved instance
   reference link 63
resource groups 47

return on investment (ROI) 2, 61

S

SAP 1
SAP Application Performance Standard (SAPS) 99
SAP as a Service (SAPaaS) 18
SAP business suite 112
SAP business warehouse (BW) 199
SAP BW open hub 199
SAP Central Services Instance High Availability 67-72
SAP Certified and Supported SAP HANA Hardware Directory
   reference link 118
SAP Certified Virtual Machines 54
SAP cloud
   for customers 200, 201
SAP Cloud Connector 114
SAP Cloud Platform (SCP) 35
SAP Commerce
   about 149
   components 150, 151
SAP Commerce Cloud 149
SAP Commerce on AKS
   high-level architecture 152
SAP connectors
   in Azure data factory 198-201
SAP data access tools 197
SAP data hub
   about 143, 144
   cold data tiering 205, 206
   supported platforms 144
   system deployment 145-148
   system sizing 145
SAP ECC 198
SAP ERP Central Component (ECC) 112
SAP Fiori 113
SAP HANA
   about 115, 200
   integrating, with Hadoop 204, 205
   supported platforms 115
   system deployment 125
SAP HANA certified platforms
   need for 115

SAP HANA Enterprise Cloud
  reference link 25
SAP HANA Enterprise Cloud (HEC) Services Documentation
  reference link 25
SAP HANA high availability 129
SAP HANA resilience 128
SAP HANA scale-out HA
  about 130
  HANA scale-out HA with host auto-failover 130
  HANA System Replication synchronous (HSR sync) 131, 133
  on VMs 133-136
SAP HANA scale-up HA 129, 130
SAP HANA sizing
  about 116
  CPU and memory requisites 116-119
  network requisites 119, 120
  storage requisites 120-124
SAP HANA spark controller
  cold data tiering 206-208
SAP Hybris 149
SAP Hybris Commerce Architecture and Technology
  reference link 149
SAP, migrating to Azure
  about 29
  automation 18-20
  availability 11-15
  Brownfield 29
  business continuity/disaster recovery 15-17
  common misconceptions 24, 25
  compliance and security 7-9
  Greenfield 29
  insights and innovation 20, 21
  lift-and-transform, to S/4HANA 156
  Lift and Migrate to Cloud 30
  Lift and Shift/Migrate to Cloud, migrate part to HANA 30
  Lift and Shift to Cloud 30
  Microsoft Cloud Adoption Framework for Azure 17, 18
  partnership 22-24
  scalability 9-11
  Transformation to S/4HANA 31

SAP, migrating to Azure types
  lift-and-migrate migration 156
  lift-and-migrate, to HANA 156
  lift-and-shift 156
SAP NetWeaver-based systems
  about 96
  considerations 112
  supported platforms 97-99
  system deployment 105, 106
SAP NetWeaver high availability
  about 66
  application server high availability 66, 67
  database high availability 72-75
SAProuter 114
SAP S/4HANA 112
SAP Single sign-on
  with Azure AD 186-190
SAP Support Strategy, Maintenance 2025
  reference link 26
SAP systems, sizing
  about 99
  CPU 99, 100
  memory 99, 100
  network sizing 103-105
  storage sizing 101
SAP Table 199
SAP, to Azure migration
  data transfer 161
  environment, preparing in Azure 160
  exploring 155-158
  housekeeping and archiving 160
  interfaces 159
  move groups 159
  planning 158
SAP workloads, to Azure
  migration factors 26, 28
  migration order 28
  migration startegies 31-34
Scale-Out File Server (SOFS) 70, 84
scope reservations
  reference link 64
Secure Network Communication (SNC) 9, 217
Secure Sockets Layer (SSL) 9
self-hosted integration runtime 198
sequential data transfer 178
Service Level Agreement (SLA) 13, 64

Single Sign-On (SSO) 9
site-to-site (S2S) 158
site-to-site (S2S) VPN 44
sizes for Linux virtual machines, Azure
  reference link 53
sizing
  about 48, 49
  considerations 52
  new installations 51, 52
  rehosting 50
  replatforming 50
SLA for Virtual Machines
  reference link 13
SNP Group 180
Software as a service (SaaS) 1, 149, 184
Software Provisioning Manager (SWPM) 32
Software Update Manager
    (SUM) 30, 158, 175, 178
SSIS integration runtime 198
STONITH Block Device (SBD) 75
Storage Service Encryption (SSE) 8
storage services, Microsoft Azure
  blob storage 193
  Data Lake storage 193
  file storage 193
  queue storage 193
  table storage 193
storage sizing
  about 101
  application servers 101
  database servers 102, 103
Storage Spaces Direct (S2D) 67, 70
subscriptions 47
successful work team
  about 34
  internal resources 35-37
  Microsoft 38
  partners 37
Supplier Relationship Management (SRM) 5
support package (SP) 176
SUSE Enterprise Linux (SLES) 31
synchronous replication 73
system deployment, SAP HANA
  multiple components on one system
    (MCOS) 125

multitenant database containers
    (MDC) 126, 127
scale-out 128
scale-up 127
standalone HANA deployment 125
system deployment, SAP NetWeaver-based
    systems
Central services instance stacking 110, 111
distributed installation 106, 107
highly available installation 107, 108
multiple components on one system
    (MCOS) 109
multiple SAP databases, running on one
    server 109
standalone installation 106
system Export
  phases 169
system Import
  phases 169
System Move option
  Database Migration Option (DMO),
    using 175-178

T

Tailored Data center Integration (TDI) 10, 58
The Total Economic Impact™ of Microsoft
    Azure for SAP
  reference link 2
tight sizing 50
total cost of ownership (TCO) 61
Transport Layer Security (TLS) 9

U

unplanned downtime 64, 65
update domains (UD) 12
use case
  finding, for data extraction 195

V

Virtual Machines (VMs)
  about 8, 53, 160
  cost considerations 61-63
  size 53, 54

Virtual Private Networks (VPN) 7
Volume Shadow Copy Service (VSS) 86

W

Web Application Firewall (WAF) 150
Wide Area Network (WAN) 7
Windows Server Failover Clustering
    (WSFC) 111
workspace 209

Z

zone-redundant storage (ZRS) 56, 90

Made in the USA
Las Vegas, NV
09 December 2020